CW00818843

# WINNERS
## and
# CHAMPIONS

# WINNERS and CHAMPIONS

## The Story of Manchester United's 1948 Cup Final and 1952 League Championship Winning Teams

**Alec Shorrocks**

ARTHUR BARKER LIMITED

A Subsidiary of Weidenfeld (Publishers) Limited

*To the memory of my father Joe*
*who gave me his love of the game.*

Published in Great Britain by
Arthur Barker Limited
91 Clapham High Street
London SW4 7TA

ISBN 0 213 16920 7

Printed in Great Britain by
Butler & Tanner Limited
Frome and London

# Contents

# Acknowledgments

I owe a deep debt of gratitude to Tony Walker whose programmes, scrap books and patient encouragement provided much of the source and inspiration for the book. Many thanks also to Dave Baldwin who gave me my first chance to write about football in the *New Manchester Review* all those years ago; to Martin Rostron, Roger Dawe, Roy Cavanagh and Jack Hibbert who read the manuscript and made many helpful comments; to players past and present: George Edwards, Tom Finney, Jack Hindle, Ken Horton, Bert Johnson, Stan Mortensen, Dennis Mortimer, Bob Paisley, Jack Stamps and his wife Nora, Tim Ward, Ray Wilkins, and the late Sam Bartram for their interest; to supporters Richard Taylor, Don Baldwin, Frank Nolan, Peter Aldridge, Pete Boxley, Edward Shakespeare and Leo White for allowing me to share their rich store of memories; to Martin Corteel, sports editor for the publishers; to Alison Allen, Paul Brown, Colin Cameron, Alan Farrer, Jim Hall, John Hewitt, David Miller, 'Sandy' Sanderson and Jeff Teasdale for their help and advice; to Leslie Olive and all at Old Trafford; and finally to Sir Matt Busby and the players for their time and generous hospitality. They turned a daunting idea into a labour of love.

# Illustrations

Carey and Busby with the Championship trophy (*Manchester Evening News*)

United celebrate Championship victory

John Aston, Henry Cockburn, Johnny Morris and Charlie Mitten (Frank Wilson)

Jack Crompton (Frank Wilson)

Jack Rowley (Frank Wilson)

Jimmy Delaney (Alan Farrer)

Allenby Chilton (Alan Farrer)

John Anderson (Syed Kazmi)

John Carey and Jimmy Murphy

Stan Pearson (David Smith)

Sir Matt Busby and Leslie Olive (*Manchester Evening News*)

Except where otherwise indicated, the photographs in this book are from the players' own collections.

# Introduction

This is the story of the eleven players who in 1948 won the FA Cup for Manchester United, a story that did not really end until United won the First Division Championship in 1952 with a team which still included six members of that Cup winning side.

They were a famous team and even today, nearly forty years on, many can still recite their names like a litany: Crompton; Carey, Aston; Anderson, Chilton, Cockburn; Delaney, Morris, Rowley, Pearson, Mitten. Their success and popularity, at its peak during those years, lay in a combination of many factors. Ironically they were a team without a ground, and certainly just after the war their club was deep in debt. A German air-raid in 1941 had reduced much of Old Trafford to rubble, and consequently all their home games had to be played at Maine Road, the ground of arch-rivals, Manchester City.

Then in 1945 the appointment of a 35-year-old Scotsman called Matt Busby as manager began the renaissance. He gave a chance to many talented players who had lost six years of their footballing lives to the war, and his unique ability to spot where they could make better use of their abilities prompted some crucial positional changes. Very soon he had blended together a team of devastating power and balance.

Several of his 1948 side had made their League debuts before the war, others had matured in Services football, all were determined to make up for lost time. As the team began to establish itself, the taste for success started to grow, and their first claim to fame was undoubtedly the Cup win in 1948.

Manchester United's run of victories in the Cup campaign of the 1947–48 season was sensational by any standards. In every round they were drawn against First Division opposition, namely Liverpool, the current League Champions; Charlton Athletic, the current Cup holders; Preston North End, a team which was then lying third in the League and had in their winger Tom Finney, one of the most brilliant players in the country; and in the semi-final United met Derby County who had not been defeated in three months. Every one of these games was technically 'away' from home, and every game was won by at least two goals.

In the third round tie against Aston Villa (still rated as the most exciting and memorable third round tie ever played in the history of the competition), Manchester United, a goal down after $13\frac{1}{2}$ seconds, were leading 5-1 at half-time. With only seven minutes of the game remaining, Aston Villa had clawed back three more goals, but eventually United were to win 6-4 in a finale of Wagnerian intensity.

Four years later, Manchester United and its supporters had to wait until the very last day of the campaign on which they played the final game of the 1951-52 season against Arsenal – before they could be confirmed as First Division champions. So for John Carey, Allenby Chilton, Henry Cockburn, Stan Pearson, Jack Rowley and John Aston a Championship medal joined their 1948 Cup medal on the sideboard, and set the perfect seal on their footballing careers.

Furthermore, by 1952 Manchester United was showing a healthy profit; it had returned home at last to a restored Old Trafford in time for the opening match of the 1949-50 season; and thousands of spectators, fired by the club's name and growing reputation, flocked to watch Manchester United wherever they played, as indeed they still do today.

Every player in United's 1948 Cup team which beat Blackpool 4-2, in what has been described as Wembley's finest final, was a character in his own right.

The team was led by captain and right-back John Carey, one of the great figures in football at the time. United had signed him in 1936 from St James's Gate, Dublin, and this most versatile player had already featured in nine different positions for Manchester United, as well as holding many caps for Ireland and Eire. He had also captained the Rest of Europe team which had played Great Britain in the previous May. Carey was the quintessential leader, calm and thoughtful, with a matchless ability to read a game. Off the field, the dry sense of humour of this wise, pipe-smoking Irishman made him the best of company.

But if the brilliance of the side had to be ascribed to any one particular factor, most would have agreed that it lay with the five forwards, each contributing to the creation of a unique blend of speed, power and skill.

At outside-right was Scottish international, Jimmy Delaney, bought by Matt Busby two years before from Glasgow Celtic, for £4,000. Delaney was in fact Busby's only purchase in a team which overall cost only £7,750! This speedy and elusive winger had already won a Scottish Cup winner's medal in 1937, and Jimmy was keen to win something in the equivalent English competition. Little was he to know that his story would not end there ...

Johnny Morris was United's inside-right, one of six local-born players, and on his day a quick-thinking and mercurial ball player with a powerful shot. Direct and uncompromising on and off the field, he was also the team's best golfer as he so often proved at the team's weekly game at Davyhulme Golf Course. Even though Morris spent only three of his thirteen seasons as a League foot-baller with Manchester United, many would always remember him as a United player, and sadly he was the first of this great team to leave the club, in March 1949.

Leading the line was the already-legendary Jack Rowley, who as United's centre-forward was one of its most prolific goal-scor-ers. He was in the classic centre-forward mould, big and bustling, and he possessed one of the hardest left-foot shots in the game. The crowd loved to see him flatten defenders on his way to goal, but there was more to him than mere robust enthusiasm. Rowley could play anywhere in the forward line, and he was another of United's stars who had made his League debut before the war.

Salford-born Stan Pearson had joined United's ground staff as a 15-year-old also before the war. Always a gentle and modest man, he was highly respected by his team-mates as the general of the side, a constructive and hard-working schemer who could spot opportunities and exploit them to advantage.

Charlie Mitten was as fast as the greyhounds he loved to own and train. United's dapper outside-left once worked as an office boy at Old Trafford: as a player he could centre a ball on a sixpence, and as the team's penalty taker he rarely missed. He

was a bold adventurer in every sense, as a South American journey he took in 1950 was to show.

United's half-back line contained three men of strength and
skill. At 5 feet 5 inches tall, left-half Henry Cockburn was nick-
named 'The Mighty Atom': a ferocious tackler and a supremely
accurate distributor of the ball. He was the team's cinema buff,
particularly the films of Humphrey Bogart. His merit as a player
of quality had been recognised at international level: already
Cockburn was the proud possessor of five England caps.

Allenby Chilton was the archetypal centre-half: six feet tall,
physically strong and commanding in the air. A Wearsider, Chilton had survived shrapnel wounds just after D-Day, and was
another player who had made a pre-war debut for United, having
signed professionl forms in 1938.

Right-half John Anderson had spent nine years on United's
books before making a story-book debut for the first team only a
few months before the Cup final. Anderson had joined the Navy
as a stoker at the outbreak of war and had seen service all over
the world.

Partnering John Carey at full-back was John Aston. Originally
an inside-forward, John Aston had been persuaded to play full-
back in the previous season and a few months after the Cup final
was to win the first of seventeen England caps. He was a strong
and loyal member of the side, and had seen service as a Marine
during the war. Twenty years after the Cup final in which he was
instrumental in taming the wily Stan Matthews, a proud John
Aston senior was to watch his son John play the game of his life
as a member of the victorious Manchester United team which
beat Benfica in the final of the European Cup.

In goal was Jack Crompton, another one of the six local-born
players in the side, and an ace penalty-saver ... ironically until
the Cup final. He was a member of the very first United team
ever selected by Matt Busby in October 1945, as were Henry
Cockburn, John Carey and Jack Rowley. Never spectacular, but
ever-dependable, Jack Crompton was to serve the club in various
capacities until 1981.

Collectively, the team's secret lay in their quick distribution of
the ball one to the other, often using one touch only, which could
speed it in a series of flowing passes at dazzling pace from defence
to attack in a few seconds. This, coupled with the ability, espe-

cially among the forwards, to interchange positions rapidly, made them difficult to play against and exciting to watch.

Compared with the modern game more goals were scored then, and more conceded: the fear of failure was not the spectre haunting teams and their managers as it is today. In the 1947-48 season, for example, Manchester United scored 95 goals and conceded 54, compared with similar figures of 71 and 41 in the 1983-84 season.

It may still have been a time of clothes and food rationing, but the nation, emerging from the gloom of six dark and dangerous years, longed for entertainment, and our national game was to provide blessed relief from the privations of the time.

Attendances at matches grew rapidly: $2\frac{1}{4}$ million paying customers attended Manchester City and Manchester United's games at Maine Road in the 1946-47 season, and United, in those days when no ground regulations were in force, were regularly watched by crowds of over 60,000. The huge banks of open terraces at Maine Road (one shilling and sixpence [$7\frac{1}{2}$p] to get in) were packed with supporters of both teams, decked out in scarves and rosettes, many of them whirling noisy rattles and indulging in good-humoured banter, perfectly safe in each others' presence.

Team selections were often announced by way of a cramped list of names chalked on boards and carried around the ground by youngsters who always seemed to walk too quickly for the names to be read. At half-time, the Beswick Prize Band played marches and selections from popular tunes of the day. And in those pre-floodlit days, the kick-off was as early as 2 p.m. for January fixtures, and when those winter Saturday evenings were at their murkiest, the final minutes of the game were often played out in semi-darkness.

The ball was all leather which, when soaked and covered in mud and then propelled by the likes of Jack Rowley, could knock out a defender if he was courageous (or foolhardy) enough to put his head in the way of the projectile. The pitches, especially in the winter months, became bare and very heavy – sophisticated drainage provision and under-soil heating were very much developments for the future.

Teams often finished the game with only ten men, or more

usually with the injured player hobbling on the wing, because no substitutes were allowed in those days.

It was a good life, but the rewards were not great. In 1948 the players were on a maximum wage of £12 a week during the season, and £10 a week in the close season. Manchester United trained every day, except Monday mornings when they all enjoyed a round of golf at Davyhulme. The players did their football training at the still-derelict Old Trafford, usually on the waste ground where the main stand is now. By today's standards, of course, the backroom facilities were very primitive.

But the players were glad to be professionals at a time when many jobs offered long hours and poor conditions, and happy to be playing for a wage which was not much greater than that earned by an ordinary working man. These were mature men whose impressionable years had been fashioned by Services discipline. Teenage players were relatively unknown; professional soccer players were more often than not in their late twenties and early thirties, still trying to make up for time lost to the war. Many sports, in fact, were still dominated by the heroes of the 1930s, like Stanley Matthews, Don Bradman, Joe Louis, Henry Cotton and Gordon Richards.

An indispensable and often sole resource for the historian of football of that time is what was written about the game in newspapers, magazines, and match programmes.

Two local journalists, Alf Clarke of the *Manchester Evening Chronicle* and Tom Jackson of the *Manchester Evening News*, were mainly responsible for chronicling the life of the club in the 1940s and 1950s in their daily articles. They also contributed features and opinions, 'Casual Comments' and 'United Topics' respectively, to the club's programme *United Review*, along with its editor Sidney Wicks. Both Alf Clarke and Tom Jackson wrote in loving detail about United's games and their players, and the facts they discovered and described permeate much of the content of this book.

But a particular debt is owed to Don Davies of *The Manchester Guardian*. 'Old International', as he signed himself, set a new standard of match reporting. Drawing on a full range of classical, literary and historical allusions, his reports were lyrical essays which captured much of the spirit of the game as it was played at the time. For many readers of his paper, the colour and flair of the 1948 and 1952 teams were perfectly mirrored in the style Don Davies used to describe their play.

All three men had watched and reported on the 1948 and 1952 teams, and ten years later were finding new superlatives to describe the next generation of young United stars. Tragically, Alf Clarke, Tom Jackson and Don Davies, in their own way an integral part of the team which represented Old Trafford and Manchester United on their trip to Belgrade for a European Cup game, were killed at Munich Airport on 6 February 1958, along with eight of the young players they had written about with such pride and affection. The world of football was a richer place for their presence, and an emptier one for their leaving.

The 1948 and 1952 teams began a tradition of success for Manchester United, culminating in further FA Cup successes in 1963, 1977, 1983 and 1985, and First Division Championships in 1956, 1957, 1965 and 1967, and, of course, a European Championship trophy in 1968. Matt Busby continued to fashion many exciting sides full of brilliant young players, but the inspiration for the quality of football those teams were to produce in front of millions of admirers, and which made Manchester United one of the most famous football clubs in the world, began with the side which won the FA Cup that April day in 1948: Jack Crompton; John Carey, John Aston; Johnny Anderson, Allenby Chilton, Henry Cockburn; Jimmy Delaney, Johnny Morris, Jack Rowley, Stan Pearson and Charlie Mitten.

This is their story.

# The Story Begins

The very first player of the 1948 side to make a League appearance for Manchester United was John Carey. On 25 September 1937, United, then a Second Division club, played against Southampton at Old Trafford: the season was a month old and United were playing badly. The *Manchester Guardian* report on the following Monday described it as a 'A Sorry Exhibition' by the team and continued:

> Manchester United suffered a humiliating defeat at the hands of Southampton (2-1), and a long-suffering crowd at Old Trafford was driven to vivid profanity. It was not so much the defeat, as the startling ineptitude and futility of United's performance that made the faithful speak not so much in sorrow as in wrath. The one bright feature of the game from Manchester's point of view was the play of Carey, a black-haired Irish youngster at inside-left. He was the one man on the side who used the ball thoughtfully, and for forty minutes he played so well and so ardently that he created the illusion that United were winning. Carey, at all events, did not deserve to have so disheartening an introduction to the Football League.

John Carey's black hair soon began to thin - the sight of his balding pate was the first thing that caused the devoted thousands to roar out their welcome at Old Trafford, as 'Captain' Carey led his team out at the trot. Any hair that remains now is snow white, but his memory is crystal clear as he recalls the events of more than forty years ago in his famous Irish brogue. He had always wanted to be a professional footballer, but owes his life-long involvement with Manchester United to one of those incredible quirks of fate which put him in the right place at the right time:

Louis Rocca, United's chief scout, came over one Saturday to sign up a player called Benny Gaughran who was playing centre-forward for

Bohemians at the time. Scott Duncan, United's manager, had already been over to watch him and wanted him for United. On that Saturday, however, Benny Gaughran signed for Glasgow Celtic. So Louis Rocca was persuaded by United's Dublin scout Billy Behan to stay until Sunday afternoon and have a look at me. I was playing inside-left for St James's Gate against Cork Athletic. So he stayed over and watched the game. I scored in the first minute and by half-time Rocca had made up his mind that he wanted me to go to Manchester United. That was only my sixth game for St James's Gate in the League of Ireland. I was only seventeen years old and still at school. I was studying to be a Civil Servant, but of course when the opportunity came along for me to be a professional footballer I was very pleased. I signed for United in November 1936 and started in the third team. Then I played a few games in the second team, only a few, then I got into the first team next season.

It was really between Stan Pearson and myself as to who was going to play inside-left - it used to work out that if the ground was heavy I'd play, and if it wasn't Stan would play. After a while, we were both in.

So even though initially United were pursuing Gaughran they captured Carey, and began a partnership which was to last even far beyond the time when John Carey ended his playing career with them in 1953. Together, United and Carey were to achieve much - and yet again United's 'Irish Connection' had produced another talented young footballer. Many years later, of course, it was to unearth another black-haired genius called George Best . . .

When the youthful Carey agreed to become a Manchester United player he was joining an unglamorous Second Division club, and when he arrived at Old Trafford there were enough people around who would have been able to tell him stories about the club which might have shaken the confidence of a lesser man.

There had been many bad moments for United in the 1920s and 1930s - between the First and Second World Wars the club suffered continual financial crises and was relegated and promoted three times. And all this drama was fought out in the long shadow thrown by Manchester's premier side, City, who reached (but lost) the FA Cup final in 1926 and 1933, finally beating Portsmouth 2-1 in the 1934 final. Students of coincidence would later note that playing right-half for Manchester City that day was a 24-year-old Scotsman called Matt Busby . . .

The 1937-38 season had opened badly for Manchester United

– Second Division football was bad enough, but poor Second Division football was intolerable. The supporters were demanding better football and more goals, which is why the appearance of young John Carey on that September Saturday in 1937 gave so much hope to the loyal but frustrated followers. The lad looked a useful forward . . . maybe he could score goals as well . . .

A few weeks later the headlines on the sports page of the *Manchester Evening Chronicle* read: 'United sign a new outside-left: Rowley from Bournemouth'. The report continued:

> He is nineteen years of age, stands 5 feet 9 inches and weighs 11 stones 7 pounds. He joined Bournemouth from Wolverhampton Wanderers and scored ten goals in eleven League games for them. He may play tomorrow against Sheffield Wednesday at Old Trafford. He is a notable capture – from all accounts he promises to develop into a star, and is described as a fast go-ahead winger.

Jack Rowley did play and got a warm reception from the crowd of 20,000 who saw United beaten 1–0 by the Yorkshire club. He played well in the first half but an injury to his inside-left partner meant that he had to forage alone on United's left flank. John Carey, despite his impressive debut game a few weeks before, was back in the reserve team.

Jack Rowley's legendary bluntness only emerges when he talks about the modern game, but he looks back with affection on the memories of his earliest days as a player, and his debut game for United:

I started my professional career at Wolverhampton Wanderers on the ground staff and I was playing in the reserves at the age of sixteen. In 1936 when I was eighteen and just before the season started, I had to go into hospital for a hernia operation. As I was recovering from the operation Wolves let me go to Bournemouth Football Club (which at the time was a nursery club for Wolves), as I thought on loan. I went straight in the first team but I was only there five months, playing outside left or outside right.

The Chairman of Manchester United then was Mr James Gibson who had a house down in Bournemouth. He used to be a frequent visitor to the Boscombe ground and he'd watched me a few times and fancied me. We were returning from Holland where we'd been playing, and fog at sea held us up a day, so instead of getting back on the Thursday morning we didn't get back until the small hours of Friday morning. Then the landlady of the digs woke me up and said, 'The manager wants to see you – will you get up and go to the ground straight away.' At the time I knew a few of the clubs had been watching me and one of the interested ones was Arsenal so I thought it might be them. I saw the manager and he said, 'Manchester United are very interested in you, are you interested in them?' At that time I was so dumbfounded I said, 'Where's Manchester and how far is it from Wolverhampton?' Then I said, 'Are you prepared to let me go?' and he said, 'Yes'. So I went and saw Scott Duncan who was in Bournemouth at the time. He said, 'I want you to come up today and play in the first team tomorrow.' 'Fair enough', I said and signed there and then. We caught the Pines Express which left Bournemouth at about ten past ten on the Friday morning and we got up into Manchester about six o'clock in the evening. We caught a bus and got off at Old Trafford. Mr Duncan put me up in the Trafford Hotel and I stopped there overnight. On the Saturday I met the rest of the players and went out and played outside-left. I'd only been playing about ten minutes and Ronnie Ferrier, the inside-left and a schoolteacher, got injured and was carried off, so my introduction to United was playing inside *and* outside-left. There were no substitutes then, of course. We finished the match and I went back to Bournemouth to pick up the rest of my belongings.

From then on I played outside-left and if the outside-right was having a bad game they'd switch me to outside-right. We had another two wingers at the time: Billy Bryant who was the outside-right, and Billy Wrigglesworth who came from Wolves like me and who could play on either wing. That's how I started . . .

Although no one knew it at the time, a third outstanding player was about to be introduced to the United supporters – a player who after the war was to develop into one of the most exciting inside-forwards ever seen at Old Trafford.

Sharp-eyed readers of 'Nomad's Sporting Gossip' column in the *Evening Chronicle* on Monday 1 November 1937 would have noticed a short paragraph which ran: 'I hear that Pearson who made his debut in the Central League team on Saturday was the outstanding forward against Chesterfield.' Later that week the paper reported that Stan Pearson, an 18-year-old Salford player, after only two games in the Central League team, was to get an early chance of proving his worth. He did not have long to wait. The young 'United-mad' Stan Pearson was picked for the first team against, ironically, Chesterfield, only a fortnight after

'Nomad's' prophetic note. It was a dream debut. Next Monday's *Manchester Guardian* report sang his praises:

> Pearson, a Salford-born inside-left who had previously made only two appearances for the Central League side, played the chief part in Manchester United's 7-1 win at Chesterfield. For four years United have 'nursed' him and the result is a young footballer with the self-possession of a veteran player. He was the key man in United's success, for he dribbled and combined in such a delightful way that not only did he provide the passes which led to four of the goals, but he knitted the usually ragged United attack into a smooth working machine. His abilities have been known at Old Trafford for a long time; only a belief that he might be too young for the hurly-burly of Second Division football has kept him relegated to the 'A' team.

United's left-half that day was Bert Whalley who of course, after the war, was to return as a player, then stay on at Old Trafford as a coach. Ten years after United's Cup success in 1948, Bert Whalley was to die at Munich with so many of another generation of United footballers.

Even though Stan Pearson made 304 appearances for United and played eight times for England, he remembers his first days as a United player with great clarity. Later he was to reveal an impressive memory for players and games and goals, although he was always characteristically modest about his own contribution to United's eventual success.

As a teenager Pearson played for Adelphi Lads' Club and Salford Boys, which is where United first spotted him and signed him as an amateur on the ground staff at seventeen years of age. Continuing the story, he said:

I'm one of the few people in this world who've been across the pitch at Old Trafford on my hands and knees getting weeds out with a little dibber and a bucket. They used to put string lanes about a yard wide across the pitch and about four or five of us used to have to do the weeding. Old Scott Duncan was the manager then and he used to come behind you and if you missed a weed he used to say, 'Hey, lad, come on, there's one here'.

I played a year in the 'A' team and finally made my debut in the first team on 13 November 1937. Funnily enough, the week before I'd made my debut in the United reserves against Chesterfield at Old Trafford and

the following week they pushed me into the first team against Chesterfield again and we won 7-1, not because of me though! It was a good
debut. I played quite a few games in the remaining part of that season
which was the season we won promotion to the First Division.

In that season John Carey made 16 first team appearances, Jack
Rowley 25, and Stan Pearson, still being nurtured carefully,
played 11 times. It was, in fact, a highly successful season. Despite being knocked out of the FA Cup by Brentford in the fifth
round, United scraped into second place in the League, in front
of Sheffield United on goal average, and managed thereby to gain
promotion to Division One with Aston Villa, and the tally of 82
goals they scored was helped by 9 from Rowley, 3 from Carey
and 2 from Pearson.

The next season, 1938-39, was very ordinary by any standards.
United were knocked out of the FA Cup in the third round by
West Bromwich Albion, who beat them 5-0 at Old Trafford,
having drawn 0-0 at The Hawthorns a few days beforehand.

The team that season usually read: Tapken (or Breedon); Redwood, Griffiths; Warner, Vose, McKay (or Manley); Wrigglesworth (or Bryant), Wassall, Hanlon, Carey, Rowley.

By now, John Carey and Jack Rowley were established first-
team members with 32 and 38 appearances respectively, but Stan
Pearson with only nine outings was still waiting for the chance to
establish himself fully. Rowley scored 10 goals, Carey 6 and Pearson 1 in a total of 57 – but the team that season conceded 65, and
finished fourteenth in the League, a mid-table position they had
occupied for most of the season.

One of the few encouraging signs that season was that United
won the Central League championship – reserve-team football at
Old Trafford before the war attracted the kind of interest and
support which many Second Division teams today would envy –
with a team that contained many names that were to play such a
significant part in the United story which was to follow, including
Allenby Chilton who was to make his first team debut next season.

The *Manchester Guardian*'s football reporter, writing about the
last match of the season, a 2-0 victory at Old Trafford against
Liverpool, perhaps glad that a dull season was over (and obviously looking forward to the cricket) waxed lyrically and pro-

phetically about the contribution of Liverpool's right-half to the game. This was to be the last game of any significance for six years (though nobody knew it then) and the man who played so well against Manchester United was ironically to find himself occupying an even more prominent role at Old Trafford and guide the club to hitherto unexplored pinnacles of success. The report concluded:

> Hardly a Liverpool attack that mattered did not owe its origins to one of those beautiful passes of Busby's, every one made with strokes that seemed to belong to cricket rather than to football – drives up the centre, square cuts to his right wing, mighty hooks and pulls to the left. Even the die-hards at Old Trafford must have been a little saddened by the sight of these gifts being wasted. Perhaps even Busby himself, the gentlest-mannered and most philosophic of footballers was moved to the point of remonstrance; at all events once in each half he suddenly made a most exciting single-handed attack on the United goal and these gave Breedon his only moments of real anxiety.

In the long hot summer of 1939 the nations of Western Europe flexed their muscles and once the holidays were over, the Government announced that children from the more vulnerable cities were to be evacuated 'as a precautionary measure'. But life had to continue. 'Everything As Normal' ran the slogans. There seemed to be no good reason why the football season should not start again, though even the greatest optimists could not be certain that it would be completed.

United's season got under way with a fixture against Grimsby, one of the previous year's FA Cup semi-finalists, at Old Trafford on Saturday, 26 August. The United team was: Breedon; Redwood, Griffiths; Warner, Vose, McKay; Bryant, Carey, Smith, Pearson and Wrigglesworth. United won 4–0 in front of 20,000 spectators, Carey, Pearson, Bryant and Wrigglesworth each scoring a goal. On the Wednesday of the following week United went down to Stamford Bridge and 15,000 spectators saw them draw 1–1 with Chelsea.

Nobody was to know that Manchester United's next game on Saturday, 2 September at Charlton was to be the last official League game they were to play for six years, and young Allenby Chilton wasn't to know that he was about to be picked for his first game for the first team, and that the next time he would play for them officially would also be six years later!

On Friday, 1 September United announced four changes in their team to play Charlton in London the next day: McKay, Vose, and Carey were injured and Johnny Hanlon was dropped. Both Allenby Chilton and 'Beau' Asquith were selected to make their debuts for United.

That same Saturday Jack Rowley, recovering from injury, was having a run-out at centre-forward with the reserves against Newcastle United reserves at Old Trafford, supported by a centre-half called Walter Winterbottom ...

The Friday newspapers declared that 'Football will be as usual tomorrow', but arriving at Euston that evening the United team found London blacked out, and it took them an hour to get by tube to their hotel in Marylebone. Ordinarily, the fixture would have attracted 40,000 spectators but only 6,000 had sufficient appetite to watch Charlton beat United 2-0 – when they were not watching the barrage balloons which swayed high above the Charlton ground.

Allenby Chilton, after a distinguished career with United and Grimsby, is now back home on his beloved Wearside. He recalled the events leading up to his debut game:

I was playing football in the Wearside League for various clubs, then for Seaham Colliery, then as an amateur for Liverpool. I was there for a month's trial and probably I could have signed for them (there were a few clubs after me at the time actually), but I was only eighteen or nineteen years old and I said, 'No, I'm going home'. However, the scout for Manchester United, Louis Rocca, had also seen me. It was on a Thursday, and my mother and father had a little pub in South Hylton and they were out and my brother and I had just come in from work and opened the bar and this chap came in and said, 'Would you like to sign for Manchester United?' and I said, 'Look, I'm already on amateur forms for Liverpool'. He said, 'If I can get you clearance from Liverpool, will you sign?' I said, 'On professional forms? Straight away!' And within a fortnight I was down in Manchester and I signed for United on 26 November 1938.

I played in the reserves – along with Walter Winterbottom and Bert Whalley, Billy Porter, George Roughton, Bill Bryant, Jack Smith, Tommy Manley, Johnny Hanlon ... he was a boy there, Johnny ...

I got a Central League medal in my first year. The standard of football at that level was very high and we used to get terrific crowds.

In the summer of 1939 I tore my ligaments and I came up here to Wearside. I stayed at home and every day I went into the sea to strengthen my leg up.

At the start of the 1939 season it was much better so I started to train ... then I was picked for the first team in place of George Vose and we played away at Charlton and we got beat 2-0 and I had quite a good game. War was declared next day and I came home. All football was suspended immediately and players' contracts were cancelled. I had already registered with the militia and after about seven weeks I was called up. My second official League match for United was nearly seven years later - against Grimsby Town on 31 August 1946!

If Allenby Chilton had cursed Hitler on the Monday after his first game for Manchester United, eleven other players from a Third Division team would have joined him. On the same afternoon that Chilton had made his debut, Bournemouth had beaten Northampton Town 10-0 at Dean Court. It was the only occasion in the club's history that they had reached double figures in a League game, and because war was declared the following day, the score was not officially recognised!

So as the country made preparations for war everybody connected with Old Trafford could now only speculate about what might have been that season. The early signs had been promising. After three games United were tenth in the First Division with three points - Blackpool headed the League with six points. The team was playing well - Pearson, Carey and Rowley were gaining in confidence and experience, and the tall, strong Chilton promised much.

Events were to dictate that six troubling and uncertain years were to pass before the team could form itself again. When the players regrouped at the beginning of the 1945-46 season a few faces were sadly missing. Old Trafford had been badly damaged in a German bombing raid and the pitch was unplayable. Scott Duncan had gone, and in his place was a young Scotsman called Matt Busby ...

# The War Years

On Sunday, 3 September 1939 Britain declared war on Germany. By then most clubs had played only three games of the new season, but the Football League competition was abandoned immediately, and the English and Scottish Associations cancelled all professional contracts.

Conscription had started as early as May 1939 for men aged twenty and twenty-one, and on the outbreak of war was extended to apply to all able-bodied men between eighteen and forty. Clubs realised that their young footballers would soon be in uniform and posted anywhere, and in acknowledgment of this difficulty the Football Association and League decided that regular competitions would be abandoned in favour of regional competitions played home and away on consecutive weeks. The Association and League also agreed to the principle of 'guesting' - so clubs fortunate enough to be near military establishments could use any League players posted near them as 'guests'. Some clubs were better favoured than others. Lucky Aldershot were able to call on the services of a total of thirty-one international players to assist them in wartime football!

In those first few tense weeks after the declaration of war, clubs were urged to play friendly matches until the fixtures could be reorganised. Already more than $3\frac{1}{2}$ million people had been evacuated from the major cities, and attendance in the early wartime regional leagues was limited to 8,000 in the more vulnerable areas. So only a couple of weeks after Chamberlain's sad message to the people of Britain, 4,600 managed to watch Manchester United beat Oldham 3-1 - digging over the allotment or helping the wife to measure black-out curtains could surely wait for a couple of hours. United also played friendlies against Manchester City (at Old Trafford) and away at Stoke City and Blackpool before the regional competition which started for Manchester

United on 21 October 1939 against Manchester City at Old Trafford. To pad out the fixture list, clubs were also encouraged to
arrange 'friendlies'.

Allenby Chilton, along with other United players, returned
home to await the inevitable call to arms, but Rowley, Pearson
and Carey managed to make quite a few appearances before they
were needed.

A young outside-left called Charlie Mitten also managed to
play a few games for the United seniors in the early months of
the war. He had been on United's books as a boy, and later was
to emerge as one of the great characters of the side, and was part
of the brilliant forward line that won the Cup for United in 1948.

Everybody who saw or played with this popular outside-left
seems to have their favourite Charlie Mitten memory, but nobody
at this time could have foreseen the extraordinary development of
his career after the war – even his boyhood was a little out of the
ordinary:

My father was an Englishman and in the Royal Scots Regiment and he
married my mother and she went with him when he was posted to India,
which is how I came to be born in Rangoon. Being English and born in
Rangoon causes great confusion when I apply for a passport!

We returned home when I was about five and went to live in Glasgow.
My father had been a Physical Training Instructor in the Regiment and
he was an amateur international hockey player and boxer and my mother
was also a good tennis player. He left the Regiment and took a job in
Dunblane in Perthshire as a sports instructor at Queen Victoria Boys'
School. I joined the school when I was twelve or thirteen. It was a
military school and run on military lines . . . you lived in dormitories and
had parades and promotions. And you were taught skills like playing a
musical instrument. I actually played bagpipes in the pipe-band march-
ing up and down at Murrayfield when Scotland played the All Blacks
round about 1935–36! They also taught us shoemaking, shooting, how to
live off the land, map reading. And the school was hot stuff on sports –
athletics, rugby . . . it was a very good rugby school.

When I was about fourteen I was playing football for a little team
called Strathallan Hawthorns – a little village between Dunblane and
Stirling. I played every Saturday and got ten shillings for expenses! I
was spotted there by a United scout who asked me if I'd like to come to
United and so I came as one of the juniors at fifty shillings a week. We
paid thirty shillings for digs which were run by a charming lady called
Mrs Elliot in Stretford, near the Quadrant pub. Also in our digs was a

member of the first team, a chap called Jack Wassall. We became good friends.

I played in the United 'A' team with people like Stan Pearson, Sammy Lynn, Ruben Scott, Johnny Hanlon, and John Carey came to join us later. I always thought John Carey was very cumbersome in those days, leggy, like a bloody big colt. He needed time to develop his strength. The further back in position John went the better he got. Rocca and Behan obviously knew how good he was going to be. He was also a good goalkeeper and a good centre-half. He made his name as a right-back of course but he'd learned his skills up front. You never saw John wildly kick a ball . . . he always did something sensible with his passes.

When I was seventeen they called me into the office and they said they'd like me to sign full-time: 'ten pounds now and ten pounds when you play your first game in the first team'. The war came and I played for the first team before I joined up, so as soon as I got back to Old Trafford I went up to Walter Crickmer and said, 'Now, Walter, you owe me a tenner and I'm not kicking a ball until I get it!'

By the end of his career John Carey was regarded on the field as the quintessential captain full-back - thoughtful, consistent and a true sportsman. But as a vigorous 19-year-old Irishman he was to suffer the ultimate punishment in a League War Cup match at Old Trafford against Blackburn Rovers on 4 May 1940. 'Old International' wrote:

This week 'my cue is villainous melancholy with a sigh like Tom o'Bedlam'. Carey, of Manchester United, our black-haired gentler version of the incomparable Doherty, was requested by the referee to accompany Guest of Blackburn Rovers to the dressing room, presumably for conduct unbecoming sportsmen and gentlemen. Three minutes only remained for play in a brilliant match. United were winning handsomely; then our eyes fell upon two of the gladiators mixed up in a private scuffle. Carey and Guest were soon identified and arraigned as the culprits. An Irishman, coming away from the match, described them as 'poor craythurs that couldn't do anybody any harm - a couple o' game cocks breastin' wan against the other' and he voiced the feelings of many. Carey and Guest had transgressed, beyond doubt, but they were shocked, as we were, when the blow fell!

By all accounts the referee's decision seemed unjust, and most reports were fulsome in their praise for Carey's display of footballing skill that day – after all, he had scored one of the goals in the United's 2–1 victory.

One young player on United's books had reconciled himself to not being able to try for a first team place until after the war, whenever that was going to be. John Anderson, at seventeen years of age, had realised that famous guest players were ruling out any chances he might have of playing wing-half for United. But John got his chance earlier than he expected, and there was a twist to the story.

Born and bred in Salford, he had signed for United as an amateur of sixteen in 1937, having played for Adelphi Lads Club, Brindle Heath Lads Club, Salford Boys and Lancashire Boys. He continued the story:

Football of one kind or another ran in the family. My dad played professional Rugby League for Swinton and Warrington so he was quite pleased when I signed for United. When I was seventeen I signed as part-time professional. I was working in the evenings but I trained during the day with all the pre-war players ... men like Breen and Breedon the goalkeepers, Griffiths, Porter, Vose, Brown, McKay, Manley, Billy Wrigglesworth, Jack Griffiths, Billy Bryant, Harry Baird, Jack Rowley, of course. As a young lad I used to go into the dressing-room when we were training and wait until all those lads had got their pegs and then I used to creep in and hang my stuff up! Then I played 'A' team football ... along with Charlie Mitten and Johnny Morris and Allen Chilton.

In 1940 I was working nights on the *Manchester Guardian*. One Saturday in May, United were playing Stoke City away and I was in bed on the Saturday morning and Stan Pearson came round (he lived in Salford as well) and said, 'You're playing away against Stoke this afternoon!' I was up like a shot and out with him. I was just eighteen then, and I'd been picked for the first team. Stoke City had a great side then ... Herod in goal, Frankie Soo, Steele, Stan Matthews, of course. Anyway I had a good game and Walter Crickmer said he was very pleased with me.

The next game was the last of the season and I got a postcard saying 'You are selected to play against Everton at Old Trafford ...'.

The Chairman then was Mr Gibson and as soon as I reported to the ground he came up to me and put his arm around me and said, 'Johnny, you won't be playing this afternoon'. I could have fallen through the floor! The United forward line that day had Matthews again (this time he was guesting for us) and Alec Herd in it ... I had thought it was going to be wonderful to have a chance to play behind Stan Matthews.

Mr Gibson said, 'With you being a young lad, we've got to have a more experienced wing-half to play behind Stan Matthews to spoon feed him so we've brought in a Liverpool player called Matt Busby to play in your place.' He added, 'Don't worry, you'll get your money.'

I was very upset not to be playing but Mr Gibson said, 'You come up into the directors' box and watch with me.' So I watched the game from there.

By the way, the man I should have marked, that Matt actually had to mark, was a chap called Stevenson, a little inside-left and he scored all three goals, and United didn't get any so I didn't feel too bad then! Anyway I was so fed up at being dropped I went and joined the Navy!

Fate was to play another trick on John Anderson – it was 21 December 1947 before he was asked to turn out again for Manchester United's first team. After the war there was great competition for places in United's half-back line, and Anderson's selection on that day in December was to take place in fairly dramatic circumstances. He played brilliantly but made only fifteen appearances that Cup winning season – even his selection for the 1948 Cup final was a last-minute affair, as in fact was his goal for United, nine minutes from the full-time whistle.

The Football League's plan for the 1940–41 season was that in the place of the many small regional divisions of the last season, the new tournament was to have only two divisions, North and South, each with thirty-four clubs.

Guesting continued to be a feature of life in the leagues at that time and team selection was often chaotic. Players tried to get away from camps and depots in good time but often trains were held up or connections were missed.

But, like the previous season, it was a good opportunity to blood young players. The inside-right of the United team picked to play against Rochdale at Spotland on 31 August 1940 was a lad called John Aston, who later gave such devoted service to the club for many years as a player, coach and scout. He recalls:

In 1937 I was playing local football, I'd be about sixteen at the time. There was an article in one of the Manchester evening papers saying that

a group of Manchester schoolteachers was thinking of forming a junior
team to be supported and sponsored by Manchester United, and they
invited local lads around the age of sixteen to write in. The overall
intention, of course, was to create a sort of nursery of young players who
would eventually, if they were good enough, get into the United first
team. They would be amateurs but would be duty bound to sign for
United if they were thought good enough to be professionals. Unknown
to me my father wrote in and I was invited for trials at the end of the
1937-38 season. I had played for Crossley Lads, then Clayton Method-
ists. I helped to organise this side and I was very happy playing for them
... I'd got together some good youngsters from where I worked, and one
or two lads from the chapel I went to, and it was a very good side.

In the meantime I'd left them, of course, and having gone through the
trials had started to play for this Manchester United Junior Athletic
Club team and we were very successful straight away, I remember, in
the Chorlton Amateur League. It was a well-organised League and ran
three Divisions. Because we were a new team and a Junior side (the
League was all-age) we had to begin in the Third Division. We skated it
... we were winning in double figures every week and soon got promoted.
We also reached the semi-finals of the Cup. Three teams were the first,
second, and third in the First Division ... and the fourth team was us!
We were beaten in extra time (we were playing men, remember) by the
eventual winners who won the League also. But that MUJAC team was
good and well-organised and I dare say that half the team would probably
have signed professional if the war hadn't come along just then. In that
first season we scored about 300 goals, I think. I could rhyme that team
off now. The centre-forward was a lad called Jack White ... he lived in
Trafford Park ... he was a big, strong, raw-boned lad ... an ideal
centre-forward ... he got ninety-odd goals. The inside left was called
Stanley Mears, the son of an ex-professional ... he lived in Ardwick and
died during the war – I think it was of TB – round about 1943 ... he
was a great player ... very similar in style to Stan Pearson. Stan Mears
and I got sixty or seventy goals apiece ... so it was a good trio. And I
remember particularly two excellent goalkeepers named Higgins (he was
a Clayton lad like me) and Stafford, and they used to play alternate
games.

Actually it was Louis Rocca, the old United chief scout who got us to
sign professional forms ... and we were supposed to get a ten pound
signing on fee ... I never got that ... and me and a few others had to
claim that off Matt Busby a few years later. Louis had done us. He was
a shrewd old beggar, old Louis ... what a character he was!

I was the first member of the original MUJAC side to break into the
United 'A' team. We were all about sixteen or seventeen. All the time,

trials were still going on for MUJACs and that's when Johnny Morris appeared on the scene. He was brilliant. He was only about fourteen ... about three years younger than me, and you could see he was going to be a player. He was a little chubby-cheeked lad with dark curly hair ... he looked a picture of health.

Then war broke out and football stopped ... then after a few weeks they organised regional football and players were being drafted into the Services and they started guesting for clubs all over the country.

At the beginning of the 1940–41 season I was picked for the first team against Rochdale at Spotland ... on the wing and I scored. I was picked because nearly all the first team players had been drafted or were working in the munitions factory at Trafford Park and they couldn't get off. I played ten first team games that season then United started getting guest players.

The first match I played at home was against Bury I think it was ... I hit the post and overall I thought I'd played well but blow me, the next game they dropped me for some big name. I was so upset! It was difficult to get a game anywhere then because even all the Cheshire League clubs like Hyde United and Droylsden and Ashton United and Altrincham were giving games to senior players and young professionals from League clubs who were guesting for them because they'd been posted locally.

Anyway I went to play with Hyde United, along with Charlie Mitten and another young United player called Georgie Curliss, a brilliant full-back who was later killed ... quite early in the war ... he went in very young. There were some City players in that side as well ... like Joe Fagan (the former Liverpool manager) and Billy Walsh. We had a smashing team and I was better off than when I was at United! They were giving me three pounds a week with a bit extra if we won ... my wages at work were a pound a week ... I've never been so well off in my life!

The 'Phoney War' on the Western Front was now over, and the realisation was deepening that the conflict was going to last a long time. Nearly 350,000 British and Allied soldiers had been rescued from under the noses of the Germans at Dunkirk, but national morale was at a low ebb. Winston Churchill tried to rally the nation with brave words, but the country knew that nothing would ever be quite the same again. Even when City and United met at Maine Road in October 1940 there seemed nothing left of the old spirit of rivalry: United fielded five guest players and Rowley, Pearson and Chilton were 'not available'. At the time John Carey was still around and Charlie Mitten and John Aston were only getting the odd game yet 'improving noticeably' as a newspaper of the day reported.

Clubs did their best to provide a show – making up their teams from young players, guests and often volunteers from the crowd, who for ninety minutes could live out a fantasy which only a true football fan would be able to understand. 'Old International' reported a game played between United and Blackburn Rovers at Stockport on Monday 30 December 1940, which United were to win 9–0.

> At three o'clock Blackburn Rovers were still four players short, so a friendly press-gang went round the Stockport ground and invited members of the crowd to step inside the dressing room and try on 'the clobber'. Presumably those who found a pair of boots to fit them got their places. Anyway, the hero of this match was 'little Hallam', the Rovers right-half, on loan from the crowd. No queue of club managers will jostle for his signature, but the crowd will remember him. At first they sniggered at this unknown novice, with the short squat figure of a Welsh miner; legs nicely bowed; hair rough; cheeks hollow; but eyes bright with the light of battle; and fighting to the last ditch. Then they realised his worth and paid him a ceaseless tribute of mingled laughter and cheers. Here was a type they could understand – one of the world's nobodies doing his job with uncomplaining gallantry and spirit yet doomed to go under. If the ball struck him it knocked him flat. If he kicked at it he turned a somersault. Yet after each encounter he scraped himself together, as he would in a ten-round contest with Joe Louis, rose shakily and waded in for the next.

The war had now moved to a more intense phase: from September 1940 until May 1941 the Germans carried out their plan to 'blitz' Britain into submission. The whole population was in danger, and the citizens of large urban areas like London, Coventry and Manchester were particularly vulnerable.

On the night of Tuesday, 11 March 1941, the inevitable happened. Old Trafford, on the edge of the industrial complex of Trafford Park and Salford Docks, received a direct hit from a bombing raid.

Wednesday's *Manchester Guardian* carried a report of chilling brevity, not least because newspapers of the day were not permitted to be specific about details or locations:

> High explosive and incendiary bombs were dropped by enemy aircraft during a fairly heavy attack on inland areas in North-West England last

night ... Slight damage was done to dwelling houses in one or two working-class districts and slight outbreaks of fire were reported from a football ground where incendiaries fell on the main stand, and the dressing rooms were damaged by high explosives.

Walter Crickmer, the United Secretary who was also a member of the Police Volunteer Service Reserve, reached the Old Trafford buildings when they were blazing and remained there until next morning. 'It was heartbreaking to see our main stand ablaze. I tried to reach the dressing rooms to save the kit but could not get anywhere near', he told reporters.

When dawn broke on that Wednesday morning and the smoke finally cleared, Old Trafford lay in ruins. The kit and boots, as Crickmer feared, had been lost. It was plain that there would be no more football there 'for the duration'.

Near neighbours Manchester City immediately offered United the use of their ground at Maine Road (each playing their home matches there on alternate Saturdays) and City also loaned them boots and kit.

United, under the War Damage Act, later submitted a compensation claim for damage 'caused to their ground by enemy action estimated at £45,000', but it was to be nearly ten years before Old Trafford was to hear the roar of welcome as the first team emerged to play its first game at a rebuilt stadium. By then, of course, they had gained a new manager, and won the FA Cup and a reputation which was to make them one of the most famous football clubs in the world.

Meanwhile the Football League continued to encourage a multitude of cup and trophy competitions. The League North, in which United played, had its League Championship and Cup, but Manchester United never featured as winners at any time during the war, although Blackpool, with its strong contingent of guest players serving in the RAF at Squires Gate airfield a few miles to the south, won the North Regional Cup and League competitions several times. United, however, did manage to seal the 1940–41 season by beating Burnley 1–0 in the final of the Lancashire Cup at Turf Moor with a team which read: Breedon; Topping, Roughton; Warner, Porter, Whalley; Smith, Carey (who scored the only goal), Rowley, Pearson and Mitten.

Don Davies had the last prophetic word in his report of the

match: 'The new Pearson–Mitten wing is one of the treasures United are hoarding for us against the advent of a just peace.'

At this time newspapers carried as much detail as they could on the wars being fought on many fronts all over the globe, and football reporting suffered from the consequent lack of space. Even the *Manchester Guardian* could often only spare a single column in Monday's edition ... and there were the competing claims of Rugby Union and Manchester University sports activities to satisfy. League matches were often summarised in a line or two, and the players' names were not always given. A little was better than nothing, and the newspapers sent from home would be read eagerly and any details would be relished by the United fans, many of whom were by now in uniform and thousands of miles from Old Trafford.

Manchester United's first game of the 1941–42 season at Maine Road saw Jack Rowley ('ludicrously dominant') scoring seven goals in a 13–1 rout of New Brighton. Jack was beginning to emerge as a goal-scoring centre-forward of formidable power, spoken of in the same terms as the legendary Dixie Dean. He was now serving in the South Staffordshire Regiment:

I still got off occasionally to play for Manchester United and if I didn't play for them I played for Wolves or Walsall. We were posted to Worcester and I had to play for the depot on Saturdays or they used to let me off to play for Manchester United. Then I was posted to Northern Ireland and I used to play for Distillery over there. After Northern Ireland we were on invasion training at Folkestone and Dover and while I was down there I used to go up to London and play for Tottenham.

Jack went over with the invasion forces in 1944 and at the end of the war was posted back to his original depot at Worcester, where he was able to play for United until he was demobbed. He was picked many times for representative sides, once as inside-left for an Army team which included Frank Swift, Stan Cullis, Joe Mercer and Tommy Lawton and beat an FA XI 5–2 at Stoke on 11 March 1944. Two months later he was a late replacement in an England side which earned a 2–0 victory against Wales in Cardiff.

A report of the 1941–42 season also mentions Johnny Morris

as 'a promising young stylist who gave a nice display in United's
7-1 victory over Stockport'. Morris had been given a chance to
play for the first team before he was seventeen years old, and
John Aston in particular had already noticed the sharp brilliance
of the stocky young Radcliffe lad when they had played in the 'A'
team together before the war. Morris was soon to become a
trooper in the Royal Armoured Corps and be posted abroad very
near the end of the war (and therefore be one of the last to return
home), but in the few games he managed to play for the first team
he left an impression on the minds of spectators and football
reporters as an exciting, aggressive player who would be bound
to figure in Old Trafford's post-war forward line. In November
1944, Alf Clarke, the senior football reporter of the *Manchester
Evening Chronicle*, wrote prophetically in a programme note: 'The
more I see of Morris, United's soldier inside-right, the more I
realise that, in him, United have a potential post-war star.'

Johnny Morris, still dark-haired and twinkle-eyed, remembered how it all began:


Arsenal was always the big team when I was a lad, but Manchester City
always did well. When United asked me to play for them I didn't know
where Old Trafford was ... I had to ask the way to the ground. As a kid
I'd never heard of them. It was always Bury, Bolton and Manchester
City.

I was recommended to United by a man who was manager of Bury
FC at the time. His name was Norman Bullock. He had a friend
who was manager of Manchester United called Jimmy Porter, who
looked after the club between Rocca and Scott Duncan. I had just left
school.

When I was fifteen Bert Whalley and I were loaned out to Bolton
Wanderers as guest players for a season. Then I went back to United at
sixteen and I travelled with them mainly as a reserve player and eventually I played for the first team before I was seventeen.

At eighteen of course I had to go into the Forces. It was 1942 then. I
came home at weekends to play occasionally. Then I went to Germany
and didn't play for fifteen or sixteen months, and then I went out to
India. I played some football in a touring side ... there were two ...
actually Stan Pearson was in one and I was in the other. When we were
out in India, Stan and I would talk and he used to say, 'What are we
going to do when we get back? United are doing quite well and they've
got about twelve inside-forwards there already!'

Meanwhile John Anderson, after his single senior appearance, was now in uniform. He was determined to continue playing football but did not find getting a game quite so easy:

I joined the Navy in June 1940. Because I was a volunteer they said I could have a choice – a seaman or a cook or a telegraphist – all at two shillings a day, or a stoker at two shillings and sixpence a day. I said, 'I'll be a stoker' ... true professional you see, do anything for sixpence extra! After my initial training I was sent to Devonport and I thought I'd try to get a game of football so I went to see the chief PT instructor. I said, 'I've come to see if you'll fix me up with a game of football.'

He got his pen and a form and started to ask all the normal questions ... name ... rank ... mess number ... official number (DKX109392 ... you never forget that!) ... what position do you play ... who did you play for ... I said, 'Manchester United'. There was a pause. He threw his pen down using a bit of naval language. He said, 'Every bugger who comes in here, they've either played for Manchester United or Arsenal or Chelsea or West Brom ... eff off!' So I off'd in a seamanlike manner!

I thought, 'This is good this, where am I going to get a game of football now?' So I went across to Plymouth Argyle's ground. Jack Tresardern was the manager at the time and welcomed me with open arms. He said, 'We're playing Exeter away on Saturday, would you like a game? We don't get many pro footballers in the Navy, they all seem to join the Army or the Air Force.'

It was two pounds a match I think, which wasn't bad ... because I was getting less than that a week in the Navy! I got a good write-up in the local paper, we'd beaten Exeter and I'd scored a goal.

On the Monday morning I got a message: 'Stoker Anderson to report to the Chief PTI's office at once'. When I got there and saw him he said, 'Oh, so you *are* a pro footballer. That's good ... you can play for the barracks now.' I said, 'I'm sorry I can't, I'm playing for Plymouth Argyle.' He said, 'Listen, son, if you don't play for the Navy you'll not be in barracks very long!' He obviously meant he'd get me drafted. I think I only played three or four times for Plymouth and then I was posted. I only got the worst draft there is in the Navy ... they sent me to Freetown in Sierra Leone, West Africa, right on the Equator! I spent twelve months there. I was in the Navy for six years, and I played for them in West Africa, South-East Africa, Italy, Egypt, Ceylon, China, Hong Kong, Australia, even in the South Sea Islands against Fiji. Out of the six years I was four years eight months abroad ... that PTI really did for me!

Les Olive has been Manchester United's Secretary since his predecessor Walter Crickmer was killed in the Munich air crash in

1958. His memories of Old Trafford began when he joined the
staff as a 14-year-old office boy in 1942. Three years later, and
only a few weeks after Matt Busby arrived as manager, Les Olive
was called up and returned to Old Trafford in July 1948, having
listened to the radio commentary of the 1948 Cup final in Egypt.
Today, he is responsible for overseeing the administration of one
of the most famous football clubs in the world, but the weight of
that responsibility has not dulled the memory of events forty
years ago:

I left school at fourteen in the summer of 1942 and was working as a
telegram delivery boy with the Post Office in Manchester. I wanted to
continue playing football so I wrote to United asking for a trial as a
player. Just at that time the lady in the office wanted to give up her job
because she didn't want to face the winter here, and so Walter Crickmer,
the Secretary, offered me an office job, as well as a chance to play in the
Colts team. I'd only been working at the Post Office three weeks but I
handed in my notice and came to work here at Old Trafford. At that
time there were only two office staff here, me and Walter Crickmer.
Walter was the Secretary, but because the war was on he worked only
part-time here ... the rest of the time he had a job in the Chairman's
company, Cornbrook Cold Air Stores, which handled lards and frozen
foods and fats. The stores were on Hadfield Street, around the corner
from the Northumberland Hotel where the old City Road and Chester
Road meet. It was only five minutes on the bike from here and both
Walter and I went to and from home and the ground and Cornbrook by
bike. Because of Cornbrook's connections with United it used space at
Old Trafford for storage as well, and we also rented space beneath the
stand over at Maine Road. Very often, I remember, they'd get a delivery
there in the late afternoon and they'd get on the phone to me to see if I
could cycle over and give them a lift to yank these 28 lb blocks of fat and
lard into the store!
By the time I joined, Old Trafford had been bombed, of course, and
all you could see inside the ground was the twisted metal girders and the
overgrown weeds where the main stand is now. The pitch itself was
alright, but of course we couldn't accommodate spectators back here
until 1949.
During the war it was a bit of a scramble to get a team out but Walter
Crickmer was in touch with all the local Army and RAF units so we
could draw on some of their players. We had certain players who were
in the munitions works at Trafford Park ... they trained here Tuesday
and Thursday nights ... and one of my jobs was to send out postcards
to the players giving them the arrangements for the weekend match. The

players got thirty shillings a match plus expenses. At the same time we ran an 'A' team and a Colts team and I acted as their Secretary. Occasionally we'd have a practice match at the ground here. I remember that one of Walter Crickmer's jobs was to cut the grass and keep it under control, although we also had an old groundsman called Bob Roberts who lived in the end house on Warwick Road, number 24.

Louis Rocca was around at the time. During the war he worked only part-time as a scout, but when I got back to Old Trafford after my National Service he was back here full time. He was quite a character. I think he was a diabetic and he had a restricted diet of sandwiches and a glass of milk at lunchtime. If I was around he'd always offer me bits of these strange-tasting sandwiches. Another thing I remember about him was when he put in his expenses. It was sometimes one shilling and sixpence to go into the game and threepence for a cup of tea and a bun ... or if he went mad and was going a distance he had a meal which was two shillings and sixpence and a tip of threepence for the waitress!

Walter Crickmer had been here since 1918 and had seen the club through all its hard times, and the years of strikes and unemployment. During the war he'd call in the club in the morning, go to his job at Cornbrook and then call back in the evening at about 4.30 just to see what had been going on and to sign any letters. Louis Rocca and a chap called Jimmy Porter dealt with the playing side and Walter would keep the wheels turning and liaise with the directors. He was, as they used to say, 'Mister Manchester United'. He was a short man and had tremendous energy ... even at the time of the Munich accident - he'd be about fifty-eight - he used to run up and down the stairs here two at a time. He couldn't just walk up, he had to be there in a hurry.

I lived in Salford and even before I came to work here I occasionally used to watch United at Maine Road, when I could afford the bus fares and the sixpence or so admission. I also watched them at Maine Road when I came on leave from the Air Force. I always used to stand in the crowd behind the left-hand goal. I remember that during the war Jack Rowley came up and played here fairly regularly. Stan Pearson played occasionally ... John Carey I think went overseas fairly quickly and I don't recall him playing a lot. I can also remember some of the younger players beginning to emerge. Henry Cockburn was only on the small side but he always did extremely well in the air for the size he was, and also in the tackle ... he timed them so well that he would often come out with the ball against somebody twice as big as he was. He was a lovely character ... bubbling all the time. Johnny Morris had come through the 'A' team and then at eighteen went off in the Army ... he played first team football occasionally. He was obviously an extremely good player and everyone was counting the days till he got back ... as they were doing for all the players.

I left the club for National Service soon after Sir Matt arrived and in those days it was still a hand-to-mouth existence. It was only a couple of years later when you saw the team together that you began to be hopeful and think they were going to go places. By all accounts we were beginning to get the nucleus of a good side together when war broke out, because the players we've been talking about were round the twenty mark, but the club was unlucky that they missed those five or six years when these players could have got together so much earlier and had a longer time together and made a name for themselves and the club much sooner.

The Football League and Football Association continued to satisfy the beleaguered nation's appetite for football by organising international matches and representative games, usually against Services sides. Wartime and 'Victory' internationals did not count as full internationals, and caps were not awarded. England played Scotland and Wales many times, especially during the latter part of the war, and were rarely beaten, mainly because players like Stan Matthews, Raich Carter, Tommy Lawton, Joe Mercer, Jimmy Hagan and Frank Swift were at their peak.

On 3 February 1944 England beat Scotland 3-2 at Villa Park in perhaps the most exciting football international of the war in front of 66,000 fans. The man of the match, it was generally agreed, was Matt Busby, Scotland's captain and right-half who apparently played like two men. Scotland's goal in the 1-1 draw was scored by a little right-winger from Glasgow Celtic called Jimmy Delaney who later was also to have such an important part to play in the story of the 1948 United side.

Matt Busby and Jimmy Delaney had always featured prominently in Scottish wartime International teams (and Johnny Carey had played many times for Ireland during this period), but a minor controversy was caused by Charlie Mitten, now a 23-year-old PT instructor in the RAF.

When the teams were announced for the Scotland versus England clash at Hampden Park on 22 April 1944, Charlie Mitten had been picked as a reserve for Scotland. The Scottish FA said Mitten was a Scotsman, but the English FA (who had been keeping an eye on him as a future England prospect, not least for his brilliant displays for Chelsea) said he was English. He had been

born in Rangoon, but his father was English, even though he had
served in a Scottish regiment and was living now in Scotland. It
was revealed at the time, incidentally, that Charlie Mitten's
mother was Irish!

The Scottish FA had apparently always regarded Mitten as a
Scotsman, because they had understood Mitten's father and
grandfather had been born in Scotland. As it happens, Charlie
Mitten did not get a game, and England beat Scotland 3–2 in
front of a huge 133,000 crowd at Hampden Park. Sadly, Mitten
was never to win an International cap, although he did play for
England in the unofficial 'Bolton Disaster Fund' international at
Maine Road in 1946.

But the story has run ahead of the characters. What was happening to those promising young players whose careers had been
so cruelly interrupted by a war which had to be fought?

At the outbreak of war John Carey decided to stay in Manchester and look for work whilst waiting for his call-up:

I went to Metrovicks, the aircraft factory in Trafford Park. The year
after the war started I got married and then I was called up and I served
in the Army in North Africa and Italy and I was there for three and a
half years before the war finished and I was repatriated.

During the war I remember being selected for Ireland thirty days
before the match and everybody said this was a record because they
didn't usually select teams thirty days before a match. They did this
because they didn't know whether I'd be able to get home or not since
I was in Italy at the time. Actually I don't think I managed to get home
for that match! But eventually I managed to restart my International
career, because I was first capped in 1937 against Norway for the Republic of Ireland, and I more or less stayed in the team until 1953 when
I retired. I won caps for both Eire and Northern Ireland because at the
time Northern Ireland felt that it had the right to choose players from
the whole of Ireland so they often picked players from the South like
Con Martin, Peter Farrell . . . I suppose there were five or six of us from
the South who played for Northern Ireland. I got seven caps for them
and twenty-nine for Southern Ireland.

As a professional of course I was obviously prepared to play for both.
I once played against England on the Saturday in Belfast for Northern
Ireland and against them on the Monday for the Republic of Ireland. I
got two fees so I was alright!

Stan Pearson, who had made such a promising debut in 1937, continued to develop his footballing skills far from the smoky streets of Salford:

I was very fortunate in that I got to play a lot of football during the war. I joined up and was eventually posted to India. The drill was that after the boat docked in Bombay the troops went to a holding camp in a place called Doolali for about three weeks then they were pushed up to where all the fighting was in Burma.

I'd been there about ten days and the Adjutant sent for me and said, 'We see from your records you're a professional footballer. We're sending a team to Bombay to take part in two knock-out competitions. You'll be in Bombay as long as you're in both competitions. As soon as you're knocked out of them both it's back here and God knows what'll happen then – you could go anywhere.' He thought that if I could play for Manchester United I must be better than some they'd got! We won both competitions. Of course they wouldn't let me go then – and I was given a soft job in the stores. Then a month after that we turned the Japs and started driving them out of Burma and then a couple of months later they asked different regiments to recommend footballers to go for trials in Delhi with a view to forming two touring parties. I finished up with the party that went north into Burma and ended up in Rangoon playing matches for the troops. Dennis Compton was in charge, I remember.

John Aston was also able to play football and see the world:

When I joined up I guested for a couple of clubs. I was down near Plymouth for a while. Then I moved to Portsmouth and guested for them for a few matches. This would be about 1943. Andy Black, the City and Scotland player, was also guesting for them. Jimmy Guthrie, who was the Players' Union Secretary, was playing for them ... and Mike Summerbee's dad ... I was very impressed with him ... he was a nice chap. I also guested for a few matches with Hamilton Academicals when I was posted up in Scotland after coming back from Africa and Sicily. Then I was posted to Australia to establish a base ... the war was over then and they sent us home.

Being able to guest for teams brought Charlie Mitten and Allenby Chilton together again. Mitten remembers:

Allenby and I played against each other during the war in the Southern Cup final. He played for Charlton and I played for Chelsea, both as guests.

I had actually played against Matt Busby in the semi-final of that Cup, when he was playing for Reading (we beat them 1-0) which brought us to the final.

But before that, when war broke out, I went to Metrovicks as a semi-skilled engineer ... six in the morning to six at night and never seeing the daylight. That was no good for me so I said, 'No, I've had enough of this' and I went and joined the Air Force. I went down to Cardington which was the centre for all the rookies to be kitted out.

The first night there I remember I had a quiet cry to myself under the blankets, and thought, 'What the bloody hell am I doing here?' I'd got married just a month before. I was nineteen years old and I thought, 'She might never see me again!'

Then I went on a wireless operator/rear gunners' course at Blackpool and I met Stan Matthews and he said, 'You're mad going on this course, Charlie, get yourself on a PT instructors' course.' So I applied for that and got on to it. Those aircrew lads were marvellous but after a raid there was often not much left of them ... sometimes they had to hosepipe and sweep out the turrets. I suppose I was one of the fortunate ones.

I met Freddie Simpson the boxer, he was a PTI, and he and I were posted to a new Air Force station at Brockenhurst. I had a couple of years there and played for Southampton and then Chelsea with John Harris and Jack Stamps and Tommy Walker, and that's how I came to play against Allenby in the final.

I was then posted to the Azores and was there when D-Day happened ... it took a good few months before I was eventually flown home and demobbed.

Perhaps the most dramatic wartime memories of all belong to Allenby Chilton:

During the time I was in the Services I was fortunate to play for one or two clubs. While I was in the Durham Light Infantry we were training down in Norfolk. I was with a friend of mine called Billy Robinson who played for Sunderland and Charlton and eventually West Ham. We travelled down there and played for Jimmy Seed's team, Charlton Athletic, and we won the Southern Cup. We beat Chelsea and Charlie Mitten was playing for them. I remember we were presented to General Eisenhower ... I've got a photograph of me shaking hands with him.

Then I went on commando training up in Scotland and I played a few games for Airdrie as wing-half ... nice little ground ... that was the first time I met Jimmy Delaney, when Airdrie played Celtic. Then I had a couple of games for Newcastle United when I was stationed in the area. Then I was posted to Iceland for a couple of years. I did quite a bit of boxing in Iceland and when we returned we went to Hereford where I was picked to fight for the Western Command. I was beaten on points so I thought I'd better stick to football. It was a good way of keeping fit though!

I was wounded in Normandy a few days after D-Day. I was hit by a piece of shrapnel which broke my arm. We had come under attack from mortar fire and I dived into a hedge and I heard the shrapnel come buzzing through the grass and a piece hit me in the arm and the side. I went to the field hospital and was then flown back to England.

I've had some trouble with sciatica in my hip and the doctor once asked me if I'd been hit in the war at all and I said, 'Yes, I got hit in the side with shrapnel', and he said, 'There's still a bit embedded in there', and I said, 'I wouldn't get a pension for it now, would I?'

I was lucky I suppose, but not as lucky as some who seemed to spend all the war in uniform but playing football every week, or being in the Home Guard looking after the Woodhead Tunnel!

The 1944–45 season began on a note of genuine delight when Manchester United revealed that a profit of £960 had been made in the previous season!

No less importantly, the Allies had landed in France in June 1944 and were beginning to sweep steadily across Europe towards Germany and Berlin. It was to be the last winter of the European War; surely, people said, it would all be over by the summer.

In this last season of the wartime period, two more young players of the 1948 Cup winning side started playing for the first team. Henry Cockburn was a diminutive 21-year-old half-back from Ashton-under-Lyne who began his rise to soccer fame with a famous local side called the Goslings:

I began playing football for the Goslings, an amateur side in Newton Heath ... at the time Jack Crompton was also playing for them. The team was run by a local fruiterer, Mr Abraham Gosling. It was a good side and we won lots of cups and medals. We never got paid, of course, but Mr Gosling used to pay us in kind - instead of putting money in your boots he used to put onions, which were scarce, and all kinds of fruit, and even a rabbit now and again if we did well!

At that time Blackpool seemed interested in signing me - and one Saturday one of their scouts called Cyril Edge came around to the house to get me to sign, but I was in bed with the flu. He said, 'Oh, I'll come again if he's not very well.' Before he'd come around again though, Bert Whalley came along and asked me would I sign amateur forms for Manchester United, which I was willing to do because it was a club near to home. That was August 1944.

Mr Crickmer was running the United side then, but he couldn't fit me in ... he couldn't find a regular place in the team for me. United had lots of Service lads who were stationed in the vicinity playing for them.

I was working as a fitter at Platt Brothers, a textile engineering firm in Oldham. After work on Tuesday and Thursday nights I used to go training at The Cliff. Then United loaned me out to Accrington Stanley. They had a decent side then and I really enjoyed playing for them.

Also at the beginning of the 1944-45 season, another quietly spoken young fellow-Gosling called Jack Crompton made his first team appearance as a goalkeeper for Manchester United.

When I was a boy I never really wanted to be a goalkeeper, I wanted to be an inside-forward. Then one day the YMCA team I was playing for was short, so I had to play in goal. They never let me out after that! I never really knew whether it was because I was shaping fairly well in goal or whether they were glad to get rid of me upfield! So you could say I was pushed into goalkeeping. I'd played for Manchester Boys, and the Goslings, then I signed for United as a junior in 1942, then as an amateur, then as a professional on 30 December 1944. I don't think too many people know that I even played for Manchester City as an amateur sometime in 1944, before I signed for United. At United I used to play in goal when Jack Breedon wasn't available.

I then joined the RAF but was invalided out because of a leg injury. I'd passed the medical with an injured leg ... they said, 'We'll see how it goes', but it didn't get any better so they turfed me out. Even an orthopaedic surgeon at Ancoats Hospital I went to see said, 'You can sell your football boots, lad, you'll never play again.' It's a good job I kept my boots because I think I've done reasonably well over the years, don't you?

As the war neared its end, the Manchester United board decided that it should try to find a manager - no longer could a team be picked from an office and trained haphazardly. Professional football was now bound to demand higher standards all round. Surely someone knew of a manager, or even a player who could manage, a man who knew about fitness and tactics, with an ability to mould a team from youngsters who had been developing with the club during the war, and blend them with former play-

ers, some of whom had been able to play regularly, and others
who hadn't seen a football for months.

Louis Rocca, United's scout, wrote to Matt Busby telling him
'about a great job I have for you if you are willing to take it on'.
He then asked Busby to get in touch with him 'and when you do
I can explain things better, when I know there will be no danger
of interception'. Rocca was worried that someone at Liverpool
FC might get wind of the fact that United were interested in
talking to Matt Busby about the managerial vacancy at Old Trafford.

Busby's considerable ability as a player was well known in
Manchester. He had played for City between 1928 and 1936 as a
stylish and skilful half-back and won a Cup medal with them in
1934, and a Scottish cap in 1933, before joining Liverpool in 1936
for a fee of £8,000.

Busby had spent the war as a physical training instructor where
he was obviously able to refine his ability to organise and direct
training methods. He had guested for many clubs and made eight
wartime appearances for Scotland, several times as captain. Near
the end of the war, Liverpool, anxious to retain the services of
their wise and popular player, had offered him a five-year contract
as player-coach and assistant to George Kay who was manager at
the time. Other clubs, also quick to recognise his value, offered
him team managerships or coaching jobs. However, Matt Busby
accepted Liverpool's offer, but only verbally.

When Mr James Gibson, the chairman of United, interviewed
Busby, he was impressed by the 35-year-old Scotsman's ideas and
his honesty of purpose, even though Busby himself had some
doubts about the difference between managing the fitness of
squads of soldiers and running a First Division side. There had
been no time to serve an apprenticeship. Matt and Jean, his wife,
talked it over and made the decision. They had good friends in
both cities and could have continued to live happily in either, but
Busby felt that Manchester offered the better opportunity.

Busby and Manchester United had not broken any legal agreement, but Manchester's happiness at the 'capture' was matched
only by Liverpool's anger at the 'betrayal' (because technically
Busby was still a registered Liverpool player), and the relation-
ship between the clubs was strained for a while.

On Monday, 19 February 1945, Matt Busby returned to Old

Trafford to accept the post as Manchester United's manager. As Gibson and Busby shook hands on the deal, the former City player remembered that way back in 1931 City had nearly sold him to United, but the club he was now to manage could not afford the £150 transfer fee! Walter Crickmer, who had run the team during the war made the obligatory but masterfully accurate statement to the press: 'He will build up the team and put it right where it belongs, at the top.'

Matt Busby's appointment was initially for five years only, for a salary of £750 per annum, 'his duties to commence a month after his demobilisation from the Services'. He was still in uniform, a Company Sergeant-Major Instructor with six months or so to serve before he could begin his job at Old Trafford. On 7 May 1945 the Germans signed the unconditional surrender before General Eisenhower at Rheims. The war in Europe was over. In that same month Busby was asked to take a British Army football team out to Italy, Egypt and Greece to tour and entertain the battle-weary troops who yearned to see good football as much as those lucky folks back home.

In Busby's squad were players like Tommy Lawton, Joe Mercer, Frank Swift and Jack Rowley; and it proved to be a tour full of incident. VE night took place while they were away, and Jack Rowley was taken ill with fever in Naples and had to miss a fortnight of the tour. At Bari in south-east Italy, Busby met up with Jimmy Murphy against whom he had played before the war when Murphy was a wing-half for West Bromwich Albion. He was now running all the sporting activities at a Services Sports Centre there. Matt Busby was aware of Murphy's fifteen Welsh caps and his rugged ability as a player and a coach, and told him that if he ever fancied a job when he was demobbed he should look Busby up at Old Trafford.

Matt Busby was demobbed in September 1945 and a month later began his job at Old Trafford. In 1946 Jimmy Murphy joined him as trainer. It was a partnership which was to prove its strength many times in the next twenty-five years.

# 1945-46
# Out of the Shadows
# and into the Sun

When the Football League Management Committee met in the summer of 1945 it knew that few clubs were in a position to resume normal League and Cup football.

The country needed time to take stock and lick its wounds: many players were still abroad and demobilisation could not happen overnight. Clearly, another year's breathing space was needed.

It was therefore decided that the 1945–46 season would be one in which a regional programme would operate: all First and Second Division clubs would be grouped into two Leagues, North and South; Third Division clubs would be divided into two regional Leagues also, East and West. There was to be neither threat of relegation nor promise of promotion, and while the struggle for League positions would be missing, it gave clubs a chance to regroup their players and begin building up and preparing for the following season. It was also decided to restore the FA Cup competition, each round up to the semi-final being played on the home and away principle which had proved so popular and successful during the war.

Football fans would also be able to look forward to a programme of 'Victory' international soccer. The Secretaries of the four national Associations drew up a fixture list and also passed a resolution that players would now receive £10 for an international appearance.

Back at Old Trafford, secretary Walter Crickmer and trainer Tom Curry realised they would have to continue picking the teams, because Matt Busby was not able to take up his managerial responsibilities for a couple of months or so. The familiar problems still remained. Many of the registered players were still missing: Johnny Morris was now a young soldier in the Royal Armoured Corps and had been posted abroad in the summer of

1945 and was not expected home for a couple of years; Stan Pearson, John Carey, Charlie Mitten, John Anderson, John Aston and Jack Rowley were all still in uniform, and all but Rowley stationed overseas.

Allenby Chilton played left-half in the second game of the new season against Huddersfield Town at Maine Road. He remembered:

At the end of the war I was still in uniform, waiting to be demobbed, and I actually went 'absent without leave' to go to Burnden Park to play for United against Bolton in the Northern Regional Cup in May. I stayed with my old landlady in Stretford and Matt said, 'Will you be coming back permanently, Allen?' and I said, 'Yes, if you want me back ... I'm waiting to be demobbed in the "25" group'. Within a fortnight of being demobbed I was back in Manchester and playing again.

Clubs could still include guest players this season, but there would not be quite the same need for them as there used to be. Some United players had not seen Old Trafford since 1939, others had been lucky enough to make the odd appearance during the war, and there were now youngsters who were ready to fight for places in the senior team.

After six years in the dark shadow of war men emerged gratefully into the sunlight of that autumn day to watch the opening game of the season. The world would never be the same again – but how had the game the nation loved to play and watch survived?

Nearly half a million football-starved fans, paying one shilling and sixpence (7½p) to get on the terraces, turned out to watch League soccer on that first Saturday, 25 August. The biggest crowd of the day – 35,000 – watched Newcastle United beat Sheffield United 6-0, and Manchester City beat Middlesbrough 2-1 in front of 25,000 at Maine Road. Stanley Mortensen, who was to play such a significant part in many of United's games (not least the 1948 final), scored the first hat-trick of the season (three in 33 minutes) in Blackpool's 4-1 defeat of Bury.

The side that Crickmer and Curry sent to Huddersfield for United's first League game of the 1945-46 season still had a very rough and ready look about it. It was: Crompton; Walton, Wilson; Warner, Whalley, McKay; Bryant, Smith, Hanlon, Koffman, Wrigglesworth.

A crowd of just less than 3,000 watched the Yorkshire side beat United 3-2, and the handful of United fans who had saved

enough petrol to struggle over the Pennines were particularly
interested to see how centre-forward Johnny Hanlon fared. Hanlon was a former Manchester schoolboy who had played his first
senior game for United in November 1938, ironically against
Huddersfield Town. Then, as an Eighth Army 'Desert Rat', he
had fought in the North Africa campaign and in 1943 was taken
prisoner in Crete and sent to prisoner-of-war camp Stalag 48 in
Germany. Still officially Sergeant Hanlon (expecting to be demobbed by the end of the year) he was desperate to learn how
the privations of the last couple of years had affected his footballing skills. After only a few games a still-weak Hanlon had to
ask to be allowed to drop out of the team in order that he might
build himself up in the reserves. He reappeared in the middle of
November on United's right wing and held his place until Busby
signed Jimmy Delaney at the beginning of February, but was able
to fit in a few more games at centre-forward before the end of the
season. Sadly, Johnny Hanlon was never really able to establish
himself as a regular on United's forward line, such was the competition for places, yet he was expected to be one of United's
post-war stars. Fifteen appearances during the next two seasons
and one only during 1948-49 was sufficient proof that there was
no longer a place for him at Old Trafford. United lost by the
same score in the return game at Maine Road on the following
Saturday. Several changes had been made and the team now contained Jack Crompton, Allenby Chilton and Jack Rowley, all of
whom were to play such a vital part in the side which won the
FA Cup several seasons later.

In the early part of the season United were not playing particularly well, and after eight games were sixth from the bottom of
a League of twenty-two. Matt Busby watched United draw 1-1
with Barnsley at Old Trafford on 29 September: he was to be
demobbed on 3 October and would be able to start his job a few
weeks' later.

On Monday, 22 October Matt Busby at last took over officially
as manager of Manchester United. He met Walter Crickmer at
the club's temporary offices which were in the Cornbrook Cold
Stores in Hadfield Street, Old Trafford, and then Busby told
waiting reporters that he was going to spend the next few weeks
quietly assessing the club's present playing material and investi-
gating scouts' reports of promising youngsters. 'With so many

good players not yet available because of Service requirements', he told them, 'it will not be easy to start building up, but I hope I may form some concrete plans for team strengthening later in the season.' He added ruefully, 'United have a first-class side if I could only get them together in one place!'

On that autumn morning, dressed in the obligatory 'demob suit', Busby gazed over the Old Trafford terracing which was covered in weeds and rubble and twisted girders, and the magnitude of the task facing him sank in. He was the manager of a League club without a pitch or dressing rooms, the club had an overdraft of £15,000, the club's offices were a mile from the ground, and there was nowhere to train at Old Trafford except the cinder car park.

Still, the job had to be done – and one day, Busby mused, United would be the best club in the country. But meanwhile next Saturday's team had to be picked: United were to play Bolton Wanderers at Maine Road. Making use of advice from Walter Crickmer and Tom Curry and what he saw in training Matt Busby picked his first Manchester United team.

United beat Bolton 2-1 in an exciting game in front of a crowd of 30,000 to secure their first home League victory that season.

United were then occupying sixteenth position in the League and John Carey, who scored United's equalising goal, was home on leave and playing his first match for United for two years. By all accounts he played brilliantly and justified Busby's decision to make him United's captain that day. Both men – wise, deep-thinking Catholics – took to each other immediately, but any immediate hopes Busby might have had of being able to build a team around Carey were in vain, because the popular Irishman had been told to return to Italy directly after the game, leaving Busby with only a faint promise of an early demobilisation. Even so, he had enough time to squeeze in another game and play a major part in United's 6-1 victory against Preston North End on Saturday, 3 November: as a consistent scheming inside-forward he knitted the team together and was an influence behind nearly every goal. John Carey had already spent two years in Italy and the Middle East. As a Southern Irishman he could have returned to Eire at the outbreak of war but decided to stay 'and help in the war for the country which has provided my living', as he said at the time. Even the Irish FA selectors found it difficult to prise

Carey away from his Service responsibilities in Italy. They had selected him a month before he was due to appear for Northern Ireland versus England in Belfast on 15 September but found even then that he couldn't get leave to play.

As the year drew to a close, United proudly announced a profit of £133 6s 3d for the 1944–45 season. Other figures were declared: gate receipts brought in £24,845, but the entertainment tax bill was £11,391. There had been £4,707 allotted to players' benefits, and the wage bill was £1,542. The club also paid £1,455 for the hire of the Maine Road ground and confirmed that arrangements had been completed for the continued use of the ground for the following season.

Optimistically, reports from Old Trafford at the time suggested that United would be able to play on their own ground next season. The stand had been demolished in preparation for rebuilding, and the club was waiting for grants and materials for the rebuilding work to begin. What the complete repair of the ground would cost was not known, but the expectation was that it would be above the £6,000 which was the ceiling figure the Ministry of Works would allow for the present. Repairs would probably cost four or five times that amount. All the hopes were premature, of course, for repairs only began in February 1946, and it was August 1949 before Old Trafford could stage first team football again.

United were beaten both times in the Christmas double against Sheffield United, then found themselves drawn against Accrington Stanley in the third round of the FA Cup, to be played for the last time on a two-leg, home and away basis.

Over the years United had enjoyed good connections with Accrington Stanley: United's Cockburn, Briggs, Wilson and Roach had been loaned to them a year or two beforehand. Accrington's manager was Jack Hacking, a pre-war United and England goalkeeper, whose son was now actually Stanley's current goalkeeper.

As the Reds took stock at the end of 1945 they found themselves thirteenth in the League table, which was headed by Chesterfield, and of the 23 games they had played 6 had been won, 9 were drawn and 8 had been lost. John Carey, at last free of Service responsibilities, was back in the side permanently: the defence and half-back line looked fairly sound, but the attack was not scoring goals ... perhaps, Busby will have been reassured, it was because many of the forwards hadn't yet returned.

On 5 January, in the first leg of the third round tie on Accrington's famous sloping field, United (who were leading 2–0 at half-time) eventually had to be content with a 2–2 draw, Stanley's equalising goal coming only two minutes from the final whistle.

On the following Wednesday afternoon at Maine Road United overwhelmed their visitors 5–1. Jack Rowley, obviously responding to Busby's plea for more efficient finishing, scored three good goals. Like all United's forwards he would also have been aware of the need to establish his place in the front line, because Stan Pearson, Charlie Mitten and Johnny Morris could be heading home any time now.

Encouraging reports were reaching Old Trafford that Stan Pearson was playing particularly well in Dennis Compton's touring side in India and was the leading scorer.

The Press and the supporters speculated about who would have to make way for whom. Where would Jack Rowley play? He said at the time that he preferred inside-left, but lots of people thought his best position was centre-forward. And what about Jack Smith, United's leading scorer with twelve goals in seventeen appearances? And what about Charlie Mitten? Everybody had read that Charlie, now stationed in the Azores, once scored thirteen goals in one match over there. And don't forget young John Aston ... and there was Johnny Hanlon, John Carey, Ted Buckle and Billy Wrigglesworth, all useful players and always hungry for goals. Matt Busby might even buy a forward or two. He still could never be sure who would be available for any particular match: players continued to rely on sympathetic foremen or depot commanders to get time off to play. As he had promised, Matt Busby was still experimenting with the side, moving players about with the canny ability of a man who could spot strengths and weaknesses even the player himself might not recognise. Once Allenby Chilton had returned to the centre-half spot, Bert Whalley was tried at left then right full-back. Henry Cockburn claimed the number 6 shirt as his own for this and many seasons ahead, but John Carey who always seemed to play at inside-right at the beginning of the season looked as though he could also be a very useful wing-half, or even full-back ...

The draw for the fourth round matched United with Preston North End. Early in November, United had gained their biggest victory of the season (6–1) against North End and had drawn the return fixture. However, United were warned not to rely too much on past form, as Preston were now a stronger and better side. The pundits were correct. United won the first leg 1–0 at Old Trafford but then fell 3–1 to the Deepdale side a few days later. Bill Shankly scored first for Preston from a penalty, even though Jack Crompton had at first parried it, but the little Scotsman, following up, had scored from the rebound. Preston's second goal, just into the second half, put them 2–1 ahead on aggregate, but Johnny Hanlon replied for United which meant extra-time had to be played. With only two minutes to go Mac-Intosh, Preston's left-winger, headed the winner.

Six 'Victory' internationals among the home countries had been arranged this season (as well as informal international matches against Switzerland, Belgium and France), before the official international programme began in the autumn of 1946.

No United player had featured in any of these matches so far, but on 2 February John Carey played for Ireland against Scotland at Windsor Park, Belfast. He had been picked as centre-forward (another testament to his versatility) but actually played the game at inside-left because of injuries to some of the selected players. Ireland lost 2–3 before a crowd of 53,000, but John Carey was hailed as 'the best forward on the field'.

Suddenly, Manchester United added another international to its ranks. Matt Busby announced that he had bought his first player, Jimmy Delaney, the Celtic and Scotland outside-right, for £4,000, and the signing would be in time for Delaney to play against Liverpool at Maine Road on 9 February.

Jimmy Delaney, a slight, balding figure, had been with Celtic since 1934 and had made nine appearances for Scotland before the war. Busby knew all about Delaney's qualities, because only a year before he had played behind him in the Scottish team against England at Villa Park and had seen Delaney's speed and skill on the wing and was aware of the Celtic player's ability as a centre-forward. It was a good time to sign Delaney, not least because just a fortnight before the signing he had scored two goals in Scotland's draw with Belgium at Hampden Park.

But what about this reputation he had for being brittle-boned? And hadn't he had some time out of football with a shoulder injury? Apparently Sunderland had wanted him in 1938 but their £10,000 offer had been turned down. Now that player was six years older, and £4,000 seemed a lot of money to spend on a 30-year-old who might injure too easily in the hurly-burly of English League football.

Busby, however, did not think that Delaney was past his best, and persuaded his directors that even if United only got a season or two out of him, Delaney's enthusiasm and experience would be bound to rub off on the side. In fact, Delaney played six seasons for United and the club sold him for only £500 less than they paid for him!

Jimmy Delaney was delighted to have a chance to reminisce about the circumstances which led him to Old Trafford:

I signed for Celtic in the 1933–34 season and won a Scottish Cup and a League Championship medal with them before I joined United in 1945.

In 1939 I broke my arm and I couldn't play football for two and a half years. But there were two surgeons in Glasgow who performed marvels on the arm – I had a bone graft – it was like a jigsaw puzzle. They told me that if I hadn't been a footballer they would have amputated it.

Even when it had been fixed they wouldn't give me the all clear – it was still suspect. I tried to start playing football again. Every time the Scottish selectors picked a team there were crowds outside shouting my name but they couldn't get anybody to insure me. Then some insurance man took the risk and I got cover.

So I went back and played with Celtic, about 1941: they'd almost given me up as a player because I'd been injured for so long.

When the war ended I'd fallen out with Celtic and I wanted away. I was actually in Ireland on holiday and I got a telegram telling me that Manchester United were interested in signing me so I got the boat next morning and went back to Glasgow, met Matt and signed.

I didn't know Matt all that well even though we'd played together in the Scottish national side. Actually Matt was born in Bellshill, only about five miles from here [Cleland] – him and the great Hughie Gallagher.

All eyes were on Jimmy Delaney as he and his new team-mates trotted out on to the Maine Road pitch to face Liverpool that Saturday afternoon. He got a big cheer from the 33,000 crowd when he first got the ball and on his first run forced the left-back to give away a corner. The crowd quickly got to like his deft touches and his willingness to cut inside, but the game, which had opened brightly enough, was turning out to be a dull affair.

Liverpool scored first when Balmer headed in a corner from Liverpool's left-winger, a sprightly north-easterner called Bob

Paisley, then United drew level on the hour. Suddenly, drama. With fifteen minutes to go Delaney was brought down in the penalty area and decided to take the spot kick himself. To score on your debut game for your new club is every footballer's dream, but the normally cool and deadly Scotsman blazed the shot over the bar! However, inside-right Jack Smith saved United's blushes by ramming home the winner with only two minutes remaining.

Despite the penalty miss, the fans who streamed away from the ground rated Jimmy Delaney highly ... it was just that the other forwards didn't play very well ... Delaney had played forcefully enough when he had the ball, but a winger like him needed lots of service ... if Jack Rowley's train from Wolverhampton hadn't been delayed and *he'd* played it might have made a hell of a difference ...

But things change quickly in football and consistency is rare. In the return fixture a week later United won 5-0, which was the score at half-time. This time Jack Rowley *did* play, brilliantly by all accounts, and scored two goals. Not even the famous Billy Liddell, Liverpool and Scotland's winger, could get a look in because he was so well policed by Joe Walton.

It was also a nostalgic, if subdued, return to Liverpool for Matt Busby who was making his first appearance there since he left Anfield to take charge at Old Trafford.

The prospects at Old Trafford seemed even better when a few days later the headlines of the *Manchester Evening News* announced 'Stan's Back!' At long last, Stan Pearson had returned to Manchester after six and a half years' military service. After a few days' recovering from the long voyage from India he turned up at Old Trafford, re-signed his professional forms and began training at The Cliff, United's training ground at Broughton. Matt Busby felt that Pearson needed a week or two to settle in, but Stan travelled as twelfth man to Bury for the League fixture on Saturday, 23 February and played in the Central League side on 2 March and scored. He looked fit and had put on weight, and was desperately keen to start playing again. 'I shall take a holiday when the football season has ended', he told reporters.

Pearson actually made his triumphant return on Saturday, 9 March against Blackburn Rovers at Maine Road, his first League appearance for two years. United trounced Rovers 6-2 (Rowley 3, Hanlon 2 and Delaney, scoring his first goal after a long solo run). Jack Rowley scored his three in 9 minutes and United were 3–1 up at half-time. Jimmy Delaney had a brilliant game, and Stan Pearson found his feet very quickly. He was impressed by all the players around him and singled out Henry Cockburn for special mention as one of the best half-backs he'd seen for years and one who would surely reach international standard in the not-too-distant future. Pearson's ability to size up players was never more accurate: Cockburn was rapidly learning all the skills of half-back play from his manager and was becoming a polished player who was, in fact, to be awarded his first England cap in seven months' time. Henry Cockburn was even doing extra training: realising his lack of inches he and Matt Busby had developed agility exercises with a view to getting an extra inch or two in his leaps to head the ball and perfect his timing.

Even though the war was over, military obligations still affected civilian life, as Manchester United learned to their cost.

In mid March, at the request of the FA, United had arranged to entertain troops by playing a Services XI in Hamburg. Twelve players and Matt Busby, Walter Crickmer and Tom Curry left Manchester for the fixture, but their plane had to land at Manston Airport in Kent because of bad weather. A reception for the party in Hamburg and a tour of the docks to see the bomb damage was cancelled. The United party had to land seventy miles from Hamburg and continue their journey next day in an RAF three-ton lorry, reaching the ground only two hours before the kick-off. After losing 2–1 in a fast, clean game before a crowd of 25,000 they were told that no plane was available so they were forced to make the return journey by rail and sea, and there was every danger that they wouldn't be able to make their fixture against Bradford on the Saturday. Tired out after their long journey, the United party got back to Manchester late on Friday evening. The angry club chairman, J.W. Gibson, said later: 'If we had known our players were facing such an unfortunate experience we would certainly have given the matter more consideration before agreeing to the tour.'

On Wednesday, 27 March John Aston was selected for the number 9 shirt in place of Johnny Hanlon in the team to meet Blackpool at Bloomfield Road on the Saturday. John Aston had been recently demobbed from the Royal Marines and had been playing in the reserve side. This was to be his first League game under normal conditions, although he played once or twice in the senior side at the beginning of the war in regional matches. Blackpool were routed 5-1. Reports said it was because Stan Matthews (a Stoke player but guesting for Blackpool that day) was a passenger for all but the first few minutes of the game with a strained ligament in the left knee. What was much more apparent though was that John Aston led the line well and Stan Pearson was described as a 'star performer'.

John Aston's return to Old Trafford from service abroad had gone unnoticed, but the player who came back was still young and strong and the war years had given him a maturity and introspection which Busby was quick to notice.

I came out of the Forces ... I was twenty-four years old then ... six years had gone ... we'd all lost six years. I'd got married during the war and we'd got a youngster – a daughter – and I started wondering what I was going to do. We're an engineering family ... I had three or four brothers in engineering and I thought I'd go back to that because I was an engineer as well. So I started to look for a job. I didn't think of football as a career.

Actually, when I was on the way home from Australia I'd heard that Busby had taken the manager's job so I wrote an airmail letter to the club explaining who I was and saying that I was on my way home and hoped to be demobbed soon. I didn't know really whether I was going to be good enough. I was home two or three weeks looking for a job and I never bothered about Old Trafford and then I thought, Blow it, I'd better see what's doing down there. I didn't have much confidence about things. So I went down to see Matt Busby and he made me welcome and said, 'Come down and we'll give you a game in the second team'. I was fit and sun-tanned. But I said, 'No, I'd better start in the "A" team', and I did. Within a couple of weeks I was in the first team. I wasn't a regular choice but I did get two or three games with the first team. I used to play inside- or centre-forward, although I wasn't really big enough to be centre-forward. At that time I used to go on the field without much confidence. I think it was because I was married ... that was a responsibility. I used to worry a lot about that, silly really ...

By now Busby was overstocked with inside-forwards, but at the back of his mind he had the thought that John Aston might make a very useful half-back ... or perhaps even full-back, but both John Aston and Old Trafford had to wait another few months before the idea became reality.

Meanwhile, another Old Trafford favourite was home. Charlie Mitten had been stationed as a PT instructor in the Azores and was home on compassionate leave and expected to be demobbed in May.

Unlike Charlie Mitten, Stoker John Anderson's return at the end of the season went unheralded. Other players were drifting back in ones and twos, many had retained their old strength and enthusiasm for the game, for others the war had taken away their best footballing years and their priorities were to get a decent Civvy Street job and settle down. John Anderson, still only twenty-three years old, had seen the world and he returned to Manchester keener than ever to continue his life as a professional footballer. He remembered:

I was on the first ship, a destroyer, into Tokyo Harbour when the Japs signed the surrender on 2 September 1945. By then I was upper deck stoker, doing jobs like dipping tanks and looking after the fresh water supply . . . upper deck stoker was a good number in the Navy.

Then we went showing the flag in Australia, Fiji, Samoa, South Sea Islands and Hong Kong. I kept thinking, It's about time I was at home, but I didn't manage it until the summer of 1946.

I arrived home just in time to play the very last Central League game of the 1945–46 season, against Leeds United I think it was.

Everybody was looking forward to next season well before this one was over, especially when in January the League Management Committee recommended a return to normal League championship football with the usual system of promotion and relegation: now the real competitive spirit would be back in the game.

It was clear that Matt Busby was a wise and industrious manager who was constantly searching for the right blend and balance in the side. He realised he had several first-class players on the books, but a championship side needed eleven first-class players. Charlie Mitten remembers Busby telling him, 'Let's start from the beginning, we're all newcomers.' Mitten added, 'It was just by sheer good fortune for Matt that in his first year as manager he'd seven or eight really good players who'd all got their experience during the war playing in different countries.' Mitten was right, there were good players, or in Busby's words 'a group of top-class talents' but he did not inherit a team, as his critics were to claim. For the next couple of seasons Busby brought in a few more players and juggled them around until they fell into their right positions: he was constantly experimenting – moving players into different positions – wanting to give men who had lost six years of their footballing lives a chance, but knowing deep down that some would have to be replaced very soon, and that the real key to success lay with younger players.

During the season nearly forty players had made first-team appearances (compared with twenty-one in the next season when the League proper began). Matt Busby was determined to give pre-war senior players, and those who had shown particular promise during the war years, a chance to prove themselves this season.

Matt Busby was always searching for the perfectly blended side, and if he could have looked into the future he would have gained great satisfaction from knowing that all but one (Johnny Morris) of his 1948 Cup winning side were back safely and playing by the end of the season.

Busby never regarded a man's position on the field as sacrosanct – his own personal experience as a player at Manchester City had shown him how a move from inside-forward to half-back created a player of international standard from one who was seriously considering packing in the game and returning to his miner's job in Scotland.

John Carey and John Aston (inside-forwards to full-backs) and Allenby Chilton (wing-half to centre-half) were the three most obvious results of Busby's ability to find a better position on the field for an already good player: Carey and Aston were soon to become the best club pair in Britain and Allenby Chilton was United's pivot for the next seven seasons and achieved international status in 1950.

In this season the team usually read: Crompton (or Tapken); Walton (or Whalley), Roach (or Walton); Warner (or Carey), Chilton, Cockburn; Hanlon (or Delaney), Carey (or Smith or Pearson), Smith (or Hanlon), Rowley (or Buckle or Pearson), Wrigglesworth (or Rowley or Mitten).

The much criticised forward line of the early part of the season now had an exciting look about it and Jimmy Delaney in particular seemed to have regained his old confidence. When he led Scotland against England at Hampden Park on 13 April, in front of a colossal crowd of 139,468, he scored the only goal, in the 89th minute, which gave Scotland the 1945-46 Championship title.

That Saturday was highly significant for another United player. John Carey had been forced to move to right-back in one of seven positional changes in the United team which beat Manchester City 3-1 at Maine Road. He was a striking success and occupied that position for the rest of the season. The skilful Irishman could play anywhere on the field but maybe this was his true place ...

Tony Walker, a Manchester United fan for many years, was a schoolboy in 1946, and wrote to Alf Clarke of the *Manchester Evening Chronicle*, hoping that Clarke might know where he could get a football for his school team. Footballs, like sweets, were difficult to obtain. Clarke's letter not only showed how helpful and friendly he was, but the last sentence contained a superbly accurate prophesy:

> Thanks for your letter. Glad to hear you confirm my opinion about United's play. They'll be the team of next season, and I hope to see them at Wembley. Had they been there last Saturday they would have beaten Derby and Charlton together. I am sorry I cannot help you regarding footballs. They are difficult to get. United have three of four teams to keep supplied each week, and they are under quota, of course. In fact, I've just been talking to Matt Busby, on the phone, and he has been relating to me the difficulties he is having in getting stocks of all kinds. You may be interested to know that I have just received a letter from the Middle East telling me how well Johnny Morris is playing out there. How do you fancy this forward line for next season: Delaney, Morris, Rowley, Pearson, Mitten?

The papers reported that Manchester United had drawn 270,000 spectators in their last six matches, and predicted the side to be 'next season's most exciting team'. Even their reserve team playing Newcastle United reserves on Easter Monday was watched by 25,000 followers!

When United played Stoke in the last League game of the season at Maine Road there was obviously nothing at stake, yet nearly 38,000 turned up to pay an enthusiastic compliment to the men who had provided such entertainment and excitement this season, and who had taken the team to fourth place in the unofficial League table behind Sheffield United, Everton and Bolton Wanderers.

In the team which played that day only Crompton, Whalley and Wrigglesworth remained of the eleven who had turned out against Huddersfield for the very first League game of the season back in August. Now Chilton, Aston, Cockburn, Delaney, Pearson and Rowley had settled into the side which had lost only three League games since February and was beginning to combine together very successfully. Every man was eagerly anticipating next season's conflict.

There were of course other players who showed as much promise that season as those who eventually formed the 1948 Cup winning side.

Jack Warner, a United player since the 1937-38 season, was the team's regular right-half in this and the next few seasons, and was eagerly pressing his claim for another Welsh cap to add to the two he had won before the war. He was in fact selected to play right-half for Wales when they met Ireland at Cardiff on 4 May in a 'Victory' international.

Also a prominent player this season was Joe Walton, a plumber's assistant from the Bradford area of Manchester and a brilliant young full-back who was tipped for future England honours.

Busby also had many talented forwards to choose from; as well as Jack Rowley, Stan Pearson, Charlie Mitten and Jimmy Delaney, he had Johnny Hanlon and a 20-year-old Croydon lad called Ted Buckle who scored a goal on his debut and had found the net on many subsequent occasions.

At the time much was made of the fact that eight of the current first team had cost nothing. True, Chilton and Carey had come to United for small 'donations' – acts of appreciation by United to the clubs concerned – but Cockburn, Hanlon, Mitten, Pearson, Walton and Crompton were young 'home grown' stock. Their collective current value, it was proudly estimated, was about £48,000.

A few international games remained to be played that season: United's Jack Warner and John Carey wore the number 4 shirts for Wales and Ireland respectively in the last of the 'Victory' internationals on 4 May at Ninian Park, Cardiff which Ireland won 1-0 in front of 45,000 spectators.

Later that summer a United player called Walter Winterbottom was appointed director of coaching and England team manager. He had made a few wartime appearances for United and Chelsea at centre-half before becoming an officer in the RAF. Up until then, England's teams had been selected by an international committee (just as many League teams were picked by the directors), but young Winterbottom, a native of Oldham who joined United in 1936, had the personal and professional qualities that the FA were looking for. He had been a teacher, then superintendent at Oldham Juvenile Inspection Centre, then PE lecturer at Carnegie College in Leeds, and was a qualified coach and expert tactician.

On 11 May, Manchester United enjoyed a last slice of success when they beat Burnley 1–0 in the Lancashire Senior Cup final at Turf Moor. Jack Rowley at outside-left scored with a classic left-foot drive a few minutes before half-time.

A week or so before the season finally ended, Jimmy Murphy, demobbed at last, joined Matt Busby at Old Trafford as coach to the club's young players. He had remembered Busby's offer in Italy in the previous year and was now looking for a job. The visionary Busby had always been keen to implement a youth policy as soon as possible, but he needed help to find likely youngsters, get them to Old Trafford, and fit them into a team which would take Manchester United to the top.

Busby and Murphy knew that the streets and parks of Britain were full of eager, talented young lads who loved the game and would play all day for nothing. Somewhere out there that talent was waiting to be discovered and nourished. Both men had the confidence to realise that their instincts and knowledge of the game had conferred on them an ability to recognise exceptional footballing skill and they wanted to bring that skill to Old Trafford. But where to start looking? In that summer of 1946, hundreds of miles from one another, Bobby Charlton aged nine, Duncan Edwards aged eight and Dennis Law aged six played happily, unaware of the triumphs and disasters fate had in store for them. And even Busby and Murphy could be forgiven for not beginning their search in Belfast, but unknown to them, that summer on 22 May at the Royal Infirmary, a tiny dark-haired son, to be christened George, was born to Ann and Richard Best.

# 1946-47

## The Foundations are Built

When the players assembled on 24 July 1946 for pre-season training at Manchester University's playing fields in Fallowfield, their
optimistic mood was tempered yet again with an awareness of the
many difficulties which faced them at the beginning of another
season.

Matt Busby firstly had to tell his squad that there was not
enough training kit for them, so Tom Curry announced that he
would be having a 'whip round' among the United players for
clothing coupons to provide jerseys, stockings and boots for training purposes. Busby also had to make several appeals in the local
press and in the first few match programmes for clothing coupons
– reminding them that 'the club had just enough match kit for
our four teams'!

Old Trafford was still not ready despite all the promises that it
would be available for first-team football at the beginning of this
season. Repairs were slow, and building supplies (like just about
everything else) were restricted, and the estimated costs of repair
were beginning to rise alarmingly. Manchester City had agreed
again – for a seasonal payment of £3,000 – to allow United to
play its home games at Maine Road, a concession it was to have
to repeat annually until the end of the 1948–49 season. In return,
both sides' reserve teams were to play their games on alternate
weeks at Old Trafford: the pitch itself was fit for play, but as yet
there was nowhere for more than a few spectators to watch the
game. Manchester City were still in the Second Division, having
been relegated from Division One at the end of the 1937–38
season and only reaching fifth place in the last full season of
football before the war.

Matt Busby also confirmed that the first game of the season
would start on the last Saturday in August and that the fixtures
would be identical to those of the abandoned 1939–40 season.

Seven years of friendly regional soccer were over: the battle was now really on!

For their part, the spectators learned that this season they could watch soccer from the popular side of League grounds for 1s 3d (6p), and the club announced that because they were unable to issue season tickets for their League games at Maine Road in the coming season, the 1,100 people who had bought tickets for games at Old Trafford seven years ago would have their money refunded. When the 1939–40 season was cancelled at the outbreak of war, the club had promised each season ticket holder free tickets for the 'first season of normal football' but the Luftwaffe had put paid to this generous arrangement. Some die-hard United supporters were warmly praised by Walter Crickmer 'because in spite of the hard times, many have said they don't want their money back, but will wait until normal football is resumed at Old Trafford'.

Despite all these worries, training got under way, and Matt Busby, one of the first track-suited managers, could be seen working with the squad at the Firs, and apparently getting as much enjoyment from it as the younger players. Everybody was eagerly looking forward to the new season.

A treat lay in store for local soccer fans a week before the League season began. On Saturday, 24 August an unofficial 'international' match was played between England and Scotland, in aid of the Bolton Disaster Fund, set up to help the dependants of spectators killed in the previous season's accident at Burnden Park. A sell-out ticket-only crowd of 70,000 (proceeds £12,000) watched England (which included United's Charlie Mitten and Joe Walton and City's Frank Swift) draw 2-2 with 'the Old Enemy'.

Unaccountably, this was to be Charlie Mitten's only 'international' appearance and reports of the game indicate that he was outshone by Stanley Matthews on the other wing, but in any case 'was not given enough of the ball'. Charlie Mitten, with a wry smile, agreed with the verdict:

I didn't have a good game, I knew that myself. I look back on that game and I think, Charles, you were inexperienced for that level at the time. I was only just out of the Forces and Matt had pushed me ... 'You'll be all right, lad! he said, but I wasn't, I was just playing with a lot of strangers. I think they should have allowed internationals to play together for four or five games so they could get to know one another ... it's no use picking someone and dropping him after one game. If only I could have played in an England set-up which had Stan Pearson and Henry Cockburn and Jack Rowley and John Aston in it. We'd have been permanent!

Charlie Mitten was soon to emerge as a brilliant outside-left for his club, but unfortunately he reached his peak years at the same time as Tom Finney who was to make 76 appearances for England, 33 of these at outside-left. Even so, at the time the verdict was that Mitten should have been given another chance to show his true worth, but sadly that chance was never offered to him again.

However, there seemed to be universal agreement that Manchester United's prospects for the 1946–47 season looked very good. Only Morris and Anderson were missing from what was to be the team which won the FA Cup in 1948: most of the players had found their right positions and the team was beginning to blend together and play the kind of swift, flowing football that the crowds loved to see. Matt Busby was an effective manager and popular with the players, and the team was determined to pick up where it left off the previous season with the same settled side.

The disciplined team work was initially as much a result of the players' wartime experiences as it was of Busby's developing knack of being able to bring out the very best of a man's ability to combine with others. Ten years later Busby's 'Babes' were to underline the merit of gathering together a team of brilliant youngsters, but the first post-war United side had very few men under twenty-five in its ranks. The players had already shown towards the end of last season that they were beginning to play with the urgency of men who were making up for lost time.

United's opening game of the season was on Saturday, 31 August against Grimsby Town – and 40,000 fans packed into the 'home' ground at Maine Road to watch them defeat the 'Mariners' 2-1. Jack Warner, John Carey and Stan Pearson were the only United players who had appeared in the same fixture just before war was declared seven years ago, and Allenby Chilton, it could be said, was making his second appearance for United, his first being seven years ago in the last game of the official 1939–40 season.

United began the season's campaign in excellent style. From the whistle the United attack stormed the Grimsby goal and after a few minutes Jack Rowley headed against the cross-bar from a Jimmy Delaney centre. The Reds' defence looked secure enough and newcomer Bill McGlen was giving a particularly good account of himself. Then, just before half-time, the lively Charlie Mitten slid the ball past the goalkeeper for United's first goal, but five minutes into the second half McGowan, Grimsby's inside-left, fired in a shot which flew past Jack Crompton for the equaliser. With ten minutes to go Jack Rowley again came to the rescue and headed in United's second goal, from yet another Delaney cross, although it was actually deflected in by the Grimsby right-back Vincent (and credited to him as an own goal).

The papers next day were full of praise for United's performance, and particular mention was made of the accuracy of Jack Rowley's crossfield passes and his co-operation with Charlie Mitten, of Jimmy Delaney's 'hanging' corner kicks, Henry Cockburn's craft and Billy McGlen's confidence and zest.

The praise was well-founded, because after five games United were top of the First Division with a maximum of ten points, and playing with a power and balance which the team and Busby always knew they could achieve – but perhaps not quite so soon.

Don Davies, back reporting for the *Manchester Guardian*, wrote a typically eloquent report on the United versus Liverpool game which contained more than a strong hint of the emerging brilliance of the Old Trafford side:

The ever-popular Liverpool side (which on this occasion certainly took the palm for sartorial elegance) met Manchester United at Maine Road last night, and as a result of their meeting received a lesson in football craft which they are not likely to forget for many a long day.

The first twenty minutes was an almost ceaseless bombardment of the Liverpool goal. Wave after wave of red shirts rolled over and round the Liverpool defenders at will; in the twelfth minute Pearson converted a lob by Warner and soon afterwards Pearson slammed a 'shot-cum-centre' from Mitten high into the Liverpool net. This was progress indeed, and soon a feast of football entertainment which the 41,657 operatives who had called in on the way home to tea seemed to find ample compensation for meals deferred. Still the attack went on; and when Delaney was floored by a charge heavy enough to buckle

the plates of a submarine, Rowley collected the resulting free kick and
scored a handsome third goal.

That Liverpool were surprised and bewildered there is no gainsay-
ing, but one expected a less pettish approach to their problems than
some of them showed. In football, as in boxing, the only hope of a
recovery lies in preserving a philosophic outlook and a cool head.
Early to talk, of course, but hard to achieve when goals come as easily
as Manchester United's fourth did, four minutes after the interval,
when a deflected ball put Mitten on-side and Mitten's trusty boot did
the rest. Even when United eased up, as they obviously did with a
lead of four clear goals, they still had the whip hand of Liverpool and
treated the crowd to a taste of the quality which has taken London by
storm.

In a team so strong and perfectly balanced there is little need to
discriminate; but one cannot forgo the view that the acquisition of
Delaney was one master stroke and that the playing of Carey at right-
back is another. One cannot recall an occasion when Liverpool play
was so undistinguished. Apart from one beautiful shot by Fagan, and
a few stupendous throws by Paisley (left half) they made not a single
move of consequence throughout the entire match.

Until the closing minutes, that is, when Paisley drove in a ball
which forced Crompton, the Manchester goalkeeper, to reveal his
whereabouts and prove to the crowd that he had not gone home from
sheer boredom. United's apt retort to Paisley's impudence was to walk
the ball upfield and invite Pearson to score the fifth, which Pearson
most willingly and conclusively did. Taken all in all this was a mas-
terly performance and one which even Manchester United will not
easily repeat.


United were already beginning to build up a reputation for the
speed of their attack, their fast open play, and the rapidity with
which their attackers changed positions. Opposing defenders,
looking for a face or the number they were supposed to be marking, often saw their man forty yards away on the other side of the
field and in trying to follow him were thereby drawn well out of
position.

Then, inevitably, injuries and international calls forced Matt
Busby to make changes, and United's powerfully smooth start
began to falter, although they were the last team in the First
Division to be defeated. This first half of the season also saw John
Aston, after a number of brilliant reserve team games as a for-
ward, introduced into United's first team attack against Chelsea

on 18 September, but his was an undistinguished performance and he had to wait until the end of December before he was given another game (in amazing circumstances), this time as full-back where he was then to remain for the next seven seasons.

Johnny Morris returned home at the end of September, having spent sixteen months of his four years of Army life in India. After a month's training he was in the first team, the final piece in the forward line which was now ready to perform brilliantly for the club. Ironically, a couple of seasons later (and under somewhat of a cloud), Johnny Morris was also the first to leave that famous front line.

After twenty-one games United had dropped to seventh in the table, but huge crowds were continuing to turn up and watch them: the games against Middlesbrough and Arsenal both attracted crowds of over 62,000; 57,340 saw United beat Cup holders Derby 4-1; and 57,186 left their firesides to watch them defeat Bolton Wanderers 1-0 on Boxing Day at Maine Road.

Despite their modest position United were playing well and many of the stars of the 1948 side were already permanent fixtures. Even the 'quiet man' of the side, Jack Crompton, had distinguished himself by saving the three penalty kicks which had been taken against him so far, by Don Welsh of Charlton Athletic, Tommy Lawton of Chelsea and Jimmy Hagan of Sheffield Wednesday, all, as the local papers were quick to note, England internationals.

But fate conspires even against the most noble of men. Early in November, after a game against Sunderland, Jack Crompton tried to leave Maine Road quickly to escape a rush of autograph hunters and slipped on some steps, spraining his ankle. He was not able to play again until Christmas Day. Later that month right-back Joe Walton, who was still pursuing his plumber's trade (he was still only a part-time professional), slipped off a plank, fell twelve feet and broke his wrist. It was an injury which cost him his place for many weeks.

By reputation and results England were still regarded as the supreme soccer nation of the world. They had never been beaten by any visiting foreign side and during the war had completely dominated the home international fixtures, not least because forwards of the calibre of Stanley Matthews, Raich Carter, Tommy

Lawton, Jimmy Hagan and Wilf Mannion were in their heyday during this period. After the war England was to enjoy a further eight years of supremacy before a game against Hungary at Wembley on a murky day in November 1953 marked the end of an era.

So from the moment the season began there was eager speculation about who would be selected for the England team, because the first fixtures were to be as early as 28 September against Northern Ireland in Belfast, and two days later against Eire in Dublin.

Players who luckily struck form right away were able to catch a selector's eye and because United began their season so well, several of their players were strongly fancied for selection. Stan Pearson, Jack Rowley and Charlie Mitten were the main contenders, but in most match reports Henry Cockburn's name cropped up constantly, surrounded by glittering compliments.

An FA selector, Mr Drewry, watched Cockburn's display in the opening game against Grimsby Town, and Walter Winterbottom and another FA selector, Mr Oakley, were at Stamford Bridge to watch United beat Chelsea and see Henry Cockburn, an integral part of United's powerful left flank, play another immaculate game.

Even though Henry Cockburn was only 5 feet 6 inches tall and weighed a mere 10 stones he was able to tame opposing inside-forwards by his fierce tackling, and initiate attacks from midfield with superbly accurate distribution. Spectators loved the sight of Cockburn snapping at the heels of an opposing forward, eventually pinching the ball from him and then racing off on his own with it. 'Terrier-like' was the phrase which was invariably used about him throughout his career, and all that extra practice he had put in on his heading technique was beginning to show. Matt Busby, himself a masterful half-back, had added extra polish to a player with a great deal of natural talent.

John Carey's selections for Northern Ireland *and* Eire for the fixtures against England were by now almost automatic, and were announced on 17 September. Two days later, when the England team for Belfast was declared, Henry Cockburn had been picked at left-half. His selection was truly remarkable because up until then he had only played six times for United in this first official season, and only two seasons beforehand had been playing in a Manchester Amateur League with Goslings AFC. He could not even be regarded as a full-time professional footballer either, because he was working as a fitter in a textile works in Oldham, a 'reserved occupation', which meant that he was not eligible for National Service, but instead had to work a full day in an essential industry.

So now Henry Cockburn, the pride of Ashton-under-Lyne, had been picked for England:

I was very fortunate because at the end of the war I was around and I got into the side straight away ... lots of others were still in the Forces or getting demobbed. I'm sure that's why I got my first international cap so soon ... I was picked for England in 1946 after only six League games. My first international match was at Windsor Park, Belfast ... on 28 September 1946. I'll never forget it. We won 7-2. Just before we went out I was all keyed up. I'd only had a few League matches, remember, and I was reading Braille half the time! I was only a little lad and I was trembling like a leaf. I'd had telegrams from all over ... one from the Lord Mayor of Ashton, even. I thought to myself, What *am* I doing here? I was in a line with Frank Swift, Tommy Lawton, Raich Carter, Wilf Mannion, Billy Wright and George Hardwick. I thought, Well, I've nothing to lose, I'll have a go anyway. I knew I was fit enough ... I'd always prided myself on my fitness, you see. So the bell goes, and we starts to go down the tunnel, but a policeman holds up his arms and stops us. 'Sorry, lads, the crowd's invaded the pitch, you'll have to go back to the dressing rooms.' That was even more tension! We had to wait another five minutes ... I just wanted to get cracking. You see, the crowds were so vast at the time (and there was never any trouble) ... they'd been starved of class football during the war.

In fact football fever had spread across the Irish Sea and a fifteen-minute delay was caused by the need to control some of the 57,000 spectators who had spilled on to the running track around the pitch.

According to one newspaper report Cockburn played 'a storming game' in the victory, but neither he nor the side were able to reproduce the quality of the Belfast game, and when they played in Dublin two days later were lucky to win 1-0.

Henry Cockburn was picked for the next fixture against Wales at Maine Road on Wednesday, 13 November, but even though England won 3-0 he had a poor game, and the predictions that he would soon have to make way for Harry Johnston, the Blackpool half-back proved to be correct. Cockburn's next appearance in an England shirt was to be towards the end of next season, but he had done well to achieve what he did with relatively little experience. He was warmly welcomed back to Old Trafford where the rest of the side could now bask in the reflected glory of being able to play alongside Manchester United's first post-war England international.

Football is full of coincidences and one occurred early that December when United crushed Brentford 4-1 at Maine Road. Trying vainly to cope with the wily Stan Pearson that day was Brentford's right-half George Wilkins, father of one-time United midfielder Ray!

At the end of the year Manchester United were seventh in the League having survived a busy period against Bolton Wanderers on Christmas Day, a return fixture against the same side at Old Trafford the next day and then drawing a game up in Grimsby on 28 December.

Because all the recognised full-backs, Carey, McGlen, Walton and Worrall, were injured, a party of thirteen was selected to travel to Grimsby, including the 23-year-old John Aston who had made only two first-team appearances that season, at left-half and inside-right. For a long time Matt Busby had thought that John Aston, after some uncertain performances in the forward and half-back line, would make a good full-back, and now perhaps was a good time to try him out in that position. The decision about whether to play him at left- or right-back arose from an incredible series of events. Stan Pearson's memory of the episode was very clear as he described what happened when the team made its way up to Grimsby's South Humberside ground:

We took Johnny Aston with us and another full-back was Bert Whalley who could also play half-back, and we had a meeting on the Friday before the match and we finished up by asking the commissionaire at the hotel who was the best winger they had. This fellow said, 'The outside-left is the better of the two', so Johnny Aston says to Bert Whalley, 'Right, you're playing right-back and I'll play left-back!' Johnny was an inside-forward really but Busby converted him to a full-back. Believe it or not, six or seven months after that Johnny Aston played for England. The positional change really settled him as a player.

John Aston's placing at left-back was a fortunate accident and his memory of it was naturally more detailed:

Midway through the 1946-47 season the half-back line of the second team was Anderson, Whalley and myself. The first team weren't having too good a time ... then suddenly both full-backs got injured. United were to play Grimsby round about Christmas time, so all three reserve team half-backs were taken up to Grimsby with a view to two of us playing as full-backs for the first team.

On the Saturday morning we were told that Bert Whalley and I had been picked (Bert was older than me – in his thirties – and a great pal) and he said, 'Do you want to be left- or right-back?' He was being very kind about it ... we could both play either side and he was giving me first choice. I didn't know which I preferred really. By then my daughter was two or three years old and Bert and I went into a shop to get things for a doll's house I'd made for her as a Christmas present. I wanted some special brick paper. The shop-keeper recognised our accents and said, 'Are you up for the match, lads?' ... thinking we were supporters, and I said, 'Yes,' and he said, 'I'd go but I saw them last week and I said if they pick that bloody outside-right again I'm not going!' So when we came out Bert Whalley said to me, 'Are you playing left-back then?', and I said, 'I am that!' That morning everybody in the side was asking around about who was the best winger, which is why Stan Pearson told you the story about asking the porter at the hotel!

Because I thought I wasn't expected to do well in this new position I wasn't worried, so of course I found it easy and all the lads were raving because I'd played so well.

The Press described Aston as 'the best defender on the field' and praised him for 'playing brilliantly throughout'. Even the Grimsby officials asked how much United wanted for Aston when the other full-backs were fit again!

But their enquiries were in vain, because John Aston held the left-back place until March, then moved over to right-back until the end of the season. As Stan Pearson remarked, Aston became an England player a few months later, and remained United's automatic choice at left-back until 1953.

Once the Christmas and New Year festivities were over, the players turned their minds to their next big hurdle – at Bradford Park Avenue against Bradford on 11 January in the third round of the F A Cup.

Second Division Bradford were not expected to provide much

opposition, but long experience of the unpredictability of football ensured that Matt Busby prepared his men thoroughly for the fixture, telling them also to ignore the reports that Manchester United had been tipped as favourites to win the Cup. In the game, which began in heavy rain, Bradford were outclassed, conceding a goal by Ted Buckle and two by Jack Rowley.

'How did the others get on?' was United's first question when they reached the dressing room, and the joyous news soon spread that five First Division sides, Aston Villa, Sunderland, Huddersfield, Blackpool and Leeds had been knocked out of the Cup by Second Division sides!

When the draw for the second round was made on the following Monday, United learned that they were to play Second Division Nottingham Forest 'at home'. Somebody remembered that the last time the two sides had met in the Cup was, ironically, in the fourth round way back in 1935 when a 0-0 draw was followed by a 3-0 shock defeat for United in the replay at Old Trafford a few days later. There seemed to be general agreement though that this season Forest were not good enough to create a surprise, as their position half-way down the League table would seem to indicate.

So a fortnight after their third round victory, and in front of a crowd of 58,641 United lined up against Nottingham Forest at Maine Road full of confidence. It did not even matter that they were playing with a reserve goalkeeper, Bill Fielding, because Jack Crompton was still suffering from the effects of concussion sustained in the previous week's game against Middlesbrough. The match was played at a furious pace and Forest's forwards took every opportunity to unsettle newcomer Fielding by firing in long-range shots from all angles. Suddenly the game did not look easy any more for United. The Forest defenders kept the United forwards at bay with some strong tackling, and even the redoubtable Jack Rowley was held in check by Forest's six-foot centre-half Ted Blagg. Both Jack Rowley and Ted Buckle hit the posts, but the first goal was scored by Forest's centre-forward Barks on the half-hour, and half-way through the second half Forest scored again through outside-left Lyman, with the United defence spread all over the field. Nothing would go right for the Reds and the harder they tried the less effective they became.

The headlines next day blared, 'The Cruiser Beat the Battle-

ship' and 'United Lost in a Forest', and Matt Busby in the next
home programme described the defeat as 'a great shock to us all,
none more so than the players themselves. There is never a
second chance in the Cup, and that's what makes the competition
such a thrilling affair.' Busby generously wished Forest the best
of luck on the trail to Wembley, but in spite of that, after drawing
2-2 with Middlesbrough at home, Nottingham Forest fell 6-2 in
the replay at Ayresome Park. The defeat had been a chastening
experience for the United team and every player must have taken
Busby's wise words to heart, because next season's Cup story was
to have a very different ending.

In the next match, a League game against Arsenal, Manchester
United crashed 6-2 to the Gunners, their heaviest defeat of the
season. Somehow the memory of the 5-2 victory over Arsenal at
Maine Road earlier in the season was of little consolation.

United's very next League game also created a record. The
Reds met Stoke City on 5 February, a Wednesday afternoon, in
a rearranged fixture, and the coldness of the day (and the fact that
many who would have watched were working) resulted in Manchester United's smallest recorded gate since the war, a figure
which still stands today. Only 7,800 watched United draw 1-1 on
a hard, icy pitch. There was little to keep the crowd warm, except
perhaps the excitement generated by the award of three penalties,
two for United (one unsuccessful) and one for Stoke.

Life in Britain was brought to a standstill for nearly two months
as the population suffered one of the coldest winters on record.
Football pools were cancelled for Saturday, 15 February because
21 of the scheduled 44 League games were frozen off, and that
had not happened since February 1933. By the time the thaw
came nearly six frozen Saturdays had passed and the system was
about 200 fixtures in arrears.

The Football Association announced that because so many fixtures had been affected by the weather, the season would have to
be extended to 10 May (later adjusted to 14 June). The situation
was so desperate that serious discussion was given to proposals to
play League games on Wednesday afternoons behind closed doors
(so industrial production would not be affected) or Sundays,
although the administrators realised that government legislation
would have to be introduced to legalise Sunday games. Neither

proposal became reality however, and when the thaw came in early March (and even when many pitches became waterlogged where they used to be frozen) most of the nation forgot their worst experience of the winter and enjoyed what was left of spring. Footballers, however, could justifiably lament the lengthy dislocation of the natural rhythm of training and playing, although the Manchester United players at least could count themselves lucky. They had escaped the worst of the bad weather with only games at Maine Road against Portsmouth and Sheffield United, and away to Preston North End to be rearranged.

At the end of March, Manchester United were delighted with the news that John Carey had been included in a squad of fifteen players (whittled down from an original list of fifty) from whom a Rest of Europe side would finally be chosen to play a Great Britain team at Glasgow's Hampden Park on 10 May.

The game had been arranged as a welcoming show-piece celebration of the British Football Associations rejoining FIFA from which they had seceded in 1928 on the question of 'broken time' payments for amateurs. Nearly twenty years and a world war later it was time to forgive and forget. The quality of continental football was a mystery to most British fans but the immense popularity of soccer, and the Moscow Dynamo visit the season before, guaranteed excited interest all over Britain.

John Carey remembers:

At the time there were competitions in the papers to let the readers give their opinions on which players should represent Great Britain, and I was very pleased to see that a lot had voted me into that side. When the time came to select the side though, it was found that I wasn't eligible to play for Great Britain, but I was qualified to be considered for the European team. I thought to myself, 'Well, that's it ... I'll never get into *that* side.'

Then I was very surprised to learn that I had been picked for the Rest of Europe squad of fifteen players. I was also notified that I should go over to Amsterdam, then to Rotterdam where there was to be a trial match against a Dutch team.

The Great Britain side was announced a month later and comprised: Swift (Manchester City and England); Hardwick

(Middlesbrough and England), Hughes (Birmingham and Wales); Macaulay (Brentford and Scotland), Vernon (West Bromwich Albion and Northern Ireland), Burgess (Spurs and Wales); Matthews (Stoke and England), Mannion (Middlesbrough and England), Lawton (Chelsea and England), Steel (Morton and Scotland), Liddell (Liverpool and Scotland).

The Rest of Europe side was to be: Da Rui (France), Petersen (Denmark), Steffen (Switzerland), Carey (Eire), Parola (Italy), Ludl (Czechoslovakia), Lambrecht (Belgium), Gren (Sweden), Nordahl (Sweden), Wilkes (Holland), Praest (Denmark).

Carey continued:

There was only a little difficulty with the language in that team – many could speak some English and I could speak a little Italian because I'd been over there in the war. I was absolutely amazed when just before the practice game the President of FIFA came over to me and said, 'We want you to be the captain.' It was a tremendous honour for me, and we beat Holland 2-1 in front of a crowd of 60,000!

I can remember all the players, particularly our very small goalkeeper Da Rui. My word, I was surprised how small he was, only about 5 feet 5 inches, but very agile. I thought he might be struggling because there were some big strong fellows knocking around in the Great Britain team, like Tommy Lawton and Billy Liddell.

As expected the Great Britain players, on a fee of £20 for the match, overwhelmed the Rest of Europe side 6-1 (after leading 4-1 at half-time) in front of a massive 134,000 crowd.

Carey concluded:

So we didn't know too much about Continental players, and this was the problem with the Rest of Europe side. We were a mixture, and while we were all fairly good players we weren't together as a team at all. The whole thing was a beautiful spectacle though, and such a convincing win for Great Britain. Britain, and England in particular, were masters of football in those days and it wasn't until 1953 when the Hungarians came over that we were shown what it was all about.

Manchester United enjoyed a powerful run of success during the last quarter of the season in a bid to capture the Champion-ship of the First Division, and won all but one of their last twelve games, including a 3-1 home victory over Leeds United who were to go into the record books that season as the first Division One club to suffer 30 defeats and earn only a scant 18 points in 42 games.

United's single defeat was unfortunately at the hand of Liverpool, who beat them 1–0 on 3 May. Only one point separated Liverpool and United at the end of the season but Liverpool had to wait until 12 June, the very last game of the extended season, before they could be confirmed as champions: the defeat of Stoke City by Sheffield United on that day meant that Liverpool took the title for the first time in twenty-four years.

Although there were no cups or medals for Manchester United's team this year they, as First Division runners-up, were able to share the permitted bonus of £220. This would have been a welcome addition to their weekly seasonal wage of £12 a week, especially as summer was approaching when their close-season income dropped to £10 a week!

At the end of May, Matt Busby looked back over his first official season as United's manager and allowed himself a quiet minute to remember how, exactly twenty years ago, almost to the week, the train from Scotland had brought him to Manchester, a young 18-year-old clutching a suitcase containing his football boots and a huge slice of his mother's home-made cake.

Now as the manager of one of the most popular and successful teams in the First Division he could afford to feel well satisfied with the team's progress. They played attractive, attacking football that thousands had flocked to see. They were runners-up in the First Division, and even though the Championship on which they had set their hearts had eluded United's grasp, and their Cup hopes had crashed very early on, there had been many memorable games culminating in a rousing 6–2 final-match victory over Sheffield United at Maine Road. The reserves had won the Central League title but a cautionary note was sounded by the man in charge of the side.

The story is told of how at the end of the season Matt Busby came to Jimmy Murphy's house for a drink to celebrate the success of the reserves side, only to hear the shrewd Welshman telling him that even though he was pleased with the result he didn't feel that he had anyone in the reserves good enough to justify a place in the first team. An even greater determination to find young players was born out of that conversation.

Sir Matt recalled:

My main objective was to try and build a team of our own which meant embarking on a youth policy; getting skilful footballers of school-leaving age and trying to build up a team that way. The club had no money to buy players and I thought that young players who could start their careers at Old Trafford would give you all they'd got at all times, and they'd give you loyalty which I think is so important.

In fact Manchester United has always believed in the value of having junior sides playing in their name – the club could point to the pre-war successes of the M U J A C side which had nurtured the youthful talents of John Aston and Johnny Morris before the war. More than once that season Busby had alluded to the rising transfer fees, and he never lost an opportunity to reaffirm how the club was now fully committed to developing teams of young players whose aim was to win a first-team place. The footballing world had to wait only another few years before the first of his 'Babes' – the brilliant young individuals who formed the back-bone of the side that was so cruelly shattered in 1958 – appeared in the senior team.

Sir Matt continued his story:

When I first took over I was young enough to train with players and I used to enjoy it very much. I suppose I could have actually played in the side itself for a couple of years, but I felt that I'd made the decision regarding the job and the question of being a player–manager never really fitted in with my ideas anyway – but I had a lot of fun playing against them in practice games ... they'd put me in all sorts of positions, mind you, striking, midfield and everything else. It was a very enjoyable period.

I realised very soon that United already had a number of players of quality, so I was fortunate there. There were also some players I moved into different positions, like Johnny Carey, John Aston and Allen Chilton. I suppose all my training and experience in the game had given me some insight into where players could make the best use of their abilities ... I felt somewhere along the line that things came through that way to me and the positional changes I suggested seemed to work out success-fully.

Busby's inspired decision to move John Carey gave Manchester United a full-back of world-class standard. John Carey recalls:

I used to play at inside-forward before the war against Matt Busby and when he became manager I can remember him saying, 'You know, I've never pictured you as an inside-forward, but as a wing-half or even full-back.' I said, 'That's probably because I never got up into the opposition penalty area!' Actually, as an inside-forward I did tend to operate a lot in midfield. Certainly it was an inspiration on Matt's part to convert myself and Johnny Aston to full-backs ... we were both really inside-forwards. As full-backs we were the ball players and supplied the finesse, and Henry and John Anderson were the strong players and did all the work. It just worked out that way though it was contrary to the general pattern of the way defences operated at that time.

Other testing moments often awaited Matt Busby when, after training, he climbed the stairs to his office to deal with the other side of a manager's job.

Busby was now completely in charge of team selection and training, but it had not always been like that. United's chairman James Gibson had been keen to appoint Busby and it was at the interview that Busby first showed his stubbornness: he was offered a three-year contract and came out with one for five – no mean achievement against a man who liked his own way and usually got it. There had been clashes already between Busby and Gibson: the somewhat autocratic Gibson found the strong-minded Busby demanding certain rights as a manager, especially to train and pick the team and to bid for players or to reject those the directors thought should be bought. There are numerous stories about those early clashes, perhaps prompted from the outset by Gibson saying to Busby, 'Now you've got the job I hope you are not going to spend a lot of money!' But after a while Gibson could see that Busby was achieving good results and that his Celtic determination did not confine itself merely to the football field.

James Gibson found it hard adapting to Busby's demands for control of the playing side of the club's affairs. Before the war, the situation was very different. In those days teams were trained and given tactical talks by the trainer, but the buying of players and the selection of the team was in the hands of the club's directors. After all, their money usually kept the club alive (and this was even more so in Manchester United's case) which is why the directors, with advice from the manager when asked, usually decided who was going to turn out for the club next Saturday afternoon.

But Matt Busby was the first of a new breed of manager; he

was young, he had played at international level, he was acquainted with the new vocabulary of tactics, he had theories based on solid experience. He had also quickly built up a reputation with his players for wisdom and understanding and everybody's Service experiences had taught them to respect a man who gave them orders, trained with them and had a drink with them when the game was over.

There was one last moment that season for local football fans to savour. It contained a hidden poignancy, however, which became apparent only a decade later. On Saturday, 7 June at Old Trafford, Salford Boys played Leicester Boys in the second leg of the English Schools FA Trophy final. Nobody in the 30,000 crowd would have realised the particular significance of Salford's diminutive inside-left and captain from Tootal Road School called Geoffrey Bent, apart from the fact that he marshalled his team superbly in their 2–0 victory over Leicester Boys to take the Trophy.

Ten years later, and by then United's strapping reserve left-back, with twelve senior appearances and many more promised, he was one of those to die so tragically with seven of his teammates at Munich Airport.

## Worthy Winners

After probably one of the shortest close seasons in the history of the game, the first fixtures of the 1947-48 season kicked off on 2 August, one of those classic late summer days when the air is warm and the pitches never look greener or the shirts brighter.

When United met last season's Cup winners Charlton Athletic at Maine Road for their second 'home' game of the season (having dispatched League Champions Liverpool 2-0 the week before), Matt Busby's note in the programme ended with a promise 'at all times to try and serve up the class of football of which United can be proud'; and football reporter Alf Clarke reflected that this season 'in my opinion may be an outstanding one'. How right they both proved to be!

Unaccountably, after a rousing 6-2 victory against Charlton Athletic, Manchester United found themselves not winning again for nearly two months. Last season's pattern was repeating itself: a run of impressive early season wins had slowly ground to a halt in a morass of draws and defeats. Many games were disappointing – United's defeat by Sunderland on 18 October consigned them to fifth from bottom place in the League. A month before, watched by a massive crowd of 72,000, United had drawn 0-0 in a very drab game against Manchester City, the first 'derby' game the city had witnessed for ten years.

Manchester United's lack of progress in the League was probably the reason why no international calls came for Stan Pearson and Jack Rowley for England's game against Belgium on 22 September in Brussels; although John Carey and Jimmy Delaney were picked to play against each other when Eire were to meet Scotland in Belfast on 4 October. Sadly though, injury prevented Carey from turning out in that game.

The lack of good results caused even the most experienced players to lose confidence. Jimmy Delaney saw Matt Busby with a view to leaving the club and the city which had taken him to their hearts, but Busby's calm reassurances set the popular Scotsman's mind at rest. Loss of form could be restored: the solution was to keep playing and not to run away. Delaney told reporters that he had changed his mind. 'I knew I had not been playing as well as I can, but Matt Busby wouldn't listen to any kind of transfer talk. That's good enough for me. If Matt wants me to stay, I'll stay.'

Matt Busby and his team agree unanimously that the turning point of their fortunes in the season came on 1 November when, lying seventeenth in the table with only eleven points from 13 games, they beat Wolverhampton Wanderers 6-2 at Molyneux. Admittedly the week before they had beaten Aston Villa 2-0, but the victory against Wolves saw their attack hit a new level of power and penetration. United's players always believed that a goal against them, however early, brought out the best in their play and this was to be proved a few times this season, notably in the third round Cup game, and even in the final itself. Against Wolves, United were a goal down after seven minutes but were level thirty seconds later. Ironically only Jack Rowley, one of Wolverhampton's sons, did not score, but Stan Pearson and Johnny Morris claimed two each and Jimmy Delaney and Charlie Mitten brought the tally to six, the heaviest home defeat the Wolves had suffered for thirteen years.

The players and supporters were not the only ones who were relieved to see themselves on course again. England's manager Walter Winterbottom was becoming a regular visitor to United's games. Possibly as an ex-Manchester United player himself, he had to try extra hard to be objective about players from his home town, but reporters soon discovered that he greatly admired Pearson, Rowley, Cockburn, Morris and John Aston and they were 'all in his plans for places in the England team'.

The draw for the third round fixtures of the FA Cup is one of the most eagerly awaited events in football, and there was great excitement when on Sunday, 14 December it was announced that United were drawn against Aston Villa, the match to be played on 10 January.

A Manchester United supporter would have to have had a good memory to remember the last time United won the Cup. In fact, it was nearly forty years before in 1909 when they beat Bristol City 1–0 in the final which was played at Crystal Palace. In the following seasons United's Cup runs had always ended in the early rounds, apart from way back in 1926 when they were beaten 3–0 in the semi-final round by Manchester City.

Remembering the previous season's Cup defeat Matt Busby wrote in a programme note at the time: 'I am not unduly worried. I would prefer going to Villa Park than to some Second Division ground. Villa play good football and so do we, so it should be a great match.' Privately, Busby's faith in his team burned strongly, but at this stage he was prepared to share his deepest thoughts only with close friends.

At the beginning of the season I'd gone to watch a player up in Glasgow and bumped into a great friend of mine who was also a real soccer fan. We weren't doing all that well in the League and my friend said, 'What's your side supposed to be doing, Matt?' I said, 'I think they've a great future, as a matter of fact I think they can win the Cup – we're just at the stage where something's going to happen – there's so much talent there and it just wanted knitting together and us getting a break.' He put a few pounds on us to win the Cup that season, at 25–1!

Busby at least was sure the team was poised for success in the Cup or the League. He had already learned that a manager must believe that his team is going to win, and be able to transmit that belief to his players. Out of that belief springs confidence and success.

United's current form looked very promising and Busby was hoping that the team could maintain this new consistency, especially in the vital Cup games which lay ahead. The support for the team, as always, was tremendous: an average of 50,000 spectators had watched United's nine home fixtures so far this season, and since the victory against Wolves, United had slowly begun to climb up the League. The goals began to come and Jack Rowley was currently prominent among the League's top scorers with thirteen to his credit.

The third round tie against Aston Villa was regarded as the outstanding fixture of this round, but from United's point of view could not be regarded as an easy one. They had already beaten Villa 2–0 at Maine Road on 25 October, but the Midlands club was a few places higher up the League table. Predictably, there was an immediate rush for tickets 'especially on the popular side'. As the players prepared for the Christmas fixtures and the Villa cup tie, the final part of United's superb footballing machine was about to be slotted into place.

On Saturday, 20 December, United were to play Middlesbrough at Maine Road, and early that morning the reserves had set off by train to Newcastle for their Central League fixture at St James's Park. A few hours before the kick-off, John Carey told Matt Busby that he had stomach trouble and it would be impossible for him to play. Busby had to think quickly. Middlesbrough were sixth in the League and they were a class side sporting the likes of George Hardwick, the England captain, and Wilf Mannion, an England inside-forward of exceptional talent. Jack Warner, United's most likely substitute, was also ill. Only one other reserve defender would do – but he was on his way to Newcastle. There was still time to retrieve the situation. Matt Busby sent off a telegram to Leeds Station.

John Anderson remembered the dramatic incidents of that day:

On the way to Newcastle we had to change trains at Leeds, and over the station tannoy was an announcement asking our trainer Bill Inglis to go to the station master's office where there was a message for him. It was to send me back to Manchester ... I didn't know I was playing, I thought I was to be twelfth man or something. The team's boots were always on the top of the skip, so they just threw my boots out and away I went straight back to Manchester. When I got to Maine Road Matt Busby said, 'Get changed John, you're playing'.

It was a dream debut. John Anderson's patient nine-year wait for a first-team game was rewarded, and the 25-year-old from Salford played the game of his life in United's 2–1 victory. The papers were full of praise for him 'a player of rich promise ... a player with the poise and self-command of a seasoned veteran ... his play was one of the highlights of the game'. He had contained Wilf Mannion brilliantly and Matt Busby realised that here was a ready-made player who had shown himself well capable of first-team soccer. But where could he fit in?

When John Carey returned to the side for the Christmas Day fixture against Portsmouth, John Anderson was named as twelfth man, but during that game United's regular right-back Joe Walton received a knee injury. So for the return fixture against Portsmouth two days later, Carey dropped to right-back to allow John Anderson another try at right-half where he had another impressively confident game.

Manchester United had at last put together the team which was to take them to the highest pinnacles of success in this and the next few seasons. John Anderson, apart from the odd game missed through injury, maintained his place for the rest of the season, displacing Jack Warner who had given many years of loyal service to the club.

To celebrate the New Year, United hammered Burnley 5-0 at Maine Road, thus completing a run of twelve games without defeat. United turned on a devastating display of fast, open football on a muddy and waterlogged pitch (against a team which had only conceded a few goals in twenty games), watched again by Walter Winterbottom who sat next to Matt Busby, and as Don Davies reported, 'puffed his pipe with rare contentment and watched the behaviour of his old team with immense satisfaction'. Significantly, the team had yet again shown that they could turn on their most devastating soccer on heavy pitches. It was to be a crucial factor in their Cup match against Aston Villa, now only a few days away.

*Third Round versus Aston Villa at Villa Park, 10 January 1948*

MANCHESTER UNITED: Crompton; Carey, Aston; Anderson, Chilton, Cockburn; Delaney, Morris, Rowley, Pearson, Mitten.

ASTON VILLA: Jones; Potts, Parkes; Dorsett, Moss, Lowe; Edwards, Martin, Ford, Brown, Smith.

Some of the 58,683 spectators who crowded into Villa Park that afternoon would have been aware of how Aston Villa had always featured prominently in United's history. They had inflicted United's record defeat of 7-0 in 1930, and when they played United in 1920 an Old Trafford record crowd of 70,504 had watched the game.

The Villa side of that day contained some famous and remarkable players. Their centre-forward was big and bustling in the classic mould – a Welsh international called Trevor Ford whose aim, once the whistle blew, was to establish immediate superiority over the opposition's centre-half. He and Allenby Chilton were to have some enthusiastic exchanges that afternoon. At inside-left was Albert 'Sailor' Brown who had transferred to Aston Villa from Nottingham Forest earlier in the season. His goal in last season's fourth round tie with Nottingham Forest had effectively ended United's Cup hopes that season. Dickie Dorsett at right-half had one of the most fearsome shots in the First Division: legend was that his penalty kicks could stave in a barrel. If the ground was wet and muddy the soaked leather ball became heavier and heavier and, hit hard enough, became a lethal projectile. If Matt Busby could have been told that, during the course of the game, Jack Crompton would have to face a Dorsett penalty and several of his free kicks, he would have certainly have kept the news from his goalkeeper!

Sadly, Villa would be playing without their regular and experienced goalkeeper, Joe Rutherford, who had broken his arm in a game a couple of weeks before. Instead, young Keith Jones was to deputise – his home debut for Villa. The week before he had appeared for the first time at Maine Road against Manchester City where, encouragingly, he had saved a penalty. Villa would also be without George Cummings, their captain and Scottish international left-back. So how would the defence cope this afternoon, Villa supporters asked themselves, against one of the best forward lines in the country?

Meanwhile, inside the dressing-rooms, the teams were preparing themselves for the match. Little details still cling to their memories. 'One of the first things I noticed', the diminutive Henry Cockburn recalled, 'when we got into the dressing-rooms was the height of the pegs where we were to hang our clothes. I thought, Dear me, those Villa lads must be big'uns ... they must all be six-footers to have pegs that high. I had to stand on the bloody bench to hang my stuff up!' Allenby Chilton also remembers Villa Park with affection, echoing the sentiments of many of the 1948 side who said it was one of their most favourite grounds: because of the superb Victorian façade of the main grandstand side, for the pitch itself, and for those famous dressing-rooms. 'I think it's one of the finest-looking grounds in the country, you know. The dressing-rooms were beautifully panelled in oak: you had three or four pegs to a person: the floors were wooden and when you went for a bath you walked down a slope into the water, which is better than climbing up which we had to do at Stoke!'

So the stage was now set for something special: the crowd was huge, mostly standing on open terraces as the rain swept down on that cold grey afternoon; sleeves were rolled up, hands were spat on, the referee put his whistle to his lips, and the game began.

When referee Berry blew his whistle at 2 p.m. precisely to start the game, Villa's centre-forward Trevor Ford pushed the ball to inside-left 'Sailor' Brown, who quickly dribbled past the advancing Johnny Morris and John Anderson, and passed the ball out to Les Smith on the left wing. He took the ball a few yards and centred a low ball. George Edwards, Villa's outside-right, slipped in from the wing and met Smith's cross with an unstoppable shot into United's goal.

Jack Crompton had never played at Villa Park before and his first action of any significance at that famous ground was to pick the ball out of his net, 13½ seconds after the referee had signalled the start of the game, and he was the first United player to touch the ball. John Anderson remembered 'automatically looking up at that big clock they have in the corner of the ground at Villa Park as they kicked off. It was two o'clock. The ball was tapped to the inside-forward, out to the wing, across, bang – it's in the net, we're one down. I looked for the time. It was still bloody two o'clock!'

United seemed to take the loss calmly and within a few minutes settled to a rhythm which involved all the forwards who displayed their full range of skills. United's reaction to that early goal was devastating. After six minutes Jack Rowley powerfully headed in a cross from Charlie Mitten. Ten minutes later Johnny Morris headed in from a Delaney corner. After half an hour Stan Pearson scored United's third goal, a ricochet from a blistering Rowley free kick. Before the half-time whistle blew Johnny Morris headed in a Charlie Mitten cross, and a few seconds before the interval Jimmy Delaney ran the ball in after a mesmerising passing movement involving Morris and Pearson.

Amid the mud and sweat of the dressing-room at half-time, the Villa players contemplated the 5–1 scoreline and tried to extemporise a defence against United's devastating play. They had conceded nearly all their goals from wing play. How could they control Delaney and Mitten? How could they stop Pearson or Morris finding their wingmen so accurately? If United had scored five goals at half-time, might it be ten at the final whistle? Only a couple of attempts by Trevor Ford and Frank Moss had troubled Crompton in the United goal.

For United, the tie looked safe. Their lead looked impregnable and there was no reason why Delaney and Mitten shouldn't continue to torture the Villa defence for another forty-five minutes.

The second half began. Don Davies in his account of the game wrote: 'Naturally with a score of five goals to one in their favour and all going well, the Manchester portion of the great crowd of 58,000 chattered during the interval like thousands of red and white magpies. Fifteen minutes later they were silent as Trappists and ten times more scared.'

The reasons soon became clear. United, not surprisingly, found it difficult to pick up the same pace and rhythm they had achieved at the end of the first half, and the subconscious temptation to defend their lead and only free-wheel in attack was irresistible. Then suddenly and dramatically the whole course of the game changed, resulting in one of the most memorable third round ties ever played.

Only a minute into the second half the United defence, trying to stem a Villa rush, conceded a corner. Winger Edwards took it, the ball curled into the goalmouth without another Villa player touching it, and although Jack Crompton tried to smother it and John Carey tried to hook it away, the referee ruled that it had crossed the line.

John Aston still believes that the ball never crossed the line and Jack Crompton agrees with him. 'I dived on the ball which was on the line and then there was a scramble and the referee said it had crossed the line. It hadn't, never did. The conditions were atrocious and you just couldn't see the line and that's why the goal was given, I think.' He also echoed John Aston's reaction to it. 'You just accepted it though and got on with the game.'

Aston Villa continued to press attack upon attack, and a misunderstanding between Carey and Chilton, reflecting an increasing uncertainty in United's defence, gave Trevor Ford a gilt-edged chance only two yards from goal but he shot hurriedly wide.

Chilton and Ford had soon resumed their bruising battle in the mud of Villa Park. Fellow half-back Henry Cockburn remembered Chilton and Ford 'giving each other stick ... niggling away at each other all through the game. After one incident the ball had been played away and Chilli, who'd been a boxer in the army, turned round and slotted one on Ford and down he went. Nobody saw a thing. It was beautifully done, you know what I mean!'

Villa's second half plans were working: the ball was being kept from United's destructive forwards, and their defenders were being hurried at every turn. Their manager Alec Massie had told them at half-time to 'keep your chins up – your task is not impossible – just go out there and do your best'.

And Villa's best was brilliant in that second half. As the rain continued to pour down, Villa yet again laid siege on the United goal. Suddenly, a free-kick was awarded to Villa just outside the penalty area and the moment United's defence was dreading had arrived. Dickie Dorsett took the kick and banged the ball goalwards. It spung off the wall of brave but quailing defenders and fell at the feet of Les Smith who pushed it over the line. Charlie Mitten chuckled as he remembered lining up in United's defensive wall when Dorsett was shaping up to take that free kick. 'Dorsett had a shot like a thunderbolt – no finesse or anything – he just used to put his boot and his body behind it – he could bore a hole through you. We were all looking at each other and laughing, even at that stage of the match, and saying, "I hope to God he misses me and hits you, or it goes over our heads." When he hit the ball we all ducked and it clipped one of us and Les Smith stuck it in on the rebound. Anyway, we were all still glad to be alive to see the end of the game!'

Villa with three goals were now within striking distance of United's five. The Villa crowd bayed encouragement and with only ten minutes of the match remaining Allenby Chilton, whose titanic battle with Trevor Ford was one of the most enduring features of this memorable match, brought down the Welshman in United's penalty area. Allen admits giving the penalty away. 'I brought Ford down because he was being a bit naughty in that game – I maybe shouldn't have done but I did. Early on in the game he'd brought his foot up and caught me in the stomach when I was clearing the ball and it was that which had brewed up the trouble.' Dickie Dorsett, of course, was Villa's penalty-taker as well and Don Davies described it as a penalty 'most violently taken and we can only congratulate Crompton on his skill in avoiding such a murderous missile!'

Aston Villa were now only one goal behind. Few had experienced or ever were to experience again the atmosphere of the last ten minutes of that game. Roars of encouragement for more Villa attacks blended with the shouts of United supporters encouraging their team to hold on to the now very slim lead. Nine goals scored, ten minutes to go, whoever got through this round would surely win the Cup!

The action on the field was frantic. Trevor Ford forced the ball past Jack Crompton but the goal was disallowed. According to George Edwards, the Villa outside right, that could have been a certain goal which might have meant that Villa could have forced a draw. 'Les Smith crossed a beautiful centre, Trevor went up to head it but couldn't reach it, "Sailor" Brown was shouting for him to leave it, but Trevor put his hand up by the side of his head and handled the ball. We all still contend that "Sailor" would have scored from that chance and we could have levelled the score if Trevor hadn't handled!'

The deciding goal came two minutes from time. The Villa goalkeeper had just pushed a Mitten shot past the post and the attackers and defenders took their positions for what could be the last action of the game. A corner taken by Charlie Mitten sailed into the penalty area and dropped to Stan Pearson who turned it in through a crowd of players, a goal that Matt Busby was later to describe as 'one of the most valuable he has ever scored for the club'. It was also one of a number of decisive goals Stan Pearson was to score on the way to, and in the final itself. United's arms were flung skywards, Villa's heads sank to their chests. The struggle to reach the United total had sapped Villa's strength and invention, and now time had all but run out for them.

There was in fact barely time to restart the game when the final whistle blew – the game was over, a game that was to live for ever in the memories of those who played in it and those who watched it.

The United players were full of praise for the match and one another, it was truly a magnificent team effort. 'In my opinion',

said Stan Pearson, 'and I don't care who hears it, that game was
when we played the best football I've seen from anybody, anywhere, anytime. That's saying a lot, but we pinged that ball
around so quickly first time – I've never seen anything like it
before or since. We were shoving it around and darting here and
there. The lads would be moving ... taking somebody out of the
way and another would slip into space ... it was magic ... everything seemed to click.'

'We played some brilliant stuff that afternoon,' agreed Charlie
Mitten, 'we could have found each other in the dark.' Jack
Crompton remembers it 'as a hell of a game. It had everything –
goals, bags of excitement, a huge crowd, plenty of skill and it was
a good strong physical game as they were in those days. That
game took a year off your life, though, if you were one of the
players or managers.' Sir Matt Busby still claims it 'as an amazing
match to watch. Very often now,' he added, 'when I'm watching
an important Cup tie, that game comes back to me, especially if
a goal is scored early on.'

At the time John Carey thought that Villa's very early goal
'was the worst thing they could have done ... fancy taking the
liberty of scoring like that so quickly! We settled down to it immediately and set about them and the football we played was
out of this world. You know, it was an extraordinary thing
about this 1948 team – when the chips were down we could step
up our game and destroy the opposition in ten minutes. The
passes flew – everybody played all out and we could trans-
form a game where we found ourselves a goal down to one
where not long later we were leading by several goals. It happened
in the Villa Park game and it happened in many other matches
as well.'

Johnny Morris' comments echo his captain's view. 'The game
at Villa Park was one of the most exciting I've ever played in.
"Sailor" Brown scored an early goal but it was no problem – we
always went on the field one goal down. I thought the game was
too easy, after the first few minutes. It became too easy because
of the way we were playing. Villa had some good players at the
time, but we must have demoralised them in the first half. In the
second half they fought back and got a few goals, but when you
are leading 5-1 at half-time you are bound to relax a little bit. It
was a bit worrying later in the game when they fought back, but

once we picked ourselves up it was no problem. We used to like to play under pressure.'

Charlie Mitten's minor concern was that he hadn't scored. 'After the match I said to Matt, "Bloody marvellous: we win 6–4 and I'm the only forward who didn't score." "Never mind," Matt said, "we're keeping your goals for the hard games!"' Mitten also remembered how the tension of the match affected even the referee. 'It was 5–4 and the referee was a chap called Berry, a really good ref. he was. If there was any trouble he'd say, "Come on lads, stop buggering about and get on with the game." Anyway in those last few minutes when the tension was unbelievable, Stan Pearson pulled a high ball down on his chest and the ref. blew for a foul ... handball. I said, "Oh no! Mr Berry!" He said, "I know Charlie, I know, my mistake, I wish I could stick the whistle up my bum, but there you are, it's all the tension." So he gave a bounce up and soon after we went on to score another goal!'

Amid the victory celebrations there was still time to spare consoling thoughts for the Aston Villa side which had fought so hard. 'I'll never forget that game because it was close ... so close,' said Jack Rowley. 'It really was a ding-dong battle. Some of those Villa players were nearly in tears at the end. They fought back in the second half ... they really fought back. The crowd got their money's worth – it was as good as a Cup final for the people who watched it.'

George Edwards, the Aston Villa outside-right who scored the first goal and the second which began Villa's storming revival in the second half, remembered that, 'Weeks prior to our Cup tie with Manchester United we had been having an early goal scored against us, and then had to fight back like hell for a good result. We sat in the dressing-room before the Cup tie and said if only we could get an early goal it would be great. A few minutes later I'd cracked one in. We all thought, This is it! But Manchester United came straight back at us with some great football. At half-time Alec Massie said, "Well lads, we've got a hard job to do so let us let them know that they have had a football match." It was a great game, and we nearly did it.'

Thirty-five years had not dimmed the memories of some of the Aston Villa spectators who now count themselves almost as a privileged élite who saw the game. Some were merely lads.

Peter Aldridge, now living in West Sussex, was a teenager at the time:

... well-smitten with claret-and-blue fanaticism, I watched the game from the old Witton-end terrace, now replaced by the North Stand. The tie was probably the most attractive of the round. Manchester United were developing a reputation for skilful football, and Villa were having one of their better post-war seasons.

I recall being apprehensive before the game. Villa were obliged to replace their experienced goalkeeper, Rutherford, with Keith Jones, later to make his mark with Villa and Wales, but at the time an inexperienced youngster. To make matters worse, George Cummings, Villa's captain and left-back also cried off through injury shortly before the game. I thought at the time that Villa would be exposed with an untried goalkeeper and without the cool head and uncanny organising ability of Cummings. In the event my apprehension was well founded, but had it not been for the circumstances which led to the replacement of Rutherford and Cummings it is unlikely that the game would have been so memorable. Although Villa produced the first drama of the afternoon by scoring direct from the kick-off through centre-forward Edwards, before a Manchester player had touched the ball, it was what happened during the rest of that remarkable first half that lives in the memory. The United forward line scored five goals, to lead 5–1 at half-time. I probably did not appreciate it at the time, but I have since realised that I was fortunate to be standing behind the goal which United were attacking. For forty-four minutes I had a panoramic view of the most fascinating forward play that I have ever seen. The United forwards made the creation and scoring of goals appear to be the easiest thing in the world and I can clearly recall swearing to people afterwards that at half-time United had scored five goals and not one of their forwards had broken sweat! They made it look that easy.

At half-time I seriously considered leaving the ground, a thing I had never done before – or since. I had seen my team humiliated, but I stayed, perhaps because the United football was so captivating, perhaps because I hoped for better things from Villa in the second half. As it turned out the miracle almost happened when Villa pulled the score back to 5–4 before conceding a sixth goal to United a few minutes from the end.

If, from all the hundreds of games of professional football which I have watched, I could live just one game again, I have never doubted which one it would be. I would opt for Villa Park, 10 January 1948. It was without doubt the greatest game of football I have ever seen.'

Richard Taylor of Shaw near Oldham made the journey to
Villa Park as a Manchester United supporter:

In those days milk-bottles had cardboard tops and using one of those,
my wife sewed some red and white ribbon bought from Woolworths and
there I was with a home made rosette. Later on as United progressed,
larger rosettes appeared but I stayed with my smaller home-made version
throughout. The only other souvenir I still have is a pre-war Tootal's tie
which I wore for every round. I wore it again for the European Cup final
and when they eventually put me down, it's going with me.

I was standing almost directly opposite the players' tunnel and the
first Villa goal was scored at that end. The last goal, Stan Pearson's, was
also scored there two minutes from the end, but the intervening eight
were all scored at the other end. United got five before half-time with
some dream football, but when Villa got their first goal I felt like going
home. It was a very big crowd and in those days supporters of both
teams mixed, spoke to each other and indulged in leg-pulling. I was
kidded about my red and white rosette because United were playing in
blue that afternoon.

With eight minutes to go it was 5-4 and Villa had scored three from
set pieces. The atmosphere was so charged I felt that if anyone had
struck a match the place would explode. I think the Pearson goal still
rates as one of my biggest ever sighs of relief!

The only other thing I remember was that on both journeys there and
back to Manchester by Claribel Coaches it was snowing. There was no
motorway, of course, and travelling through Staffordshire a group of
workmen by the side of the road gave us the thumbs down. We were
looking for them on the way back but it was too much to hope for on a
wet Saturday night!

The Press excelled themselves, of course, on an afternoon
which had sent them searching for descriptions which could do
some justice to the game they had to describe.

Don Davies of the *Manchester Guardian* and Geoffrey Green
of *The Times* both wrote famous accounts of the match. Don
Davies selected artistic metaphors to introduce his report.

If Picasso and Matisse jointly or severally had been responsible for
the design of this match they could not have given a more original
twist to the proceedings. The Aston Villa forwards kicked off and in
13½ seconds were dancing back to the centre spot in delirious celebration of a goal which may become historic as a model of swiftness and

surprise. Villa's opening move had been so perfect in design, so precise in execution, that not a single United player could touch the ball even; it was as though one of those theoretical blackboard diagrams, used by football managers to illustrate tactical talks, had really come to life. But the odd thing was that Manchester United were not in the least degree upset or ruffled by the game's ironic beginning. Calmly and blandly they set their own incomparable machinery in motion, seized and held the initiative, and by a beauty of method which seemed like a system of logic made visible they put on five delightful goals by half-time and reduced the Birmingham populace to a state of wide-eyed wonderment, if not utter stupor.

Geoffrey Green wrote an equally vivid account in which 'deep human qualities flowered before our eyes, and if the skies wept they proved to be tears of joy. Here was an afternoon to remember; a grey, damp, winter's day touched by magic. It was a match of superlatives, in which football science was later challenged by undying courage.'

The *Daily Dispatch* report's enthusiasm was much less restrained. For him 'It was Mafeking Night, Armistice Day and VE Day rolled into one!'

When the draw for the fourth round was made next day the problem everybody hoped would not arise, did arise: Manchester City were paired at home to Chelsea and Manchester United were drawn, also at 'home' to Liverpool. The rules would not allow the fixture to be played at Maine Road on another date. A new venue had to be found for the game, and the directors of both clubs discussed the merits of staging the game at several neutral grounds. The choice was quickly made: Goodison Park seemed to suit both sides admirably, even though the away side seemed to have a distinct geographical advantage. Liverpool's team need only walk across Stanley Park, whereas the home side would have to travel from Manchester, forty miles away.

John Aston admired Busby's reason for electing to play the game at Goodison Park, at a time when everybody else thought it was too deep inside the enemy's territory.

He told us it would suit our style of play: it's a big, wide-open ground and we could really sling the ball around there. He knew it would be a full house – a third of the ticket allocation would be going to Everton, and they'd be bound to be shouting for us, so we would actually have two-thirds of the crowd on our side. Busby was always very cute at thinking about things like that.

Walter Crickmer, within hours of the draw being announced, was besieged by phone and letter requests for tickets, and the indefatigable United secretary had to implore supporters not to apply for tickets as 'the prices haven't even been fixed yet'.

Despite drawing a match away from home, again, United were confident that they could beat Liverpool, much to the alarm of the local bookmakers who stood to lose thousands of pounds should United win the cup. Before the competition had begun the bookmakers had laid odds of 25:1, and United were now joint favourites at 9:1 with Blackpool and Derby County.

Just a week after their magnificent victory at Villa Park, Manchester United were plunged again into their League programme, a home game against League leaders Arsenal.

An English League record crowd, variously quoted between 82,950 and 83,260 (no doubt attracted by the success of the Villa game and the amount of attention United were enjoying from the newspapers) watched a 1-1 draw at Maine Road. A classic thunderbolt from Jack Rowley equalled an early Arsenal goal and thereafter Arsenal's brilliant defence managed to hold out against some vintage high-powered United forward play.

This was another fine team effort which carried Manchester United to fifteen games without defeat. They were a 'united' team in every sense and their forward play was particularly brilliant, reflected in their goal tally. Around this time, it was noted, Johnny Morris (18) and Jack Rowley (18) led the First Division scorers' list (Cup and League) and Stan Pearson had also scored 11 goals. No other club came within a distance of this achievement – 47 goals by three inside-forwards alone. Roll on the next round!

*Fourth Round versus Liverpool at Goodison Park, 24 January 1948*

MANCHESTER UNITED: Crompton; Carey, Aston; Anderson, Chilton, Cockburn; Delaney, Morris, Rowley, Pearson, Mitten.

LIVERPOOL: Minshull; Jones, Lambert; Taylor, Hughes, Paisley; Liddell, Balmer, Stubbins, Done, Priday.

The Manchester United team versus Huddersfield Town, 1 September 1945. From left to right: Roach, Warner, Walton, Crompton, Whalley, Koffman, Chilton, Hanlon, Rowley, Worrall (Portsmouth), and Smith.

Preparing for the third round FA Cup tie against Aston Villa – the team watches assistant manager, Bill Inglis, do the hokey cokey! (Taken at Old Trafford, Friday, 9 January 1948.)

On the Davyhulme Golf Course, United listen to the draw which paired them with Liverpool in the fourth round of the 1948 FA Cup.

Gooch, the Preston goalkeeper, makes a flying save from Pearson during the sixth round tie, 28 February 1948.

An incident during Manchester United versus Preston North End in the sixth round at Maine Road. The United players are (from left to right) Mitten, Cockburn and Pearson.

Robinson, the Blackpool goalkeeper, watches as one of his defenders and Charlie Mitten tussle for the ball.

Jack Rowley is left with an open goal as he scores his first goal, with Robinson stranded.

Jack Rowley (on the ground) scores Manchester United's second goal in the 1948 Final.

John Carey, United's captain, receives the FA Cup from the King, as HM the Queen looks on.

Mitten and Crompton chair Carey, holding the Cup, with Rowley behind and Anderson and Pearson (holding the base) to their left.

The gates closed half an hour before the start, enclosing another huge crowd of over 74,000 and locking out as many as
15,000 according to some estimates. The interest in the game was
massive and supporters got to the game any way they could. The
*Manchester Evening News* had earlier reported that one air charter
company, flying eight-seater Rapides, was charging only four
pence per head per mile for the trip from Manchester Airport to
Speke Airport.

Liverpool began the game promisingly with a strong cold wind
at their backs, but after John Aston had kicked off the line when
Jack Crompton was beaten, and when Liverpool's inside-left
Done had missed an easy chance, the Anfield side seemed to give
up. Chilton, Aston, Cockburn and Anderson were playing magnificently and so completely dominated the Liverpool forward
line that they had time and energy left over to lend their weight
to the attack. Up front, the interchanging of United's forwards,
particularly that between Rowley, Mitten and Morris, was up to
its usual dazzling standard and Don Davies wrote in the *Guardian*
the following Monday that Minshull, Liverpool's goalkeeper, had
to deal with so many shots from so many angles 'that his fingers
must be tingling yet!'

All the goals came within seven minutes in the first half. Half
an hour into the game Jack Rowley scored the first from a pass
by Charlie Mitten; then five minutes later John Carey placed a
free kick so well that Hughes only succeeded in heading it to the
feet of Johnny Morris who drove it home from nearly thirty
yards; immediately after the kick-off Rowley beat Hughes neatly
in the air for the ball, and Mitten raced in and lobbed it coolly
over Minshull's head as he advanced to meet the United left-
winger.

It was an easy game for United: Liverpool were completely
overwhelmed and it probably would have been of little consolation to them then to have known that their greatest years were
yet to come.

John Aston recalled how in that game a Liverpool plan to
reposition Billy Liddell, a Scottish international winger, had
failed miserably. Matt Busby had played with Liddell in his
Liverpool days, and United's defence, and John Aston in particular, had been well briefed. 'They put Billy Liddell at outside-
right against me, because Johnny Carey always used to have a

good game against him, and John had caned him once or twice in League games. Liddell was a smashing bloke ... he always gave you a good clean tussle. Anyway, that game they thought they'd play him on me. Bloody easy he was ... I was surprised how easy!'

All United's defenders, as well as the forwards, had outstanding games, and the Liverpool forward line, starved of possession, withered quickly. Someone observed that the only time Liverpool's youthful left-half Bob Paisley got the ball was at the throw-in! Paisley still remembers that fourth round game in which, as a defender, he had to face the dazzling speed and control of the United forwards. His final compliments are brief but should be treasured because in his years at Anfield as a player and manager Bob Paisley has seen some of the best teams in the world in action. 'The lasting memory of that game', he wrote, 'is being soundly beaten 3-0 by, in my opinion, one of the best post-war teams I have ever seen.'

Manchester United had managed to achieve the most difficult thing of all in football – to maintain a high level of success and consistency in both League and Cup games; not for them the almost inevitable slump which most teams would have suffered after the peak they had reached in the game at Villa Park.

As the crowds streamed away from Goodison Park, the other full-time results were ready for them in the 'Stop Press' column of the *Liverpool Echo*. Blackpool had beaten Chester 4-0 (and later details revealed that Blackpool's full-back Eddie Shimwell had scored the first goal with a shot from fifty-five yards out); Charlton Athletic had beaten Stockport 3-0; non-League Colchester, who had knocked out mighty Arsenal in the previous round, had reached the last sixteen by beating Bradford 3-2; and Manchester City had beaten Chelsea 2-0 after extra time.

Would Manchester United meet any of these teams in the next round?

A week after their fourth round Cup victory, Manchester United were finally beaten 2-1 by Sheffield United at Bramhall Lane, their first defeat in over three months and sixteen consecutive League and Cup matches. However, such a magnificent run of success had to end sometime – better, as Matt Busby remarked at the time, in a League rather than a Cup game.

Manchester United had played their game against Sheffield

United knowing that, yet again, they had drawn a fifth round tie at home against a First Division side, this time Charlton Athletic – then seconds later learning that Manchester City had also been drawn at home, to Preston North End.

The FA again would not entertain the idea of allowing Manchester United to play their match just before or after City's fixture, and they were quick to remind everybody that the rules called for all ties to be played on the same day. So the task of finding another neutral ground began again. Charlton Athletic did their best to extol the virtues of Stamford Bridge and Highbury as possible venues, but United felt that as the 'home' side they were going to try a little harder to find a ground north of Watford. Unfortunately, an old favourite, Villa Park, had already been booked by Aston Villa for a friendly against Newcastle United.

At last the decision was made: the tie would be played at Leeds Road, Huddersfield Town's ground. Many semi-final ties and international matches had been staged there, and it had a crowd capacity of nearly 70,000.

Whatever the choice United could not please everyone. Even for the team itself 'home' draws were becoming meaningless – it was bad enough having to play only First Division sides let alone having to play a Cup tie in Yorkshire. Not for the first time would United have wished that Old Trafford could have been ready. A few envious glances might have been thrown in Blackpool's direction. This time the lucky 'Tangerines' had been paired at home to non-League Colchester!

To reach this round Charlton had beaten Newcastle United 2–1 and Stockport 3–0, but their current League form was not particularly inpressive. Manchester United had already beaten them 2–1 a month before at The Valley, and in only the third match of the season had overwhelmed them 6–2 at Maine Road. But there was enough experience at Old Trafford now to acknowledge that League form often had little bearing on Cup results. Charlton were a famous First Division side with an impressive record in the Cup: they were, of course, the present holders and had been runners-up in 1946. Also, they had a famous heroic goalkeeper, Sam Bartram, who eventually was to make 800 appearances for them between 1934 and 1956, and it was Sam Bartram who was to be the hero of this game. Charlton Athletic also had an interesting connection with Manchester United. Allenby Chilton had guested for them in the Football League South Cup final at Wembley on 15 April 1944. Charlton's opponents that day were Chelsea, and playing for them on the left-wing was another United guest, Charlie Mitten. Watched by General Eisenhower and a record crowd of 85,000 (the maximum permitted by wartime regulations) Charlton won 3-1. Allenby Chilton still remembers wryly the memento each player received after the match – a £5 Savings Certificate!

As Manchester United prepared for their game with Charlton, Matt Busby did his best to make as little as possible of the fact that they were now 4-1 favourites to win the Cup, although he and the Board realised that the team's run of Cup success would warrant some extra financial reward. A *Daily Express* report revealed that for the fourth round victory against Liverpool each United player was paid his wages, plus a £4 bonus. In the fifth round, the report added, the bonus would rise to £6, then it would rise round by round, eventually reaching £20 per head if United won the final!

*Fifth Round versus Charlton Athletic at Leeds Road, Huddersfield, 7 February 1948*

MANCHESTER UNITED: Crompton; Carey, Aston; Warner, Chilton, Cockburn; Delaney, Morris, Rowley, Pearson, Mitten.

CHARLTON ATHLETIC: Bartram; Campbell, Lock; Johnson, Bicknell, Revell; Hurst, Fenton, Vaughan, McCrae, Duffy.

A few minutes before the kick-off only about 33,000 spectators were in the Leeds Road ground, a remarkable enough phenomenon for any Cup tie, but especially so when Manchester United were playing last year's Cup winners. The probable causes were the rain which had begun in the morning and which was to continue all day, coupled with the fact that Charlton had brought only a small number of spectators up to Yorkshire. The police had fixed the crowd limit at 55,000 and because of this many people thought they would not be able to get in. Just down the road Huddersfield were playing Bradford Northern in the first round of the Rugby League Cup and even the prospect of seeing famous players and famous teams did not lure too many Yorkshiremen from their first love.

The heavy ground and the drizzling rain, of course, held no fears for Manchester United, nor did they take any notice of Charlton's 'lucky' white shirts – the same shirts they had worn when they won the Cup against Burnley in the previous season.

Manchester United were playing Jack Warner at right-half in place of John Anderson who had been injured in the previous week's League match at Sheffield.

The game kicked off a few minutes before two o'clock because, it transpired, it was the only way Charlton could catch a rail connection from Wakefield to London after the match.

As expected, United quickly mastered the treacherous pitch and in their usual fashion in these conditions began to dictate the play. Johnny Morris in particular was at his buzzing best and he brought several fine saves from Sam Bartram in the first few minutes of the game. United forced seven corners in twenty-five minutes and this pressure eventually led to their first goal. Jack Rowley slipped the ball to Jack Warner who fired in a speculative shot from twenty yards out. Sam Bartram looked to have it covered but it caught Charlton's centre-half Bicknell on the ankle and was deflected a few inches beyond Bartram's reach into his goal.

The pressure that United were able to apply was constant and Charlton could only defend: there was neither time nor opportunity to mount attacks. At the other end of the pitch a shivering Jack Crompton had only one good shot to save in the first half.

A similar pattern of play continued in the second half. Charlton found themselves facing the wind and the rain and seemed unable to find the impetus to reach United's penalty area. All the play was in the Charlton half – Charlie Mitten hit the cross-bar and Sam Bartram continued to make last-ditch saves from the devastating five-pronged United attack which constantly buried itself deep into the Charlton's defensive flank. Charlton managed to rally for a brief period midway through the second half and their forwards struggled to knit themselves together in an endeavour to level the scores but created only one serious chance when Vaughan slipped the ball through to Charlton's Scottish inside-left McCrae who shot hurriedly wide.

United reaction was predictable and the Charlton goal then suffered another terrible pounding, but their last defender held firm. Sam Bartram flung himself up and down and to left and right and he parried or held everything that United threw at him. The gods that watch over goalkeepers on Saturday afternoons were giving Sam a lot of attention but they looked away once again when, five minutes from the end of the match as the evening gloom increased, Charlie Mitten ran through a flat-footed Charlton defence to place a glancing header from a perfect Delaney centre high into the top left-hand corner of the Charlton net.

Charlie Mitten remembers scoring that goal, and 'how we seemed to be shooting in at Sam all the match. Near the end of the game he was so tired his goal-kicks were hardly getting out of the penalty area, some going "plop" just outside the box. When this happened I shouted jokingly, "Oh, well kicked Sam lad", and he shouted back, "I'm knackered Charlie". So I said, "So that's why you let that header of mine go past you!" You know he was so tired he could hardly put his hands above his head! Sam was a great player and a terrific sportsman.'

Predictably the Charlton side were bitterly disappointed with their showing that afternoon and even their little outside-left Chris Duffy, who had scored in extra time at Wembley with a brilliant volley, made very little impact in this game.

Charlton's right-half and captain that day was Bert Johnson, and even today he maintains that being asked about that game puts him on the spot:

My most reliable recollections of that game would adversely implicate one of our players, which I prefer not to do. However, I have only unqualified praise for that pre-'Babes' United side. Statistically Charlton were the Cup side they all had to beat at the time. We had no quarrel with our defeat at Leeds Road, nor was it a surprise that United went all the way and took the Cup. We were not as formidable on the day as our reputation made out, though that does United less than justice, and probably we were only as good as we were allowed to be. All I am prepared to say is that we all seemed willingly to accept the amount of defending we had to do that day and it remained a sore point among our players for some time.

Even Jimmy Seed, Charlton's manager, found it hard to contain his criticisms of his team's performance. It was his practice during his thirty-two years as manager at The Valley to keep notes on each match his team played. Of this game he wrote: 'If

the forwards had been as good as the defence we would have
stood a chance, but they were woefully weak. Manchester United
were a really good side without a weakness and a forward line
that always spelt danger.'

Jimmy Seed also thought that Sam Bartram's performance that
afternoon was 'brilliant'.

Sam died at sixty-seven years of age in July 1981 and was one
of football's greatest characters. Few who saw him play will ever
forget his sandy quiff and green roll-top sweater and his tremendous agility between the posts. Sam remembered thinking that
the Cup tie against Manchester United was going to go on for
ever:

... because we were so completely outplayed. The crowd gave a great
welcome to both sides – something they seemed well able to do in those
days was to appreciate the skill of the opposition as well as the home
side. Our pre-match ritual (the only way I can describe it) was the same
as it always was, in fact, it never altered in the whole twenty-two years
I spent with the club: we breakfasted together, went for a walk and then
back to the hotel for a light lunch.

Within minutes of the start United were a goal up with a shot from
outside the area deflected into the net by one of our defenders, from then
on it was one-way traffic, in fact, United against the Charlton defence.
I think if I said we got over the half-way line three times it might be an
exaggeration, so I must say against such super opposition it must have
been my best match ever. However, we held out until two minutes from
time when Delaney put in a terrific shot which I could only parry, the
ball flew to Mitten who turned it over the line to make it 2–0. I then
collapsed through overwork. The referee held up the game until I was
back on my feet.

At the final whistle the Charlton supporters rushed on to the field and
carried me off shoulder-high, the first and last time it happened to me. I
realised then that a shaky ride was better than a good walk any day, then
just as I was thinking of relaxing in a nice hot bath Jimmy Seed our
manager came into the dressing room and said, 'Hurry up we have a
police escort to the station, they are stopping a train specially for us ...
you have five minutes.' I actually finished dressing in the coach.

During the journey back to London the club doctor said to me, 'Well
played Sam', adding that he didn't think anyone had left the ground
before the final whistle and that all the people in the stand had stood to
cheer me off, also that all the ladies were crying. Actually I was a bit
relieved: I thought he or the trainer may have been about to say I wasn't
100 per cent fit if I had passed out.

They were great days, with great players and marvellous supporters, I wouldn't have chosen any other days to have played my football.

If the victory belonged to Manchester United, the game belonged to Sam Bartram. He had let in two goals, but as John Aston remarked 'it could have been double figures if it hadn't been for Sam who played out of his skin'. After the final whistle, Jack Crompton, a virtual spectator of the drama at the other end of the ground, was one of many who waited in the rain to shake Sam's hand as he was chaired off the field. Crompton, like Jimmy Delaney and Allenby Chilton, had realised before the game that Charlton posed the first real threat to United's Cup hopes – and the Reds were lucky to have caught them on an off day.

Only eight clubs now remained to compete in the sixth round, although Fulham and Everton had yet to resolve their fifth round tie to decide who was to meet Blackpool. The famous Lancashire seaside club had been having an easy competition so far, and in the fifth round they had swamped non-League Colchester 5-0 at Bloomfield Road.

When the draw was made Manchester United found that they had drawn another match at 'home', albeit with yet another First Division club, Preston North End, who were currently third in the League. This time the game could be played at Maine Road. The fixture would have an even sharper edge to it because in the last round Preston had disposed of Manchester City 1-0 at Maine Road. Of the eight clubs, Manchester United, Derby County, Blackpool and Preston North End were in the First Division, Fulham (who beat Everton 1-0 in the replay), Southampton and Tottenham Hotspur were in the Second Division, and Queens Park Rangers were the sole surviving Third Division side. Coincidentally, United's very next League fixture after their Cup-tie victory over Charlton was to be against Preston at Maine Road.

Despite the absence of the England winger Tom Finney, Preston's Cup rehearsal with United understandably proved to be a big attraction and a capacity crowd of 61,265 at Maine Road watched Preston take the lead before half-time against the run of play. United were again playing Jack Warner for the still-injured John Anderson. With only four minutes of the game remaining and United's forwards becoming increasingly frustrated by hav-

ing nothing to show for their supremacy in attack, Jimmy Delaney
at last steered in a header from a Mitten cross to equal the scores.

United's goal tally of four in their last three games was modest
by their standards and was beginning to cause concern. Preston's
goalkeeper Jimmy Gooch, like Sam Bartram, had produced one
of his best displays ever as a frustrating tribute to United's forward line, but the famine was beginning to irritate the forwards
whose appetites thrived on a constant supply of goals.

What would happen if Preston's goalkeeper played like that in
the sixth round? There seemed to be no way past him - especially as United's forwards were now tending to over-elaborate in
front of goal against a fast, quick-tackling defence.

But the next League game reassured United that all seemed
well when they beat Stoke City 2–0 on a snow-covered Victoria
Ground. Ted Buckle, making his first senior appearance of the
season, at outside-left, in place of flu victim Charlie Mitten,
scored from the penalty spot and then Stan Pearson headed
United's second goal.

John Anderson was back in the side that day after injury and
had a good game, even though his mind was elsewhere. His wife
was seriously ill and in January had been taken to Bolton Sanatorium. He and his one-year-old son had given up their home
and had gone to live with relatives. John Anderson recalled:

I had been injured when we'd played Sheffield United at Bramhall Lane.
On the way back, just before we got to Old Trafford, Matt Busby told
me that he'd got a message saying that I had to go to the Sanatorium
quickly to see my wife. I'd got married during the war on one of my
brief leaves, and now my wife had got TB. Anyway, Matt had laid on a
car for me - he told me that it would be waiting for me to take me up to
Bolton, and that it would be at my disposal when I wanted it. Matt was
always very good over things like that.

Sadly, John's wife died the day after the game at Stoke, and
was to be buried the day before the Cup tie against Preston. The
decision whether he should play or not was left up to him. During
the week John trained with the rest of the side, as usual, and then
he and Matt Busby had a talk.

Matt said 'There's nothing more you can do now, John, life's got to go on.' So I decided to play. My wife was buried on the Friday before the game: Jimmy Murphy was in the background at the funeral seeing that everything was all right. The rest of the team had all gone up to Blackpool for the day to train, and they were staying at the hotel owned by Stan Matthews. After the funeral I travelled up to Blackpool. In the hotel I roomed with Johnny Aston and they sent us both to bed early with a hot toddy made by good old Tom Curry. I had a good night's sleep and I think played quite well next day.

Preston North End were a team to be reckoned with and at this stage of the season they were playing well and winning matches. They were still lying third in the League table, two points in front of United, but ten points behind the leaders Arsenal. Their best player was the legendary right-winger Tom Finney, an England international who on his day could turn defenders inside out.

Preston had been giving some thought to a defence which was going to be able to hold the famous five that comprised the United attack. Unfortunately their regular goalkeeper Jimmy Gooch was now injured and at the eleventh hour his place was to be taken by Jack Hindle, a 23-year-old ex-sailor who was having to face the ordeal of making his first-team debut in front of a potentially huge Cup-tie crowd. Being picked to keep goal for Preston even took Hindle himself by surprise: 'On the Friday before the match I had gone to Wigan to take a couple of tickets to a pal I had been in the Navy with. I didn't arrive back until eleven o'clock to learn that Jimmy Gooch was injured and that I was playing in the Cup tie, and it was going to be my first team debut!'

At right-half (and captain) Preston had a crafty little Scotsman called Bill Shankly, and at centre-half they picked Paddy Waters, an Irish International, for only his second appearance in the first team. It was he who had kept such a tight grip on Jack Rowley in the League game at Maine Road a fortnight before. Preston could also claim to be even more unlucky than United: it was their fourth tie away from home, having beaten Millwall, Portsmouth and Manchester City to reach the sixth round. And this was the second time in the competition in a month and the third time they had to play a fixture at Maine Road!

*Sixth Round versus Preston North End at Maine Road, 28 February 1948*

MANCHESTER UNITED: Crompton; Carey, Aston; Anderson, Chilton, Cockburn; Delaney, Morris, Rowley, Pearson, Mitten.

PRESTON NORTH END: Hindle; Gray, Scott; Shankly, Waters, Horton; Finney, Beatie, McIntosh, McLaren, Anders.

A crowd of over 74,000 packed into Maine Road to see if 'Proud Preston' was to be the team to halt United's progress to Wembley. It was twenty-two years since United had last reached the semi-final stage of the FA Cup – the game *had* to be won, and by now they were firm favourites to win.

The shaking the United players had received that morning when their coach had collided with a bus filled with supporters had not affected their nerves, and within thirty seconds of the start Preston received their first warnings of United's intentions, when a shot from Jack Rowley, designed to unsettle Preston's 'new' goalkeeper, flashed over the cross-bar.

United continued the relentless pressure, as wave after wave of attacking moves, revealing perfect understanding between the forwards, sent the Preston defence scampering and lunging in all directions. John Carey, as usual, prompted the attack and steadied the defence – impressing everybody with his strength and calmness.

Jack Rowley was very closely marked by Paddy Waters, and this was to become one of the memorable features of the game. One report described how 'he set himself to mark Rowley and for half an hour his search for the jersey bearing the figure "9" was always relentless and sometimes comic. He chased him to the wing, he chased him to the corner flag and they stood elbowing each other while goal-kicks were taken. Jack Rowley had learned from his experience in the League game, and, by playing deep, and on the wings (and thereby taking his marker with him) was able to pull gaps in the centre of the Preston defence.'

Jimmy Delaney chuckled as he remembered how he and Jack had planned to confuse the Irish centre-half:

The Preston defence must have been told before the game to watch out for Delaney and Rowley interchanging positions. Jack had him all over the place which meant that he couldn't cover the middle like centre-halves were supposed to do. Every time I drifted into the centre and Jack went on to the wing you could hear Paddy shouting in this big Irish voice of his: 'Oh Jasus, watch dem, watch dem, dey're at it again!' During the game he came over to me and as I was standing in the penalty area he said, 'Jasus, Jimmy, get out of de bloody road, why don't you get back to your own position!'

Then, in the twenty-third minute, Johnny Morris centred, the Preston defence hesitated, full-back Gray only half-killed the lob, and an unmarked Charlie Mitten was able to chest it down and stab the ball home from only a few yards out.

Ten minutes later Jack Rowley fired in a thunderbolt shot which Paddy Waters tried to head away for a corner. The brave but by now completely confused Irishman lay poleaxed for several minutes, such was the force of the shot and the weight of the muddy ball. Once Waters was up on his feet Charlie Mitten took the corner, Jack Rowley shaped to shoot but instead placed a back-heel flick to Stan Pearson, who drove the ball into the roof of the net.

Preston rallied and a minute before the half-time whistle sounded their centre-forward Willie McIntosh (whose goal had knocked Manchester City out of the previous round of the Cup) accepted a pin-point pass from Tom Finney and sped past John Anderson to screw the ball past Jack Crompton who had seemingly advanced too far out of his goal.

In the second half Preston began impressively, and at the same time it was clear that some of the fire and snap had gone from United's attack. Even with such a score-line and everything to play for, the match, as a spectacle, began to tail off. Tom Finney and a now-injured McIntosh continued to try, but Preston received another body blow when Jimmy Delaney centred and Stan Pearson nodded the ball home powerfully. Jack Hindle managed to get his hands to the ball but he could only help it into the net.

Hindle remembers in the second half how 'the Manchester United forwards took command of the game, and under the wet and slippy conditions it was a forward's day. Delaney, Mitten, Pearson, Rowley and Johnny Morris were bombarding the goal and it was a bit of a hectic time to say the least.'

With only ten minutes to go, Manchester United scored their fourth and final goal. Johnny Morris zigzagged his way through the Preston defence and put in a shot which Jack Hindle could only push out to Jack Rowley, who, running up, drove the ball home.

The bare facts of the game also tell something of the story. Preston kicked into touch in their own half 48 times, United 10. United forced 6 corners, Preston 2. Hindle took 16 goal-kicks, Crompton 4. United had 25 shots at goal, 13 on target. Preston had only 6, of which 3 were 'near'. Another fact was crystal clear. Manchester United had reached the semi-finals of the FA Cup for the first time since 1926.

Next day the papers were to report that Preston had been 'out-run, outwitted and outgeneralled' and Preston's Ken Horton and Tom Finney remembered much about the game.

'First, though, I remember the gate, some 74,000', said Tom Finney. 'United I rated as one of the best sides, and they had a great forward line. We lost two early goals and were never really in with a chance after that. It was a disappointing game from our point of view as we never really played together as a team. I had a very subdued game and generally United proved too good for us on the day, Johnny Morris and John Carey having particularly good games.'

'Looking at the scrap book which my father has faithfully kept since January 1943 made the old memory tick over and thirty odd years ago became last Saturday's game', said Ken Horton. 'Having beaten Manchester City at Maine Road in an earlier round and held United to a draw (they equalised in the last few minutes) just prior to the Cup tie we were confident of success. Unfortunately, Jimmy Gooch was injured and Jack Hindle had to make his debut in goal for a vital game. Part of the Cup-tie training at that time was brine baths. What they were supposed to do I can't recall (other than shedding a few extra ounces), but our preparation was very thorough and the strength and weakness of the opposition was always analysed and a 'plan of campaign' produced. A crowd in excess of 74,000 must produce a terrific atmosphere and we had a tremendous following. As often happens the game didn't live up to its expectations and although the reports quote me as the best half-back I recall Johnny Morris giving me a roasting. I think that the Manchester United forward line at that time was the best in the country and their first-time passing and running off the ball was the outstanding feature of their play.'

John Aston looked back on that game and remembered particularly how Bill Shankly had told him that 'because I'd handled Tom Finney so well I'd soon be playing for England'. It was praise indeed (and in its own way quite prophetic), although Bill Shankly's gravel-voiced eulogies of players were not yet of the standard they were to reach when he became Liverpool's manager. Even though Shankly once said of Tom Finney that 'he had the opposition so frightened they'd have a man marking him when they were warming up before the kick-off', the England winger had been effectively neutralised in this game by John Aston's skilful marking. Preston North End and Tom Finney lived to fight another day, and Manchester United and their supporters could barely contain their impatience. Who would they meet in the semi-final?

Five teams now remained to fight for two tickets to Wembley: Blackpool, who had beaten Second Division Fulham 2–0; Tottenham Hotspur, who had beaten Southampton 1–0 at the Dell; Manchester United, of course, and either Queen's Park Rangers or Derby who had drawn 1–1 at Loftus Road.

The following Saturday, whilst Manchester United were beating Sunderland 3–1 at Maine Road in front of 55,000 supporters, Derby County overran Queen's Park Rangers 5–0 in the sixth round replay, which now meant that in the semi-finals Blackpool would play Second Division Tottenham Hotspur at Villa Park, and Derby County would play Manchester United at Hillsborough, Sheffield.

Northern fans relished the idea of an all-Lancashire Final. If Blackpool and Manchester United were to get through it would be the fifth time in the history of the competition, and the first time since Everton beat Manchester City in 1933.

It had been a very lucky competition so far for Blackpool – they had yet to meet a First Division club! For their part Manchester United had met *only* First Division clubs and when they learned that Derby County had beaten Queen's Park Rangers, United realised that they were about to face their severest test.

By 2 March more than 17,000 semi-final ticket applications (the majority requesting two tickets) had been received by the Old Trafford office, who were then faced with the task of allocating the 19,700 they had in their possession: made up 13,000 for the popular side at two shillings and sixpence (12½p), 4,000 for the

enclosure at six shillings (30p) each and 2,200 for the stand at ten
shillings (50p), fifteen shillings (75p) and a pound.

Tim Ward was Derby County's right-half – and had been
capped for England this season. He eloquently described Derby's
preparation for the game and the moments leading up to the
kick-off of a game that every team dreads losing – to be defeated
so close to the final is the hardest loss for a team to take.

Football supporters, not only from Manchester and Derby but from all
over the country, looked forward to this game between arguably the two
best teams in the land at that time; it had all the promise of a feast of
football; both teams had a preponderance of internationals and both
teams placed the emphasis on open attacking football.

The Derby team stayed at a guest house near Ashbourne in the week
prior to the game; it was a favourite retreat of the players and used quite
often before the big games. It meant that the players could still train at
the Baseball Ground but at the same time get away from the clamour for
tickets, etc. that can make the big occasion very hectic.

The journey from Ashbourne to the Hillsborough Ground at Sheffield
was quite short and the Derby team arrived at the ground in good time
to soak up the atmosphere. Normally players hate to have time to waste
before a big match but there is so much to see outside and inside the
ground that it is soon time to go on the field. It is inevitable that the
tension creeps into the dressing room and reaction sets in with most
players. We were no exception at Derby and the players went through
their pre-match rituals a bit more thoroughly than normal. Very few
footballers are not superstitious and it is interesting to see other players
doing the same things that you are doing and hoping no one is noticing.
The putting on of kit in the right order for luck, the touching of wood
around the dressing-rooms, the corny jokes all heard so many times
before, but still laughed at loud and long. Eventually, the walk down the
tunnel, in the right order again, all close friends wishing each other well
and then the noise as the team arrives on the field. Gone is the privacy,
gone is the quiet, gone is the make-believe calm. One looks around and
can't help but be impressed by the wonderful efforts of both sets of
supporters; the colour, the banners, all helping to make this the greatest
football competition in the world. Silent prayers are said by players of
both teams, 'please don't let us let them down'. Strangely, with the
kick-off comes the first real relaxation that many players have known for
several days; this is it, you tell yourself, a game of football, go and enjoy
it.

The Manchester United party of players and officials spent the Friday night before the semi-final in a hotel in Buxton, then travelled to Sheffield on the morning of the game. Mr Sidney Wicks was the editor of the *United Review*, Manchester United's official programme, and he was later to describe how he travelled with the party from Buxton and how on the journey the team 'were quiet and confident and the songs they sang on the way to Sheffield gave no hint of nerves'.

By now the team virtually picked itself. Jack Crompton had been taken off with a rib injury in United's 3–1 victory against Sunderland the week before, and Charlie Mitten ('I scored at one end and let one in at the other') had donned the goalkeeper's jersey. Crompton was now fit, as was John Anderson who had been forced to leave the field for ten minutes in the same game with a bad cut over his eye.

While they may have given no sign of nerves on the morning of the match the Manchester United players were well aware of Derby's reputation, and in their quieter moments would have reflected upon the threat they posed to United's Cup hopes. The League game they played last November had ended in a 1–1 draw and currently Derby were lying just below United in the League table. They had won the FA Cup in 1946 and had several internationals in their ranks. They possessed strong defenders like Bert Mozley, Tim Ward and Leon Leuty, and a fearsome inside trio of Raich Carter, Jack Stamps and Billy Steel. But most important of all, Derby Country had not been defeated in three months. They were on a winning streak at exactly the right time, and they were determined to prove that not even the great Manchester United could deny them their chance to reach the FA Cup final.

*Semi-Final versus Derby County at Hillsborough, Sheffield, 13 March 1948*

MANCHESTER UNITED: Crompton; Carey, Aston; Anderson, Chilton, Cockburn; Delaney, Morris, Rowley, Pearson, Mitten.

DERBY COUNTY: Wallace; Mozley, Howe; Ward, Leuty, Musson; Harrison, Carter, Stamps, Steel, Morrison.

In front of a crowd of 60,000 both teams began by testing the other's defences. The opening moments were played at whirlwind speed: Derby and Manchester United each had the skill and experience to realise the value of quickly establishing an attacking momentum while offering also a resolute defence to the opposition. It was a fascinating equation.

After thirty minutes of end-to-end play Stan Pearson scored United's first goal. Jack Rowley lofted an overhead kick into the Derby penalty area, there was a moment's confusion between Leuty and goalkeeper Wallace, and Stan Pearson was there to flight a neat header into the Derby goal. Stan remembers 'the ball coming over and I was moving in on it, and out of the corner of my eye I saw the goalkeeper moving out and I headed it in so it just dropped behind him. He'd come out a little bit too soon, do you see?'

Four minutes later Pearson struck again. Jimmy Delaney floated in a cross from the right, Wallace came out of his goal again and completely misjudged the flight of the ball, and United's inside-left slipped in front of him and headed in his second goal.

Derby now knew that they had to play themselves back into the game – a goal before half-time would at least convince United that 'The Rams' were still dangerous and they mounted many attacks with Carter and Steel prominent. But the United defence, yet again, with John Carey playing his usual immaculate game, held firm.

Then, three minutes before half-time, Allenby Chilton made the one mistake the Derby side was waiting for. He failed to clear a bouncing centre from Jackie Stamps, and Billy Steel darted in, ran with the ball for twenty yards and rammed home a rasping drive on the run. It was a brilliant goal which put immediate pressure on United and even the relief of half-time left the psychological advantage with Derby. Only when Manchester United stopped attacking in order to start subconsciously defending a narrow lead did they become an ordinary side. As the United players trudged to the dressing-rooms the Wembley towers, for once, did not look quite so near.

Derby began the second half just as they did the first, pressing home attack upon attack to try and retrieve their one-goal deficit. But after only ten minutes into the half Stan Pearson dealt the final blow to Derby's Cup hopes. His third goal was one he will never forget. 'We got Charlie Mitten away on the left wing and we were all moving down fast and I just pointed to where I wanted it and he slid it right across and I never broke stride ... I just ran straight on to it and from a very narrow angle and quite far out I hit it right across the goal into the far corner.' It was a superbly taken goal and the manner of its taking was quintessential Stan Pearson.

Few teams could have retrieved a two-goal deficit against a United side which was now riding high. Their defence and attack moved sweetly together, weaving unbeatable patterns all around a now tired and demoralised Derby side until the final whistle. Manchester United had, at last, reached the Cup final!

Even though it had been a magnificent team effort the match reports singled out Stan Pearson and John Carey for their superb contribution to attack and defence respectively. Don Davies wrote of Stan Pearson in the following Monday's *Manchester Guardian*:

> Nothing could have been more appropriate nor more warmly approved, than a hat-trick for this great-hearted player. He is rarely in the limelight, since the strategy of the side requires him always to shoulder the heaviest burdens in mid-field, but the players know his worth. He is, in a way, the Pollard of the Manchester United side – 'the owd chain-'orse'.

Fellow half-back Henry Cockburn emphasised that United were perhaps lucky to meet a class side on an off-day; but his real admiration was for Stan Pearson's goals. For him, however, the real drama began in the dressing-room before the game.

> We were obviously a bit keyed up. I was having a 'Jimmy Riddle' before we went out to play ... it's the tension you know ... and Stan Pearson appears in the next stall to me. He was always a nice steady lad but suddenly he's as sick as anything. I thought, Oh hell, what's up with Stan? He's always played in front of me as inside-left and I thought, He's not well ... I'm going to have a rough time today because he won't be playing so well. I said, 'Come on Stan, what's up?' He looked up and said, 'By,' he says, 'that's better. I'm a bit nervous, that's all.' He went out and scored bloody three ... a hat-trick. I said to him after the game,

'Hey Stan, do you think you could arrange to throw up before every match!'

In contrast to the game against Charlton, where he was a virtual spectator, Jack Crompton had spent the whole match parrying the sharp thrusts of the Derby attack.

It was a hard but entertaining game, often semi-finals are dour games: you're so near to Wembley that everybody's concerned about winning, not how they play, the result's the important thing. At one stage it looked as though we might not win it – they had two or three dangerous breakaways and I remember having to go down quickly at Jack Stamps' feet to get the ball ... he should have scored really but he held on to it just a bit too long ... if it had been Carter or Steel, they might have stuck the chance away.

Sadly, Jack Stamps, the Derby centre-forward that day, is now blind, but his voice is strong and his memory sharp. Jack's passion for the game is undiminished, and he still goes to Derby's matches and listens to the commentary provided for him.

I remember firstly that it was a nice day and a good crowd to play in front of. From then on it was all about goalkeeping, I think. Goalies do make a difference ... Vic Woodley was our goalie in the 1946 final ... he made all the difference and he was the reason we won the Cup. Jock Wallace was our goalie in the semi-final ... he'd just been bought from Blackpool because our regular goalie Townsend had broken his thumb. After half an hour or so there was a move down the right, Jack Rowley sent in a high centre, poor Jock came out too far ... he sort of ran underneath it and tried to fist it away but Stan Pearson headed it in. The second goal was a replica of the first, I thought, except Jimmy Delaney crossed it and Stan, all on his own, headed it in again.

His third goal was a beauty ... Charlie Mitten sent a diagonal ball to Stan Pearson who chased it and banged it in from just inside the penalty-area but from a narrow angle. Jock Wallace had sort of half turned to face Pearson and the ball had struck him on the chest and went in.

We were dead then, even though Billy Steel had scored one for us. The United defence, especially John Carey, played so well I remember. I know I missed a couple of chances, one especially when I fired in a shot low and hard but Jack Crompton snapped his legs shut and trapped the ball between them.

Poor Jock Wallace ... he was despondent at the end of the game.

He kept saying that if only he'd stayed on his line they wouldn't have scored . . .

The last words on the game itself, fittingly, come from Derby's Tim Ward:

It would be unfair to take anything away from Manchester United because they played so well and that really was the first of some great United sides. Was it better than the 'Busby Babes'; was it better than the golden days of Bobby Charlton, George Best and Denis Law? No doubt arguments will go on for ever but one thing is for sure, over that period we had some wonderful tussles with Manchester United and enjoyed every game with them.

To say we were disappointed after the match at Hillsborough would be the understatement of all time; it must be the cruellest blow of all to lose in a semi-final and it was all summed up by a loyal Rams supporter after the game. He stood looking at the river flowing by the ground and said, 'With our luck today if I threw myself in the water wouldn't be deep enough to drown me.'

Meanwhile Jimmy Delaney and his team-mates were in the dressing-room:

. . . waiting on the result of the other game. During our match we'd heard from the crowd that Tottenham were winning, and then that Blackpool were the winners. We looked at each other and said, 'That's another bloody tough one' and you start to think straight-away of their forward line and Stan Matthews, Stan Mortensen, Walter Rickett. That boy Rickett in the League game last December was as dangerous as Matthews – he was the only winger I've seen who could give John Carey a roasting. We knew right away that it wasn't going to be easy.

Those who played and watched the game at Hillsborough were later to learn that the semi-final game between Spurs and Black-pool had produced an equally exciting match to the one they had all just been involved in. Coincidentally, it had ended with the same score-line and in each game a player called Stan had scored a hat-trick! Blackpool were having the worst of the game, and with four minutes of the match to go Second Division Spurs were leading by a goal scored by Ted Duquemin, when Stan Mortensen suddenly slotted home the equaliser to keep up his goal-every-round record.

So the match went to extra time, and Stan Mortensen scored two more dramatic goals to take Blackpool to Wembley and the club's first final. The prospects of a best-ever final, especially as it was an all-Lancashire one, looked absolutely certain!

Each of the Cup rounds so far had been played fortnightly: now Manchester United and Blackpool had to wait six agonising weeks before they could meet in the final. It was a long gap, which worried Matt Busby and his players. There was a full League programme to battle through, injuries were bound to occur in that time – but even more seriously, United might lose that vital winning impetus which had brought them so far, so successfully. The League programme was packed: the Easter holidays were to involve United in three matches in four days and in the twenty-four days before the final, United were going to have to play five League games, including the return 'derby' match against Manchester City. Nothing could be done about the problem though, except get on with the games and hope that all was well by 24 April.

So Manchester United pressed ahead with their League programme, knowing deep down that only a miracle would prevent Arsenal from winning the League championship, but there was always the chance to claim the runners-up place. Arsenal, in fact, were so far ahead that they were officially declared Champions on 10 April, with four games still to play.

Recognition for United's superb footballing displays this season came with the selection of Stan Pearson and Henry Cockburn for England, and Jimmy Delaney for Scotland, for their annual fixture at Hampden Park on 10 April – two weeks before the Cup final.

Stan Pearson, then twenty-nine years of age, fully deserved his selection, and the newspapers of the day praised the qualities which had brought him international recognition at last. His hat-trick against Derby in the semi-final would have done his claim for an international place no harm at all.

Henry Cockburn was, of course, making a return to international limelight, (after three appearances last season) having produced so many cultured displays which the selectors could no longer ignore. The dressing-room story actually goes that neither of them believed Jimmy Delaney when he told Henry and Stan that the three of them had been selected for the Hampden game, because he told them on 1 April! Stan Pearson was particularly pleased to be selected and reeled off a list of inside-forwards of the day who might have been considered for places.

There was general agreement that Stan Pearson, in his debut game, along with Lawton and Mortensen, played well enough in attack, and it was also noted that he did sterling work in defence during the danger periods, and in the second half started producing the passes which had meant so much to Manchester United that season.

Jimmy Delaney was praised as the sharpest forward of a fairly blunt Scottish attack. Even Billy Steel and Billy Liddell failed to make much headway against a solid English defence in which Henry Cockburn, Neil Franklin and Frank Swift were outstanding.

Throughout the season there had been speculation about who in the United team deserved an England cap, and apart from Stan Pearson and Henry Cockburn the names of Jack Rowley, Johnny Morris and John Aston always cropped up when these matters were being discussed. In fact, Jack Rowley scored two goals for a Football League side (a 'showcase' team for potential international players) which beat a League of Ireland side 4–0 at Preston on 14 April.

Alf Clarke of the *Manchester Evening Chronicle* frequently wrote about his conversations with Walter Winterbottom who often asked his advice about the current form of United players, and Winterbottom often dropped hints about other names he was considering. All this gossip was passed on by Alf Clarke to the players and his eager readers, and hints soon became reality for Jack Rowley and John Aston, but not before the game that everybody was waiting for had been played. The Cup final was now only weeks away . . .

The immediate response by the massive number of United's faithful supporters to the news that they were in the final was to rush to buy tickets, and the complaints about unfair allocations began a refrain which still echoes annually once the finalists are known.

Six weeks before the final and ten days before the semi-final the Manchester football public were warned by Eric Thornton in the *Manchester Evening News* that if United reached the final the club's allocation would be only 12,000 tickets. He had discovered from the FA that 41,000 (42 per cent) of the Wembley Stadium tickets would go to the County Associations; 25,000 (27 per cent) to League clubs and others in full membership of the FA; 2,000 (3 per cent) to the Council and Wembley Stadium and 28 per cent to the FA and finalists. Actually, the finalists ended up with 13,500 tickets each out of the 99,000 gate.

The first applications for tickets arrived minutes after the result of the semi-final became known. Those United supporters who could not watch their team playing Derby at Sheffield went to Old Trafford to watch the Central League team playing and beating Blackpool Reserves 1-0. Many had brought postal orders and envelopes with them to the game. Seconds after the final whistle, the word spread that the first team had beaten Derby and were through to the final – and hundreds of postal orders were duly sealed in envelopes and pushed through the Old Trafford Office letter box as the crowd made its way out of the ground.

On the following Monday, 30,000 applications had been received for the Club's quota of 12,000 Cup final tickets, and the railways announced that approximately 12,000 concession-fare tickets would be issued from Manchester at a cost of 37s 6d (1.87½p) for the return journey.

Manchester United's secretary Walter Crickmer was overwhelmed yet again with applications for tickets. On the Sunday following the victory over Derby he had received 16,000 to 18,000 letters, thousands of them stuffed through the letter box by people who had travelled many miles to make personal deliveries. Some had even posted applications through letter boxes of his and Matt Busby's own houses!

At the time Walter Crickmer was reported to have said, 'We have not decided how to distribute the tickets, and in any case it's a heart-breaking job for us to have to disappoint people, particularly if we have to leave out supporters of the team and genuine football enthusiasts.'

John Carey, like all the players, found himself surrounded by stacks of letters from all parts of the British Isles, all seeming to ask for a couple of tickets. They had about as much hope of success as a Dublin friend of his who had said to him during his last visit to Eire, 'If you do get to Wembley and shake hands with the King, have a word with him about partition will you.'

'It was ridiculous,' remembered John Anderson, 'everybody in the Navy wrote to me, often from ships I'd never been on ... they all said they knew me or had met me.'

Charlie Mitten recalled, 'that the year we were in the Cup a new rule came out from the FA allowing, I think it was, seventeen tickets per player. The clubs got "x" thousand each but the re-commendation was that every player in the final got just seventeen tickets. We said to Matt, "This is disgraceful, Matt ... we've got more than seventeen relatives each, everybody else is getting handfuls of tickets, and the people who are going on the field to play the game are getting only a few ... do you want our wives to stay at home and listen to it on the radio!" Actually we put it a little more strongly than that I seem to remember.'

John Aston also remembered all the fuss over the tickets.

I don't know what the other lads have told you, but we each got 100 tickets and I don't know what the others did with theirs, but being a Manchester lad I gave all mine away to family and friends. But we all had rows in the family about who should get tickets and who shouldn't. I used to have people coming to the door to ask for them. I remember one woman standing there crying on the doorstep saying that she daren't go home without a ticket or her husband would kick her out! We had relatives we'd not seen for years turning up and asking for tickets. On the Friday before the final we were on the train leaving for London and Busby said, 'There's a few terrace tickets left here lads, does anybody want a couple?' Well, we were so sick of bloody tickets we said, 'Keep them, Matt, keep them!'

Right up to the day of the final, a brisk barter trade was done in tickets. Some vendors had been offering one expensive ticket for two cheaper ones; others had offered a load of logs, free board and lodgings in London, golf balls and nylon stockings. Henry Cockburn was reported to have been offered a bag of coal for a three-shilling ticket!

A fortnight before the Cup final, Manchester United played Everton at Goodison Park and were beaten 2-0, but there was perhaps some excuse. Five reserve players were on show for the Reds (including two who were making their League debuts), tak-

ing the places of Stan Pearson, Henry Cockburn and Jimmy Delaney (playing in the Hampden international), and Jack Rowley
and John Carey who were injured.

But on the Saturday before their Wembley date, United selected their full side for a League game against Chelsea at Maine
Road. Characteristically, none of the United players held themselves back to avoid injury, and the result was a marvellous
morale-boosting 5–0 victory over the London side. Charles Mitten scored United's first goal from a penalty, then Jimmy Delaney
slotted United's second a minute before half-time. Then, rather
worryingly, Jack Rowley had to leave the field after fifty-five
minutes of the game with a nagging leg injury, having scored
three minutes into the second half. Obviously, with three goals in
the lead Matt Busby thought the game was safe and didn't want
to risk Jack further, and United, playing with only ten men,
coasted for the rest of the game. Even so Stan Pearson stayed
sharp as ever and scored two goals in the last ten minutes.

United's defenders worked together in a slightly different way
in this game, practising the defensive ploys which might have to
be used against Matthews and Mortensen in next week's final.
And Jack Rowley's goal from a quickly taken Johnny Morris
free kick was an almost perfect blueprint for the vital equaliser
he was to claim in the second half at Wembley.

The injury to Jack Rowley did not look serious enough to
prevent him from playing at Wembley but Matt Busby, already
realising the value of falsely raising hopes in the hearts of the
opposition by being 'doubtful' about whether his ace striker
would be playing, told the Press that 'we shall have to wait and
see'. He was, of course, delighted to announce a few days later
that the injury had responded to treatment and that Jack Rowley
would be playing! There were more, but less publicised, injury
stories to be told after the game, and even one or two that the
manager himself was unaware of.

So it was despondency not delight which Blackpool and their
supporters felt when they heard the news, especially as they had
just been beaten 2–0 by Charlton Athletic on the afternoon that
United were hammering home their decisive victory over Chelsea.
Still, as they told themselves, 'We've got Matthews and Mortensen – so watch out United!'

Six long weeks had passed since the semi-final victories, and now Manchester United and Blackpool could at last turn their attention to the game at Wembley.

Sports pages of the newspapers during the week before the final were full of facts and figures about both teams, searching among the comparisons and contrasts for clues about who might win.

United supporters needed no clues. Hadn't they beaten *only* First Division sides in away fixtures to reach Wembley? Hadn't Blackpool had the easiest of passages ever to a Cup final? Even the fine detail was only of passing interest. So Stan Mortensen had scored 20 League and 9 Cup goals so far. But Jack Rowley had scored 23 League and 3 Cup, Stan Pearson 15 League and 7 Cup, and Johnny Morris 18 League and 3 Cup goals this season. And Delaney and Mitten between them, just to confirm the devastating ability of all five of the forward line to score goals, could claim a joint tally of 15 and 4 Cup goals.

United had further cause to be proud of their team. Of the eleven players who were picked for Wembley, six were born and bred Mancunians and the remaining five, with the exception of Jimmy Delaney, had come to United as very young players.

Matt Busby had a few selection worries before Saturday's final. Jack Rowley was thankfully fit, but as a precaution Ronnie Burke was prepared to take his place should there be any eleventh hour crisis. Jack Crompton and Jimmy Delaney had taken knocks in the game the week before the final, but there were apparently no real worries about their fitness either. The only doubt in Matt Busby's mind was who to select at right-half. Should he pick Jack Warner – tried and tested in the seasons before, or should be stick by John Anderson, a young man who had made a brilliant debut last December and who had held his place and coped bravely with a bereavement only a couple of months ago? The ever-cautious Matt Busby took, by his own definition, a gamble. An experienced player is always an asset in the unreal atmosphere of a Wembley final, but Busby selected the younger, and by now established, John Anderson and chose Jack Warner as the team's twelfth man.

Matt Busby also gambled by selecting one or two established players who were not fully fit: his gambles were in fact carefully calculated risks which were to bring supreme success to the team he had put together so carefully.

As the 2.05 p.m. train pulled out of London Road Station, Manchester, bound for London, the Manchester United players had time at last to sit back and reflect on tomorrow's game.

To a man they were glad to be away from the constant attention they now attracted, and from being recognised and pestered for autographs and tickets, or with questions about who was going to win.

Matt Busby had taken great care to ensure that the settled pattern of training and tactical talks had remained unbroken in the week before the final. As well as light football training the team had as usual played golf, where they yet again marvelled at the skill of Johnny Morris on the fairways and greens of Davyhulme Golf Course, and had roared with laughter at John Anderson's and Jack Crompton's attempts to hit a golf ball without bringing up a bucketful of turf.

Together they had talked quietly and carefully about a plan to control Stan Matthews – and how to cope with the inevitable rushes of Stan Mortensen and the darting threats of left-winger Walter Rickett.

Manchester United were a superbly fit and quietly confident team and they were all relishing the prospect of tomorrow's game. One small grievance remained unsolved – and it was all to do with money. Most, if not all, the players could not believe how little they were to earn for their efforts in reaching, let alone, winning, the final. Matt Busby and the directors had been adamant about adhering to the official policy on payments: each player would receive his usual weekly wage plus a bonus of £20 each for reaching the final. A few players had probably made a couple of pounds from selling some of their ticket allocation, but there was to be no other financial reward, except for a few pounds each from a players' brochure which John Carey and the team had put together and sold for 2s 6d (12½p) a copy.

The players had argued with Matt Busby and the directors ('a crowd of 99,000 ... probably about £40,000 income from the game ... and we get £20 each') and with the Press ('surely interviews and photos should be paid for at this stage'). But the Press ('you need us as much as we need you') had paid them nothing and the team had to resort to a token gesture of protest at Euston by covering their faces as they left the station by coach for their

Surrey hotel, refusing to be photographed unless they were paid
£10 a picture.

By today's standards their financial rewards for reaching the
Cup final were derisory. Admittedly, the whole nation were suffering together in those lean post-war years, but the players could
be forgiven at this point for showing more awareness about
money than they had shown for some time. It was one thing to
be grateful for surviving the war and being given a chance to play
the game you loved for a living, but as one of the players remarked 'cups and medals didn't pay the rent'.

The last wry comment rested with Charlie Mitten, the team's
sharpest (if not always most successful) gambler and financial
entrepreneur:

Yes, we were told that if we won the final our bonus would be £20. But
did you know that the band got more than us? I was told that the military
band that played at half-time got £330, and we got £220 between us.
There's more in a band though, and I tell you what, they must have
played better than we did!

So there was nothing more that could be done, the players
reflected, but to enjoy the experience of a Wembley final, maybe
of even winning a Wembley final. The train was soon rattling
through the bleak suburbs of north London and the sight of
Wembley's twin towers caused even the strongest hearts to beat
a little faster. Some of the players remembered how the journey
had actually begun on that marvellous afternoon at Villa Park
back in January, but none of them would have known that they
were poised before a game which was to enter football history as
'the most remarkable final ever played'.

Both teams had been announced by the Tuesday preceding
the final, and the only surprise for Manchester United was that
Stan Mortensen had been picked at centre-forward and not in his
usual inside-right position to partner Stanley Matthews.

In fact three Blackpool names had to be altered on the official
match programme which had already been printed. Jimmy McIntosh, who had played in all Blackpool's Cup rounds, had been
dropped – the apparent reason being that he had not scored in
Blackpool's last six matches, and the only person who could restore the goalscoring punch, Blackpool felt, was Stan Mortensen.

George Munro was brought in as Matthews' right-wing partner, and Johnny Crosland had been selected to take the place of the injured Ronnie Suart at left-back. Crosland was an ex-Fleet Air Arm pilot and an accountant in Blackpool and had only played reserve team soccer for Blackpool as a centre-half. He was only able to train twice a week because of his professional commitments.

Despite the late changes Blackpool were as brimful of confidence as Manchester United were: not least because they had Stan Matthews and Stan Mortensen in their team – probably the best combination of creator and scorer of goals in Britain at that time.

Stanley Matthews was thirty-three years old and had been bought by Blackpool from Stoke City in the previous season for a fee of £11,500. Already hailed as the greatest player of his generation, he had first played for England in 1934 and up to now had already won twenty-one caps. On the Friday before the final he had been presented with the Footballer of the Year Trophy (Stan Mortensen had been voted into second place) by the newly formed Football Writers' Association, in recognition of his supreme genius – and the Cup final medal he might win on the morrow would be the crowning point of an already glittering career. His genius sprang from his ability to take the ball up to and around the opposition defenders in a bow-legged, side-stepping darting shuffle, a sight which was to grace England football for over thirty years.

Stan Mortensen had been a Blackpool player since 1937 and could play at inside-forward or centre-forward: both positions enabled him to make profitable use of his electrifying speed and deadly shot. He was twenty-seven years old and had scored four goals in his England debut last May and was already beginning to establish himself as Matthews' regular partner in the England forward line.

The Manchester United players took the reason for Mortensen's positional change for the Cup final with a pinch of salt: they saw it as an attempt to play him in against the strong but slow-turning Allenby Chilton. Stan Mortensen in any position was a danger, but Matt Busby and his team's defenders had been given plenty of time to work out a plan to tame this likeable but dangerous Tynesider.

Coincidentally, Manchester United would have been playing

Blackpool in a League game on the Saturday of the final anyway, and had they not been appearing in the final together that day would no doubt have been trying to break the deadlock of the 1–1 score-line which they had achieved when the teams had met last 6 December at Maine Road.

*FA Cup Final versus Blackpool at Wembley, 24 April 1948*

MANCHESTER UNITED: Crompton; Carey, Aston; Anderson, Chilton, Cockburn; Delaney, Morris, Rowley, Pearson, Mitten.

BLACKPOOL: Robinson; Shimwell, Crosland; Johnston, Hayward, Kelly; Matthews, Munro, Mortensen, Dick, Rickett.

Under a clear blue sky Wembley looked at its best as thousands of excited Manchester United and Blackpool supporters poured into the stadium after their long journey from Lancashire. The shirt-sleeved crowd whistled and sang as the Band of the Grenadier Guards played selections from *Annie Get your Gun* and *Oklahoma!*, and they cheered as the Guards wheeled and marched on Wembley's brilliant green turf to the rousing march 'Old Comrades'.

Then there was community singing led by Arthur Caiger who took the crowd through old favourites like 'Now is the Hour', and 'She's a Lassie from Lancashire', and Wembley's favourite hymn 'Abide With Me'. Suddenly red-and-white and tangerine favours were flourished, the crowd opposite the players' tunnel roared, and on to the field emerged the two teams led by Matt Busby and Joe Smith.

The teams lined up to be presented to King George VI, Blackpool wearing black shorts and white shirts, and Manchester United in white shorts and royal blue shirts, the same colour as they had worn in the third round against Aston Villa, and which a Manchester United team twenty years later, and in the same stadium, were to wear in a European Cup final. There was just time for the players to search for the faces of family and friends who were somewhere up in the grandstand along with the Queen, the Duke of Edinburgh, 16-year-old Princess Margaret, the Duke of Gloucester, the Earl of Athlone, who was the President of the Football Association, Princess Alice, Herbert Morrison,

Ernest Bevin and Sir Stafford Cripps. Also somewhere in the grandstand was the touring Australian cricket team led by Don Bradman, and seven survivors of United's 1909 Cup winning side, including the legendary 63-year-old Billy Meredith.

All over the country children were told to go and play outside as people drew closer to the radios to listen to the match commentary to be given by Raymond Glendenning. Amazingly, there were still League matches being played that Saturday, although attendances were naturally lower than usual. Even so 20,000 were about to watch Manchester City draw 0-0 with Arsenal at Maine Road, and 51,000 north-easterners scorned the all-Lancashire interest of the final to watch Sunderland beat Middlesbrough 3-0 at Roker Park.

Back at Wembley the stage was set - the match was about to begin!

Harry Johnston had won the toss and because there was hardly a breath of wind he made Manchester United kick-off into the sun. The first exchanges were watched anxiously by the supporters of both sides - their early questions needed urgent answers. How would our forwards make out? How would our defenders cope? The vast crowd saw Blackpool make the first goalwards move, and a pass inside from Stan Mortensen was neatly intercepted by John Aston. Then Stan Matthews floated over a centre, but it was headed out calmly by John Carey. Seconds later Harry Johnston took a long throw-in from the left, the ball bounced twice and Mortensen, feinting smartly, looked dangerous, but he lost the ball and the half-chance on the edge of United's penalty area.

There was no doubt that Blackpool were setting the pace and mounting the more dangerous-looking attacks, and the first real chance fell to them after only seven minutes. Matthews got the ball after a crisp bout of interpassing, rounded Aston, looked up and pulled back a centre straight to the feet of an unmarked Alex Munro who was only yards away from United's goal. Munro hurried his shot and failed to connect properly, and the ball sailed wide of the goal.

Then came the first corner of the game, forced at last by Manchester United. Jimmy Delaney took it on the right and sent it into a packed goalmouth. Jack Rowley leaped and twisted high above the Blackpool defence and headed powerfully for the far corner of the goal but Joe Robinson managed to make a one-handed save just under the crossbar and it was the Blackpool supporters' turn to gasp with relief.

Both teams had now felt the surge of adrenaline which follows near-scoring chances, and the attacking pace became even faster.

Jack Rowley, after switching positions with Jimmy Delaney, tested Robinson again with a sudden snap-shot, and Charlie Mitten and Stan Pearson also made attempts at goal which brought the crowd to their feet.

But it was still Blackpool who were applying the more sustained attacking pressure, and after fourteen minutes they broke the deadlock. A through-ball from centre-half Eric Hayward found Stan Mortensen who slipped past Allen Chilton and raced directly towards United's goal, pushing the ball ahead of him. He was well through with only Jack Crompton to beat. United's goalkeeper crouched on the line and prepared to deal with the shot. Both Allen Chilton and John Carey, who was closing in quickly from the right, were still giving chase, and Chilton, stretching to tackle Mortensen, brought down the Blackpool centre-forward in the penalty 'D', but Mortensen's momentum carried him several yards into the penalty area. Referee Barrick, behind the play and still running towards United's goal, pointed to the penalty-spot.

The protests were mild by today's standards, and Blackpool's ace penalty taker, Eddie Shimwell, stepped up to take the kick. The ball travelled hard and low under the diving body of Jack Crompton, and Blackpool were a goal in the lead, accepted by the first full-back ever to score a penalty at Wembley. Next day's papers and the Movietone film of the game were to prove that the tackle was outside the area, but at the time of the incident the margin of doubt was wide enough to convince many supporters (and even some of the players) that the penalty decision was justified.

Manchester United, who had often found themselves a goal down in the early stages of a match this season, did not allow the incident to disturb their composure. Their counter-pressure forced Blackpool to concede several corners and in one goalmouth incident Henry Cockburn, playing well up in support of his forwards, hit the cross-bar with Robinson out of position.

Both teams continued to play attacking football, but the main

initiative now seemed to lie with United. Charlie Mitten had a
blistering shot turned away for a corner, and Johnny Morris
headed narrowly wide from a Delaney centre. At the other end
the irrepressible Stan Mortensen came to scoring twice, once lob-
bing the ball over Jack Crompton's head, only to see it lodge
neatly on the roof of the unguarded net.

At last, after thirty minutes, Manchester United claimed a
well-deserved equaliser. John Carey flicked the ball to Jimmy
Delaney who, from a deep position, sent a long ball down the
centre. There seemed to be no danger as Shimwell, Hayward and
Robinson appeared to have the ball covered in front of the advancing Jack Rowley. Goalkeeper Robinson claimed responsibility with a shouted 'Right!', but perhaps the unusual perspective
of an unfamiliar stadium or the lush Wembley turf which often
'held' the ball, caused him to misread the bounce. It was too late
for the full-backs to do anything. Jack Rowley, racing forward,
lobbed the ball up and over Robinson's head, rounded him, and
side-footed it into Blackpool's yawning net.

Manchester United had little time to enjoy the experience of
being level once more, or of savouring another flashing Rowley
header which John Crosland had just managed to head away from
under the cross-bar. With only ten minutes of the first half remaining Stanley Matthews took a free-kick, Hugh Kelly headed
it forward to Stan Mortensen who darted past a surprised and
static United defence, and on the half-turn struck the ball into
the net wide of Crompton's outstretched right hand. It was a
swiftly-executed, opportunist goal which only Mortensen could
have scored.

The attacking pace of both teams did not slacken, even though
the first half was coming to an end, though Blackpool could have
been forgiven for wanting to consolidate their lead during the last
few minutes by packing their defence. Elated by their success
Blackpool launched another attack. Walter Rickett rounded John
Carey yet again and the way to United's goal was clear. His shot
on the run was brilliantly saved low down by Jack Crompton and
pushed around the foot of the post.

Later analysis defined that save as one of the turning points in
the game, and many of United's players still maintain that if Jack
Crompton had not saved that seemingly certain goal, a 3-1 deficit
at half-time might have been too large to retrieve.

The first half had been a pulsating affair, full of rich skill and played at high speed: Blackpool had used their wing-men well and had dictated the pace of the play. They were attacking quickly and taking all their chances, and the strategy of playing Mortensen at centre-forward and thereby splitting up the finest right-wing pairing in the country had not led to the disaster many had predicted.

The Blackpool defenders were tackling quickly and getting the ball away first time, and more importantly were preventing the United forwards from finding their usual rhythm and balance.

For the first twenty minutes of the second half the pattern repeated itself. Walter Rickett and Stan Mortensen continued to threaten the United goal and United's half-backs, by their own standards, were spending too much time in defence, unable to find the time to prompt their forwards as frequently or as effectively as they usually did. And, most significantly, the superb understanding which the United players had with one another was missing, and every United forward, with the singular exception of Jack Rowley, was having a very ordinary game.

With only twenty-five minutes of the game remaining even the most experienced of United's players was beginning to worry. Every missed chance or failed attack was using up valuable time. They were finding it hard to keep cool heads in the flurry of moves and counter moves, and to remember that they had faced this situation so many times already this season – and still triumphed.

Blackpool nearly went further ahead when Crosland sent a long through ball forward and as Mortensen and Crompton went to challenge together the ball eluded them both and seemed to be rolling towards United's empty net. John Aston dashed in but was thankfully able to watch it trickle slowly past the far post.

Jack Rowley and Stan Pearson found their goal efforts frustrated again and again, but flaws were appearing in the Blackpool defence and were there to be exploited. Robinson went out to collect a high cross from Delaney but it eluded his grasp and as several blue shirts closed in on him he had to make a second dive to finally secure it.

Deep in the United half, Allenby Chilton had to make a desperate sliding tackle on Munro who had embarked on a fast and dangerous looking dribble, and the Blackpool trainer had to be called on to administer the cold sponge.

From the ensuing free-kick, a move developed which resulted in United drawing equal for the second time. The free-kick was cleared to United's right wing and eventually to Johnny Morris who began foraging his way through when he was tackled unfairly by Kelly, ten yards from the Blackpool line and near the touch-line. A free-kick was immediately awarded. Johnny Morris stood up and took the kick in almost one movement, driving the ball across the face of Blackpool's goal. Jack Rowley, on the edge of the six-yard box, retreated a step or two to judge the flight of the ball, then slipped between several defenders, a couple of whom still had their backs to Morris, and dived upwards and forwards to head in the second equaliser. It was a brilliant goal, and there were twenty minutes to go.

Suddenly, United's play began to look much more fluent and relaxed. They kept the ball moving forward, piling on the pressure. The scores were equal and United now had the psychological advantage. However, they had one more fright to endure before the magic moment which gave them the lead they were never to relinquish.

Stan Mortensen might easily have put the Seasiders ahead when he again eluded Chilton, raced forward and finished with a hard angled-drive goalwards. Jack Crompton flung himself to the right and held the ball. He leapt to his feet in a flash and threw out a long pass to John Anderson who made ground and slid the ball through to Stan Pearson who was racing through on the right towards Blackpool's goal. Pearson beat Eric Hayward, and before any other defender could challenge him veered to the right and shot for the left-hand side of the goal. The ball swung away from Robinson, struck the inside of the far post and curled safely into the back of the Blackpool net. It was another brilliant goal, and so quickly executed that when Pearson's shot crossed Blackpool's goal-line Mortensen was still walking back out of United's penalty area, quietly lamenting his own near miss.

Stan Pearson's goal gave Manchester United the final boost they needed to play the kind of football everybody wanted to see from them. Their wing half-backs appeared more prominently in their attacking moves, and the forwards wove in and out of each other's positions. The passes flew quickly, and for the first time in the game Blackpool's defence looked harassed and de-moralised.

The result was finally sealed when, with five minutes to go, John Anderson found himself well forward of his usual right-half position and decided he would have a shot himself, even though he was all of thirty-five yards out. His drive glanced off the head of Hugh Kelly and sailed into Blackpool's net leaving an astonished Robinson stranded on the other side of his goal.

There was time in the closing minutes for Blackpool to force a corner, and all but Robinson crowded into United's penalty area for the last despairing attempt to score.

It came to nothing and with United back on the counter-attack the referee looked at his watch, halted, raised his hand and blew a long piercing blast to end the match.

Manchester United had won the Cup!

Within minutes of the final whistle, John Carey climbed up the steps to the Royal Box to receive the Cup from the King, and United's captain in his excitement dropped the Cup's plinth and lid back on to the table in front of the Royal party.

Behind Carey, his proud and happy team-mates were presented their medals by the Queen, while down on the pitch Harry Johnston and every member of his disconsolate Blackpool side found it hard to lift their heads as they tried to remember how they could have allowed Manchester United to come from behind twice and eventually snatch the Cup which they felt they had already won. The King had a special word with Matthews whom he had so often seen in action. 'He told me he had enjoyed the game,' Matthews later told reporters, 'but perhaps I was too miserable to catch everything he said.'

Then it was time for the Blackpool players to shake hands and congratulate the United team, and to commiserate quietly with one another as they trailed back to their dressing-room.

Among the players, reflections about their own game and the team's performances last until today.

Possibly Blackpool had relied too heavily on the magic of Matthews and Mortensen to win the game for them, and up to a certain point it looked as though it might work. But Manchester United's superior team effort won in the end and when Blackpool's energy and concentration failed them in the last quarter of the game it allowed United to brush them aside and claim a resounding victory.

All agreed that the old maestro Stan Matthews had played delightful football in the first half, but United's defensive strategy had then prevented the ball reaching him, and he had faded from the game. As he trudged off the field he might have wondered whether he would ever win a Cup medal. But Stan Matthews survived the experience and five years later on the same turf he was given the hero's part in another superb final, this time against Bolton Wanderers, and won the medal everybody wanted him to secure.

Stan Mortensen, many felt, should have been given as much sympathy as Stan Matthews – he had played his heart out, scored a goal, and joined the select band of then only four players who had scored in every round of the Cup, yet was rewarded with only a loser's medal. He, like Stan Matthews, had to battle through another two finals before capturing football's most precious prize.

Outside-left Walter Rickett had also played brilliantly, giving the lie to the accusation that Blackpool were a lop-sided team. He had beaten John Carey more often than any other left-winger had done that season and had created many good chances for himself and the other Blackpool forwards. 'Of all the forwards he played the best and most dangerously,' conceded John Carey. 'He was the one I was supposed to be marking and he had a blinder. Stan Matthews didn't do all that well in the game ... he wasn't the source of danger ... it was Walter Rickett, and if it hadn't been for that tremendous save that Jack made from him just before half-time we'd have gone in 3–1 down, not 2–1, and might have lost the game altogether.'

Looking back over the match many of United's players conceded that in the first twenty minutes of the second half they were in danger of fading away and losing the game, having lost much of their boldness and precision, and unable, until the storming finale, to summon the ability to finish attacking moves with strikes for goal. They had disregarded all the talk about favourites never winning, and they had refused to panic and even at their lowest moments had always suggested reserves of power. Teamwork had eventually triumphed and they had found the wherewithal to hit back and eventually wear down their opponents.

It is generally agreed that the greatest of United's unsung heroes that day was Jack Crompton, not least because two of his saves signalled real changes in fortune for his team.

The United goalkeeper remembered that:

At one stage in the second half they were well on top, and they certainly were at the time I saved Morty's shot and threw the ball out to John Anderson. We'd almost gone by them. Every time I meet Stan Mortensen now and we talk about the final he tells me that never in his life has he wished more that he'd missed the goal completely rather than hit the target. If his shot had gone past the post we might never have scored from the goal-kick. I suppose also if I'd have tipped it round the post, and not held it and thrown it out quickly we might never have scored. Actually I stopped another goal just before half-time when Walter Rickett cut inside John Carey and had a shot ... I think it was just as vital a save ... if they'd gone in 3-1 at half-time that would really have killed us. Actually it wasn't as vital a save as the one I made from Morty ... that would also have given them a 3-1 lead with less time for us to get back.

Jack Crompton was also involved in the first really dramatic incidents of the game – the trip on Stan Mortensen and then having to face the consequent penalty.

I never think of Allenby's trip on Mortensen as a professional foul: it was more a professional dive! He was a handful I admit, but it wasn't an intentional foul and Chilli just caught him a yard outside the penalty-area.

We knew Eddie Shimwell would take any penalties and we always talked about penalties before every game – penalties came up fairly freely in those days. Shimwell was a right-footer and he really blasted the ball and we thought he would hit it to my right so the answer was just to go when he struck it. If he'd hit it well and into the corner I'd have saved it, but because he hit it so hard and so close to me I couldn't get down ... I was flying to the right. The hardest ball for any goalkeeper to get down to from twelve yards is the one that's close to.

Over thirty-five years later Stan Mortensen still laughs about the incident: 'You know, I was going so fast I was tripped in the centre-circle (let alone the semi-circle) and I landed in the penalty-area! Actually, I don't know what all the fuss was about,' he chuckled, 'I'd have scored anyway!'

He could have been right. The Movietone film of the game shows Allenby Chilton and Jack Carey closing in on the flying centre-forward and the penalty-area was empty apart from Jack Crompton crouching on his line.

Charlie Mitten and Jack Crompton used to practise penalties together so Mitten was more than interested to see how his team-mate would cope with the challenge.

Jack was unlucky not to stop the penalty. He guessed the right way, but he dived over the ball. We used to practise together taking and saving penalties ... it taught me how to score them and him to stop them ... but not this time ... actually Jack was a magnificent penalty-stopper. Morty still laughs about that penalty, you know, he told me once that when Allen tackled him he landed two yards outside the box and skidded three!

Allenby Chilton measured his battle with Stan Mortensen against his memories of playing against other great centre-forwards:

I'd had some great battles in my time with centre-forwards ... Nat Lofthouse: working all the time, great feller, great to play against; Trevor Ford, big Duggie Reed, Tommy Lawton, Ronnie Allen from West Brom: you couldn't nail him down ... he was a hell of a good player; Roy Bentley, Dennis Westcott of Wolves. You get used to buffeting each other, it was always hard but clean, you had to be strong and go for the ball.

Doubtless, these were the kinds of centre-forwards Chilton relished playing against, but coping with the mercurial Mortensen demanded fewer obvious physical skills. Certainly the Blackpool player's speed off the mark caused Allenby many problems that afternoon:

I never kicked anybody deliberately in my life and my foul on Morty was a genuine attempt to get the ball. John Carey was having a rough time against Walter Rickett - he was having to chase him so I was having to keep an eye on Morty and watch the spaces which were opening up around me. Eventually I was caught square and Morty was past me in a flash. I clipped him a yard out ... penalty given ... he wasn't hurt but jumped for joy. It annoyed us because we could see it wasn't a penalty.

He stumbled then dived. They do it better today, mind, swallow dives and everything. Anyway, I'm glad that goal didn't decide the match.

Blackpool's gift goal to United was fair recompense for the doubtful decision by the referee arising from Allenby Chilton's admitted defensive blunder. Later the Blackpool defence also confessed to the mistake which gave Jack Rowley his equalising goal – it was caused by a complete misunderstanding between Joe Robinson and centre-half Eric Hayward. Robinson said, 'I called to Eric that I had the ball covered, but the bounce deceived me and Jack Rowley nipped in and scored.'

Few that day would have realised from Jack Rowley's brilliant performance that his mind was not fully on the game, and his modest description of United's equaliser takes no account of his speedy reactions to the lapse in concentration by some of the Blackpool defenders:

I remember very little of the final itself for the simple reason that my wife was a week overdue with our second child. I had phoned her up before the kick-off and nothing had happened and even while I was getting changed my thoughts were back home ... was everything OK ... she's missing all this. Her family were there and my family were there, but she wasn't there. So we went out and stood in front of the Royal Box and I could see the wife's people waving on one side of the Box and my own family was way over on the other side and I thought to myself, 'I'm going to be in trouble over that', because the wife's family had the best tickets. I couldn't have known beforehand because I didn't know how the tickets were numbered.

Anyway the game began and after only fifteen minutes it was a penalty ... 1-0 down. It was funny, but it never entered our minds that we'd get beaten in the final. Then a long ball was pushed through the middle to me ... I went past everybody and the goalkeeper came out and just as he went to pick it up I just lobbed it over his head, walked around him and side-footed it into the net and that made it 1-1.

John Carey's famous words in United's dressing-room at half-time merely reminded his experienced side of something they all knew instinctively:

At half-time it wasn't my place to be saying too much, but I was captain so I said, 'If we keep playing football we must win it. If we start just kicking it around we've no chance.' We had a motto in the team that 'the ball should never stop'. Only the goalkeeper in our team stopped the ball ... our game was based on first-time passes ... if we were accurate with those passes and we didn't lose the ball it was devastating. By pushing the ball around and running into open positions we made it almost impossible for defenders to pick us up.

Never in the whole game did I feel we were going to be beaten ... I knew we were going to win. I'd watched us match after match and we were always able to raise our game enough to win matches and I felt there was no reason why we shouldn't do it at Wembley. We were all experienced professionals, and knew what the game was about and this showed up in the game, I thought. It was a tremendous game and people still tell me it was the best final they'd ever been to. It had all the ingredients and was played in a tremendous spirit ... it was a competitive game and like a professional match should be.

Jack Rowley's magnificent equaliser, a diving header in truly Lawtonian style, began United's winning revival. He remembers only the barest details of the goal but his team-mates were loud in its praises. Jimmy Delaney recalled:

Jack Rowley's header was a beauty. I was very close to the incident when Johnny Morris was fouled out on the right wing and I was ready to get the ball and take the free-kick, but Johnny jumped up, shoved me out of the way and took it ... it's a good job he did because he thumped it over in front of Jack who headed a lovely goal. I'd have probably taken my time over that free-kick and the defence would have all been in position by then.

Johnny Morris, one of the main protagonists in the drama of that superb goal, began by revealing another well-kept secret that not even his manager was aware of:

I'll tell you something that's not too well known, a fortnight before the Cup final I got a very bad ankle injury. By this time, of course, we are in the final of the Cup and I didn't tell a soul about this ankle I was struggling with ... except for the first couple of days after I did it I had a bit of treatment on it. It was because I so wanted to play at Wembley. I wasn't going to miss the final just because of an injury. So in that final I played with a bad ankle, and the lads carried me that day ... I certainly wasn't able to play in the two games we had to play after the final, it was

that bad. So when you talk about my free-kick which Jack Rowley headed
to make it 2–2 ... it's the only bloody thing I did in the game!

Blackpool's defenders were later to claim that they thought the
free-kick had been awarded to them and not United, but their
excuses take no account of the superb reflexes of Johnny Morris
and the lightning free-kick. Among themselves the Blackpool defenders wondered why one of them had not kicked the ball away
before Morris had taken the kick, so that the other defenders
would have had time to get into position. Later referee Barrick
said that Morris had been pushed off the ball by Kelly, who in
turn claimed that he had merely flung his hands out to stop
himself from tripping over United's lively inside-right.

Scoring the winning goal at Wembley is every player's (and
most spectators') dream. Stan Pearson still relishes the memory
of his goal which brought the FA Cup back to Manchester:

Ten seconds before I scored I was standing in the middle of the field
with my heart in my mouth watching Jack saving a certain goal from
Stan Mortensen. And then I can see my goal to this day in great detail.
Actually, I don't think I got much credit in the papers for the goal and
I often used to wonder why, but one day Alf Clarke told me the reason.
Remember, Stan Mortensen gets a scoring chance and Jack dives and
grabs it and gets up and throws it to Johnny Anderson. He gets it and
I start moving across and shouting my head off for the ball. I get away
from Harry Johnston, collect a perfect pass from Johnny, take it in my
stride and somebody is coming for me and I manage to slip him and
have a quick look at the goal. I'm about five or six yards outside the
penalty-area in the inside-right position and there's somebody coming
... you've no time to see who it is ... you just sense that they're there
... another quick look at the goal and I hit a similar shot that Mortensen
hit – across the goal and I see it going a foot inside the post but swinging
away. It hits the bloody post and goes back across the goal-line and into
the net! I never thought I got the credit I deserved for that. Of course,
there was no TV in those days. Anyway Alf Clarke said that the reporters
all had their heads down writing about Jack Crompton's brilliant save
... and suddenly there's a bloody great shout ... we've scored at the
other end! Jack had saved the ball and thrown it out, then there was a
good long pass and in three moves we've got the ball back in their net!

Stan Mortensen lamented his missed chance which ironically
led to Pearson's goal and after the match said, 'If I had put the

ball into the crowd instead of to the goalkeeper the score would still have been 2-2, but Stan Pearson's goal was a body-blow, I have to admit.'

John Anderson, whose greatest moment was only minutes away, remembered that the goal . . .

. . . took everybody by surprise, even the radio commentators. How Jack Crompton saved that shot from Morty I'll never know. He leaped across and really he should have tipped it over but instead he held it. When Jack threw the ball out to me I made a bit of ground and thought, I've done enough here . . . looked up . . . both Stan and Johnny Morris were running into beautiful positions . . . I couldn't have missed either of them so I slung it straight through . . . Stan collected it and hit it all in one movement and it was in the back of the net.

Even the people who were listening to the wireless thought Blackpool had scored because the commentator had been describing how Mortensen had burst through and made the shot . . . he hadn't even got to the part about Jack saving it and starting to the move . . . in a few seconds it's down the other end and in Blackpool's goal. When people listening to the radio heard there was a goal they thought he was describing another one by Mortensen!

The goal Anderson scored himself illustrated perfectly how United were still prepared to take their goalscoring chances, whatever the time, whatever the score:

We could find each other in the dark with our passes . . . the only time I couldn't find anybody was when I scored the fourth goal at Wembley.

John Aston had the ball in the left-back position and I ran into the space between two players who were challenging him. I got the ball on my left foot and somebody was coming in to challenge me and I pushed it past him . . . I'd done enough running by then . . . Wembley's a big place. I looked up and thought, Who am I going to give it to now? We used to know before we got the ball who we were going to pass to, but this time I couldn't see anybody when I looked up . . . I couldn't see any of the forwards . . . they were all marked, I couldn't believe it. Matt Busby used to say, 'If they're all marked there's only one thing to do with it and that's to put it in the back of the net yourself.' I looked up again . . . I was about forty yards out and I thought, Well, here goes. This is all going through my head in a couple of seconds, of course. So it's 'bang' with my left foot. I fell over as soon as I'd fired in the shot so I never even saw it go into the net.

When the ball went in there was this big roar and the lads were all running up to shake my hand but I turned round and shouted, 'I've scored, I've scored', and started running. If those big gates at the end of the stadium had been open I'd have gone through ... I was running and running. But there was John Carey with his arms out wide saying, 'Steady, son, steady', and he managed to stop me.

The lads all told me it was a lucky goal of course, so I'll take their word for it! Henry Cockburn said, 'You know John, Joe Robinson was reading braille at the time, which is why he let it in!' Actually, Henry had already hit the cross-bar. 'I'm glad it didn't go in,' I told him later, 'they couldn't be doing with the two of us scoring at Wembley!'

A strategy to cope with Blackpool's most dangerous player had dominated United's tactical discussions in the weeks before the final. 'We felt that it was going to be a tactical win,' recalled Johnny Carey. 'If we were going to win we'd have to use the right tactics to beat them, and I think that by and large we got it right.'

Jack Crompton added:

Stan Matthews was the big danger, of course, and we'd agreed that whenever I picked up the ball I looked for him first and put the width of the field between him and the ball. We also told John Aston not to tackle him but to lay off him and let Charlie Mitten be the first to try, because if Stan felt people behind him he tended to pull the ball back and see who it was and this would give time to John and Henry to cover him. The biggest danger was him beating defenders and pulling them out of position and knocking it in for Morty or somebody.

I remember my brother saying to me, 'You didn't use the ball as well as you usually use it.' Well, I couldn't ... my first job was not to look for our side but to look for Stanley Matthews and then get the ball to the other side of the field. Even if I felt I could find somebody with a goal-kick I couldn't take a chance, I put it to the opposite side to where Matthews was standing.

John Aston also remembered that the plan to control Matthews was that ...

Charlie Mitten was supposed to come back and harass him. He wasn't all that bothered though, wasn't Charlie, he was more interested in his own game. Wait a minute, he did come back once or twice I do remember! Anyway, it was my job to keep tight on Matthews and Charlie helped out a couple of times. It worked I think, because he didn't see too much of the ball. Matthews liked a bit of space to get the ball, and the idea was that if we kept tight on him they wouldn't give him the ball. But if you left Matthews five yards of space you really had a job on.

Only after the game could all the stories be told about the injury problems which nagged the players. Johnny Morris's injury was a secret he had managed to keep to himself, but others found it impossible. Jack Crompton looked as though he might be in quite serious trouble:

The week before the final was a terrible week for me. My sister had died the week before, and then I developed an abscess at the base of my spine. It was agony and I went with Matt to Ancoats Hospital and the doctor said, 'The only way of getting him to play in the final is to take a chance and drain it and even then it might be too sore to play.'

So we did just that, not knowing how I would be. But once it had been lanced it improved quite well and from the Thursday onwards I felt all right. It was still a bit sore on the Friday and the Saturday of the final, but I was strapped up so heavily down there I hardly needed a jock strap. Early on in the game I came out for a crossed ball, stretched up, caught it then fell back, arched my back and took the force on my shoulders, but as soon as my backside hit the ground I really felt it then. I feared the worst for the moment but it soon wore off. We kept the story of the injury out of the papers ... if Blackpool had known they might have sent somebody round early on to kick me up the backside!

Jimmy Delaney also carried an injury into the final, which, as Matt Busby said at the time ... 'we kept quiet about all week. Jimmy was a doubtful starter for Wembley because the ankle injury he suffered against Chelsea the previous week was slow to mend, and although we passed Jimmy as fit there was always the risk that he would break down. We had an anxious moment twenty minutes after the start when he got up limping after a tackle and he limped for the rest of the game.' Delaney had been told by his manager to play an orthodox wing game and to steer clear of the hurly-burly in the centre of the field, which goes some way to explaining why he and Jack Rowley did not switch positions as frequently as they usually did, and why the United attack did not function in its usual classic style.

There was another special reason why Jimmy Delaney wanted to play and win at Wembley. The day of the final was his son's eighth birthday and he was determined that 'Patsy's going to get a wonderful present!' Later, he had time to spare a thought for the man who was denied the gift: 'I often wondered what Stanley Matthews thought of me winning a medal ... there's him born and bred in England not getting one for all the years he'd played there ... and I'd only been playing in England for two years and I get a Cup medal!'

The last words on this glorious episode fittingly remain with John Carey:

I don't think the final was our best display in that Cup series but it was enough to win. I think we all felt sorry for Blackpool and Stanley Matthews, and you try not to show the great joy you feel at winning and you try publicly to be a bit modest about your victory. But once the final whistle blows and it's 4-2 and you know you're going to have the Cup to bring home, that's great ... that's a tremendous feeling.

On the evening of Cup final day, the Manchester United party attended a banquet at the Connaught Rooms and on the Sunday morning, accompanied by wives and officials, travelled down to Brighton for the day. After lunch at the Hotel Metropole they spent the afternoon strolling along the promenade, then later enjoyed dinner at the hotel and a coach trip back to London, where they stayed overnight before returning to Manchester on the one o'clock train from Euston. Nowadays, the two Cup teams return to their respective towns or cities on the Sunday after the final, but the 1948 United team enjoyed the chance of a quiet day 'away from it all' before having to face the inevitable boisterous welcome when they got back to Manchester.

The team left the train at Wilmslow, then travelled by road to Hale to fulfil an important engagement before meeting the crowds gathering in the city centre to welcome them. They stopped at the home of Mr James Gibson, the chairman of the club, who seventeen years before had saved United from financial disaster, but was now under doctor's orders to rest. The players lined up on the lawn and then trooped into the house to meet him.

When the team coach at last reached the bottom of Princess Road in South Manchester the crowds were there to greet it and they lined the rest of the route several deep along Denmark Road and Oxford Road to Albert Square and the Town Hall.

The crowds shouted, 'We want Carey, we want Carey', and there was a huge roar as he appeared on the Town Hall balcony holding the Cup aloft, with the rest of the team gathered around him. After more shouting and waving the United party could at last withdraw inside to enjoy peace and refreshment which included a 'Wembley' cake, complete with goalposts made of sugar. This was to be the first of countless dinners and receptions which the players were to attend in the next few weeks. Most of them, however, were especially looking forward to Tuesday night when, after being introduced on the stage of the Odeon Cinema, they would be able to see the five-minute Movietone film of the game.

The victory had excited everybody who loved football, however young or old they were. Up in Northumberland it affected one lad who remembers it as 'the day I decided I wanted to play for Manchester United, if I were good enough'. Bobby Charlton was a sturdy 11-year-old and determined to be a footballer:

It was Cup final day 1948, and United were playing Blackpool. We played in the morning and a friend in the East Northumberland Boys team invited a few of us back to his house in the afternoon to listen to the match on the radio. Television sets were rare in those days. I was impressed by the way United fought back after being a goal down and, in the way young boys do, selected them as 'my' team for the afternoon. With astonishing strength of will we managed to suppress our mounting excitement until half-time. But then, our imaginations fired by the drama taking place three hundred miles away, we could contain ourselves no longer. Stopping just long enough to collect a ball, we rushed outside and threw ourselves wholeheartedly into a re-enactment of the 'big game'. When, at last, someone came out and told us that United had won 4–2, I danced about in delight as if I had personally scored the winning goal. From that day I belonged to Manchester. (R. Charlton, *This Game of Soccer*, Cassell & Company, London, 1967.)

Others were able to enjoy Manchester United's Cup success in more tangible ways. United's victory was a very heavy blow to the bookmakers, and backers throughout the country, it was estimated, must have won the best part of £500,000. The North in particular had seized on United's odds of 25–1 when the third round draw was announced.

One Manchester man was reported to have won £25,000 with a £1,000 early bet. A week after the final, as a gesture of gratitude, he hosted a dinner at the Midland Hotel for the officials and team. One of the players remembered the occasion, and added with a wry smile 'that he gave us a gold watch each, but we had to go into the loo to get it, because the FA had a rule that players couldn't accept expensive gifts!'

Blackpool and Manchester United met at Bloomfield Road on the Wednesday after the Cup final for their return League fixture. Neither the injured Jimmy Delaney nor Johnny Morris were playing, their places being taken by the ever-patient Ted Buckle and Johnny Hanlon.

It was an exciting first half with both sides putting tremendous energy into their play. Blackpool relished the chance of revenge against the 'team of the year', and United were anxious to confirm their last Saturday's triumph.

Stan Mortensen scored with a header after ten minutes, then just before half-time he went after a ball in United's penalty-area and ran full tilt into Jack Crompton. Both players had to be carried off deeply concussed.

Mortensen was taken to the Victoria Hospital, but recovered soon after his arrival there. There was good reason for the consternation which the Blackpool players and crowd felt for Stan Mortensen, because they all knew about a head injury he had suffered during the war. He had been serving as a wireless-operator air-gunner and one day was flying in a Wellington bomber over Scotland when it caught fire and crash-landed in a fir plantation. The pilot and bomb-aimer were killed, the navigator was to lose a leg and Stan Mortensen crawled out, virtually unscathed apart from a head wound which needed a dozen stitches.

Looking back on the game Stan Mortensen said:

It's a good job I was out cold. The ball had rolled into the net after Jack and I had collided and the crowd fully expected a goal to be awarded – it was a 50–50 ball which I'd gone for, and Jack, like all brave goalkeepers, had stood his ground. Anyway, once our bodies had been carried off the referee gave a free-kick against me! The crowd apparently went mad, as I might have done if I'd been awake!

Jack Crompton returned after twenty minutes of the second
half, playing first at outside-right then right-back, and afterwards
going back into goal in place of Charlie Mitten, his temporary
replacement.

The United forwards never got into their stride in this match
and only Johnny Hanlon came close to scoring when he hit the
post with a strong shot. Walter Rickett worried John Carey yet
again, but a subdued Stanley Matthews was again well controlled
by John Aston. Very few United supporters begrudged Blackpool's 1-0 victory that day, even though it meant prolonging the
agony until United's very last game of the season. Arsenal had
already been declared champions: but who would be the
runners-up in the First Division – Manchester United, Burnley
or Derby County?

All three teams were on 50 points to Arsenal's 57. United met
Blackburn Rovers at Maine Road on the last Saturday of the
season and beat them 4-1, thanks to another brilliant hat-trick by
Stan Pearson after a crafty first goal by Jimmy Delaney. News
soon came through that Burnley had beaten Huddersfield 2-1,
and Derby County had been defeated 1-0 by Stoke City. Thus,
by virtue of a better goal-average, United beat Burnley to occupy
the runners-up position for the second consecutive year.

A crowd of 44,439 gave the side a huge roar of appreciation as
the United players waved them goodbye at the end of a quite
superb season. Cup winners and runners-up in Division One: it
had been the most successful season in the history of the club –
Manchester United were truly 'the team of the year'!

It was now summer, but for some of United's players there was
more football in prospect. In fact, a few days before the Cup final
five United players, Morris, Rowley, Pearson, Cockburn and
Aston, were requested by the Football Association to have their
passports available in case they were picked for the England touring side which was to play in Italy and Switzerland that summer.

Only Stan Pearson, John Aston and Henry Cockburn were
picked for the final party which also included Frank Swift, Billy
Wright, Bill Nicholson, Stan Mortensen, Stan Matthews, Tom
Finney, Wilf Mannion, and a late choice: Southampton's right-
back Alf Ramsey.

The highlight of the tour (which included two representative

games in Switzerland) was to be the first game, played in Turin
on Sunday, 16 May.

A few days after the League season had ended, the England
players and officials took off for Milan. It was Henry Cockburn's
first trip abroad:

The weather was beautiful when we landed and there were crowds waiting for us and they're all shouting 'Sweeft, Matt-e-oos, Law-ton' and
they're signing autographs and getting bouquets of flowers. I thought it
was wonderful, even though you could smell garlic everywhere. We
stayed in a lovely place near Lake Maggiore called Stresa. (I'll never
forget it ... I want to go back there actually, if I can) we saw Lake
Como ... it was beautiful.

The Italians were determined to win. There was national pride
at stake, it was the fiftieth anniversary of the Italian FA. England
were still the masters of the game, but Italy were current
world champions, having won the last World Cup competition in
1938.

The excitement was intense. A national holiday was declared
and the Italian team trained in a secret mountain retreat, no doubt
inspired by the promise of an individual winning bonus of £100,
compared with England's £20 per man – win, lose or draw. Before the match the tension crackled around the huge stadium in
Turin and the sun broke through after a day of torrential rain. A
partisan crowd of 85,000 were looking forward to the inevitable
Italian victory.

Henry Cockburn was the only United player to be selected for
the England team to meet the Italians that day:

It was a night match ... a lovely warm evening ... 5.30 kick-off. I
remember they had oxygen machines in the dressing-room. Anyway,
both teams start to go up the tunnel together. I looked over to the line
of Italian players and I nearly died. They were all up here ... huge lads
in short shorts, massive thighs and short-sleeved shirts. They each had
a ball and every one of them was juggling away with it. I thought, Oh
bloody hell, what *am* I doing here? We gets on the pitch and there's a
hell of a noise. I felt even worse then. But as soon as they started to play
'God Save the King' I felt so proud. I thought, Right, we're on the line
... muck or nettles now ... I'll run 'till I'm down. We beat them 4-0!

It was a memorable game and a great performance by England. The defence played superbly and the attack of Matthews, Mortensen, Lawton, Mannion, and Finney lived up to its reputation. Looking back on their joint total of 130 internationals, both Billy Wright and Stan Mortensen later declared that the victorious display over Italy that day was the greatest they had taken part in.

Continental domination of football was only just around the corner, but on this showing English football was still supreme – and it was a fitting end to a season in which England had not been defeated.

# 1948-49

## Nearly the Double ...

The Charity Shield match (between the winners of the First Division Championship and the winners of the FA Cup) against Arsenal on 6 October at Highbury (the venue in those days being decided by the toss of a coin) resulted in a 4-3 victory for the 'Gunners' who actually scored three goals in the first five minutes. It was an exciting game and a worthy episode in the long tradition of sporting conflict which existed between two of the best supported teams in the First Division.

By the middle of December, Manchester United had played exactly half their League fixtures and had risen, as Busby had forseen, to fourth place in the table behind the leaders Derby County, Newcastle United and Portsmouth. United had won 9 games, drawn 7 and lost 5, and so far had scored 46 goals, the highest total in the League.

But the impression at the time was that the team was not playing with quite the same devastating authority as it had last season. Some thought that too often the forward play was listless, disjointed or just plain inaccurate, and many wondered why Jack Rowley was not getting the service he used to. Admittedly, the team had suffered its fair share of injuries and international calls on some of its key players. Still, there was a long way to go, and time to find that missing rhythm again. The team still selected itself and contained virtually the same players who had won the FA Cup the previous April, with the exception of Bill McGlen who was playing as many games at right-half as John Anderson, the last and seemingly least permanent of that triumphant 1948 team. Bobby Brown (in goal), Johnny Ball, Jack Warner, Johnny Hanlon, Ted Buckle and Ronnie Burke had also made the occasional first-team appearance this season.

At this point the eagerly awaited draw for the third round of the FA Cup was made. Manchester United could not have had an easier pairing - against Bournemouth and Boscombe AFC from the Third Division (South), to be played at Maine Road.

The third round was played on Saturday, 8 January, and as expected United completely outclassed Bournemouth in a 6–0 victory, with two goals from Ronnie Burke (deputising for the injured Johnny Morris), two from Jack Rowley, and one each from Stan Pearson and Charlie Mitten.

The fourth round draw matched United at home to Bradford Park Avenue, Stoke at home to Blackpool (a fixture which would bring Stan Matthews back to his home town), and Derby with Arsenal. 'Gallant Yeovil', as the papers were beginning to call them, were drawn at home to First Division Sunderland.

The largest crowd of the day, 82,771 (and the second largest gate in United's history), watched Bradford, who were apparently undismayed by the magnitude of their task, hold Manchester United to a 1–1 draw. Bradford had scored first after twenty-eight minutes, and Charlie Mitten had equalised in the second half. Neither team looked capable of resolving the draw, even with a period of extra time, although John Downie, Bradford's inside-left, wasted a gilt-edged chance of giving Bradford victory by shooting wide of the post from six yards. It was a disappointing display by United, and most agreed that Bradford, who had bustled the Reds out of their rhythm, fully deserved another crack at the Cup-holders.

The draw for the fifth round was made before United and Bradford had staged their replay. Whoever won, it was declared, would play non-League Yeovil at home!

But Bradford were far from giving in so easily to their illustrious opponents. The replay was a rough, hard-tackling match on an icy pitch in a thick Pennine fog, and United, without the injured Morris and Delaney, could only force yet another 1–1 draw. Manchester United were still 4:1 favourites to win the Cup, yet had now played for 240 minutes against Second Division opponents without being able to stamp anything like their former authority on the game. Their old magic had deserted them and every United follower longed for its speedy return.

On the following Monday afternoon the two teams faced each other yet again at Maine Road in front of 70,434 spectators for a second replay. Thousands had climbed over the walls of Maine Road or scrambled through the turnstiles, so the actual attendance was much higher than the official figure. Next day the Ministry of Labour was to ask local factories and workshops how many workers had taken 'French leave' so they could go to the game. Industry deplored mid-week matches because they disrupted production, and many firms, it was reported, intended to sack any of their work-force who had taken the Monday afternoon off to see this vital second replay. Many thousands of grannies must have been buried that day.

As soon as the game began it was clear that Bradford had used up all their chances. United, stung by Bradford's prolonged resistance, and with the prospect of meeting Yeovil in the next round, played as a team and the forwards at last found their long-lost ability to finish off attacking moves with goals. Bradford conceded one goal before half-time, but after the interval their resistance crumbled completely and United slammed in another four.

At the end of the week, again at Maine Road, Manchester United overwhelmed non-League Yeovil 8-0 in their fifth round match, watched by another massive 81,565 crowd. Jimmy Delaney was back in the side in his classic role of provider, and the Yeovil part-timers led by centre-forward Alec Stock had only courage to offer in the face of a powerful and smoothly functioning football machine containing six internationals. Jack Rowley scored 5 goals (including a hat-trick in 16 minutes), Ronnie Burke at centre-forward scored 2, and Charlie Mitten 1.

The teams now left in the FA Cup were First Division Manchester United, Derby County, Wolverhampton Wanderers and Portsmouth (the League leaders); West Bromwich Albion and Brentford from the Second Division, and Hull City from the Third Division. Second Division Leicester beat Luton 5-3 in the replay to complete the eight teams whose names went into the draw for the sixth round.

Manchester United were drawn to play Hull City, and were therefore virtually certain to be one of the teams to reach the semi-final draw. How favourable the Cup draw seemed to be this season compared to last!

A week after the victory over Yeovil, Manchester United were beaten 2-1 by Aston Villa which ended a run of eighteen consecutive games without defeat since 16 October of the previous year. And now United, after twenty-seven games, were fifth in the League behind Portsmouth, Newcastle United, Derby County and Charlton Athletic.

A ground record for Boothferry Park of 55,019 was created when Hull City and Manchester United staged their sixth-round battle on 26 February 1949. Led by their player-manager Raich Carter, Hull City were to head the Third Division at the end of the season and so gain promotion. They now relished the chance to show how good they were against one of the best teams in the country.

It began as an exciting if scrappy match, played in a blustery wind. Hull were playing well above themselves and caused their more experienced opponents several anxious moments, especially in the scoreless first half. Then United, by superior team work and that little bit of extra pace, wore down the battling 'Tigers' and so deserved the goal which eventually won them the tie. It was reminiscent of Stan Pearson's superb third goal at Wembley in the previous season. Johnny Ball, who was playing well in place of John Carey, kneed the ball off the line with Jack Crompton helpless: his 'clearance' was helped on by Ronnie Burke (who was still deputising for Johnny Morris) to Jimmy Delaney, who raced with it right to the goal-line. He screwed it square across the face of the Hull goal where it was turned in by the ever-alert Stan Pearson just before Hull's goalkeeper dived at his feet. United's captain for the day had again set the seal on another vital win with only seventeen minutes of the game left!

Two days later the draw for the semi-finals was made: Manchester United were to play Wolverhampton Wanderers at Hillsborough, and Portsmouth were matched against Leicester City at Highbury.

A week before United's sixth-round victory at Hull, a shock announcement from Old Trafford declared that Johnny Morris, at his own request, had been put on the transfer list.

Morris had been in and out of the United first team since the beginning of the year because of a recurring ankle injury. He had missed the two replays against Bradford and the ties against Yeovil, and had obviously been 'dropped' for the tie against Hull. But Johnny had played in the goalless 'derby' against Manchester City and the first tie with Bradford Park Avenue, and in both games United's normally sharp and ebullient inside-right (and still the youngest member of the team) had looked uncharacteristically subdued.

Only after the victory at Hull could the Press give the situation their full attention. But even their speculation still did not make it clear exactly why Manchester-born-and-bred Johnny Morris wanted to leave United, nor why a move should even be contemplated at this crucial time. Matt Busby was reported to have said that Morris had been unhappy at Old Trafford for some time and had requested a move. Only much later did Busby, ever the diplomat, write: 'Unfortunately differences cropped up between us which resulted in his transfer.'

The reasons why Morris himself looked likely to be the first to leave the most exciting and successful team in the country were almost lost in the clamour of offers for him. Apparently a dozen or so clubs were interested in him, but Liverpool seemed to have the strongest claim with an offer of £25,000. Morris himself seemed strangely indecisive and told the Press that he wanted a weekend 'to sleep on it', and mentioned being worried about the size of the fee. 'The public will expect £25,000 worth of football out of me all the time', he added.

On the Monday, Johnny Morris announced that he did not want to move to Liverpool. As soon as it became known that Morris was once more available, another club stepped in quickly and made United an offer they could not refuse. Derby County saw Johnny Morris as a perfect foil for their inside-left Billy Steel for whom they had paid £15,000 in June 1947. A world record fee of £24,000 was agreed upon, and on Friday, 11 March Johnny Morris became a Derby County player, ready to turn out for them against Everton at the Baseball Ground the very next day.

So Johnny Morris was the first of the 1948 Cup winning side to leave Manchester United: it was a sad, swift and unexpected move, all the more so because it took place right in the middle of an admittedly faltering, but nevertheless successful, Cup run.

Off the field, Johnny Morris had the reputation of being as direct and uncompromising as his style of play was on it, and it was well known inside Old Trafford at the time that he would often quite forcibly challenge some of Matt Busby's theories and tactics. There was not a single hint of this at the time Johnny Morris said goodbye to the friends and team-mates he had known since he had joined the club as a 15-year-old in 1939. Only much later was more to be said ...

The sports pages of the two evening papers which served Manchester at the time were full of the latest dramatic developments in the Johnny Morris transfer story, so only the most eagle-eyed readers would have spotted a tiny piece of news which attached itself to the foot of one of the sports columns. It read: 'Manchester United have signed on professional forms 19-year-old Roger Byrne, a left-back who has been playing as an amateur in the 'A' team. He is a Manchester-born boy and attended Burnage High School.'

Johnny Morris's untimely departure was to have a profound effect on the rest of United's journey in the FA Cup competition. The all-important semi-final against Wolverhampton Wanderers was now only a few weeks away, and the canny Matt Busby had realised for some time before the need to keep an eye open for a prospective inside-forward replacement for the restless Morris.

Matt Busby had liked the look of John Downie, the speedy 23-year-old Bradford Park Avenue inside-forward who had played so impressively in the three-match epic struggle to resolve the fourth round tie with United. At this stage of the season Busby knew that most suitable replacements would be 'cup-tied' and even though Busby knew Downie could not contribute to United's Cup efforts this season he saw him as a worthy successor to Johnny Morris. Busby's prompt offer of £18,000 was accepted, and John Downie became a Manchester United player. He was Lanarkshire-born and had come down to Bradford during the war as a junior before signing professional. When Downie played his first game for United a few days later he made the first of Stan Pearson's two goals against Charlton Athletic and scored one himself in a rousing 3-2 victory. On the same day, a now-fit Johnny Morris (who was still in the throes of deciding which offer to accept) turned out for United's reserves at Old Trafford against Sheffield Wednesday reserves in front of 21,000 spectators, and he headed the only goal in a United victory.

John Downie also played a significant part and scored another goal in United's next League fixture, which resulted in a 3-0 victory over Stoke City and gave the home supporters at Maine Road their first chance to see him in action with his new team.

Everybody connected with the club was beginning to regret that Downie could not play a part in United's Cup plans: there was no denying that his presence had restored something of the team's former balance and penetration.

The game before the semi-final was against Birmingham at St Andrew's and Matt Busby announced what would obviously be the team to represent United against Wolves at Hillsborough. John Anderson was restored to the team at inside-right: he had not played in United's senior side since he had been deposed at right-half by Bill McGlen.

United played badly against Birmingham and lost 1–0: Jack Rowley was injured when he caught the full force of a defender's boot on the forehead and had to leave the field with blood streaming from a gash above an eye. He returned twenty minutes later with his forehead covered by a huge square of sticking plaster.

Clearly the experiment of playing John Anderson had not been successful, and time and options had almost run out for Matt Busby. The defeat at Birmingham was the first time United's forward line had failed to score for two months and even their most loyal supporters began to have doubts about their team's prospects for Wembley. During the week before the semi-final, practice matches were held behind closed doors at Old Trafford and rumours were that several players were being tried out at inside-right.

Matt Busby eventually chose exactly the same side which had been defeated by Birmingham, namely: Crompton; Carey, Aston; Cockburn, Chilton, McGlen; Delaney, Anderson, Rowley, Pearson and Mitten. Busby was obviously making another one of his calculated gambles: John Anderson had Cup experience and in the past had shown that he was capable of scoring goals. He was definitely worth the risk.

Another capacity gate of 62,250 gave the Cup-holders a huge roar of welcome as they trotted out on to the Hillsborough turf to face Wolverhampton Wanderers, a side which had beaten them 3–2 in September at Molyneux, but which United in turn had beaten 2–0 at Maine Road a week later. Wolves were also only two places below United in the League table, and on their way to the semi-final had trounced Chesterfield 6–0; then beaten Sheffield United 3–0; Liverpool 3–1 and finally West Bromwich Albion 1–0.

Wolves were also fielding a team studded with star players. It was captained by 24-year-old Billy Wright who was also captain of England and already a holder of twenty-four caps. The daring and agile Bert Williams in goal was a wartime international; Bill Shorthouse at centre-half, like his opposite number in United's team Allenby Chilton, had been wounded on the Normandy beaches on 'D' day; tiny Johnny Hancocks the right-winger wore size 5 boots and was an England international, as was their centre-forward Jesse Pye. Sam Smyth, the inside-right, played for Ireland, and at outside-left was Jimmy Mullen, another England international, who at the time also held the record as the youngest player in a Cup semi-final when at sixteen he appeared for Wolves against Grimsby at Old Trafford before 76,962 spectators, the ground's attendance record.

Manchester United used the same dressing-room that they had occupied when they beat Derby County in the semi-final last season, and they were fielding virtually the same side. Only Johnny Morris was missing and this was probably the most vital factor in the events which were to follow.

It was a typical semi-final clash, full of pace and incident. After twelve minutes Allen Chilton committed his one blunder of the game when he aimed a poorly directed back pass at Jack Crompton and it was pounced on by Johnny Hancocks who turned it into the centre for Sammy Smyth to score. United's equaliser was just as simply won. With fifteen minutes of the first half remaining a harmless-looking pass bobbed into the Wolverhampton penalty-area, and Charlie Mitten nipped in to lob the ball over goalkeeper Bert Williams' head and into the net.

It was a very physical game. After only six minutes of play the Wolves' left-back Pritchard had been injured in a collision with Jimmy Delaney and had been forced to move out on to the left wing. The right-back Kelly was also injured with half an hour to go and had to occupy the other flank position: the injuries to their defenders had obviously upset the balance and strategy of the Wolves team, but they had coped superbly.

Manchester United had also suffered damage. Henry Cockburn had spent much of the game in a bemused state on the wing suffering from concussion, and the cut on Jack Rowley's head had reopened so he had to play much of the game with blood streaming down his face. Only Charlie Mitten, John Carey and Bill

McGlen had found their true form while those around them tried to make up in effort what they lacked in achievement. John Anderson, by all accounts, had looked very uncomfortable in his unaccustomed inside-right position.

He remembered the game very clearly:

Some of the Press thought I'd been brought into the team as an extra half-back to help look after Billy Wright, but there was no way that Matt Busby would have done that. When he called me into his office he said, 'I'm playing you at inside-right, Johnny ... let Billy Wright worry about *you* ... he's the defender, you're the forward.' In the game Henry got concussed so we had to move positions in the game. He was wandering about in a daze for a lot of the time. I even had to tackle him once when he set off with the ball ... dribbling away there ... but towards our goal!

The Wolverhampton hero was undoubtedly Bert Williams who brought off some marvellous saves in the last hectic minutes of the second half of extra time when, as the cliché has it, United did everything except score.

At the final whistle, Billy Wright jumped for joy and hugged every member of his team: his euphoria at keeping the-Cup-holders at bay with only nine fit players was understandable. They had managed to keep their goal intact after the one lapse and had weathered fourteen of United's corners when they could only force three of their own. Plucky Wolves had lived to fight another day.

When the result of the other semi-final became known, Manchester United realised that if they could win the replay they would almost be certain to win the Cup again, because Leicester City were now one of the finalists. Leicester were third from the bottom of the Second Division and obviously one of the most unfancied teams in the competition. They still were, even though they had just knocked out First Division leaders Portsmouth 3-1, two goals having been scored by their inside-right, a 22-year-old from Middlesbrough called Don Revie.

A week later Manchester United and Wolverhampton Wanderers met for the replay at Goodison Park. United had made changes: the experiment of John Anderson at inside-right had not worked, so Matt Busby moved Jack Rowley to that position and chose Ronnie Burke, United's 24-year-old reserve centre-forward, to lead the attack. Wolves had replaced their two full-backs who had been injured in the first game. At right-back and making his debut in the senior team was Alf Crook (the brother of right-half Bill) and Terry Springthorpe replaced Roy Pritchard at left-back.

A crowd of 72,500 saw another fast and exciting game, full of end-to-end incidents with United completely dominating the play in the first half. They moved the ball around quickly and skilfully, and switched positions with the dazzling rapidity which had bemused so many defences in the past. All that was missing was the ability to score. The man who foiled them yet again was Bert Williams who guarded his goal with ferocious passion. Nothing got through, and even Jack Rowley's shoulders sank as he struck a certain goal-bound shot which was parried then cleared by the Wolves defence.

In the second half the whole balance of the game gradually changed and United found themselves defending most of the time against a rejuvenated Wolves side which was playing with limitless drive and stamina.

Both defences were playing magnificently and with only five minutes to go the players and crowd were beginning to wonder what would happen in what seemed like an inevitable period of extra time.

Suddenly the Wolves centre-forward Jesse Pye, who was standing alone on the right wing, collected a long clearance and dashed forward. Aston, Carey and Chilton hesitated, certain that the linesman would be flagging for the offside they were sure it was. But the linesman was well up with the play and kept his flag down, and the nearest United defender, Allenby Chilton, set off in pursuit. Before he could make any kind of tackle, Pye turned across a centre which a diving Jack Crompton could only parry upwards, and as it bounced away Sammy Smyth, standing only a few feet from the goal-line, headed into the back of the United goal.

There was not a word of protest from the disciplined United defenders who merely looked at each other and shook their heads. They were all now very tired, and as the last few minutes were played out only the players themselves knew the awful despondency of realising they had stumbled and fallen within sight of one of football's greatest prizes. They had failed to score for the first time in fourteen Cup ties and had failed to accept those half chances that win games, and now this great team had to accept the painful consequences.

Football is full of 'what-might-have-been' incidents, but many who saw the game or reported on it believed that Jesse Pye was well offside when he accepted the pass. Some of United's players spoke of the incident and the game with voices full of regret. 'We didn't have our full-strength side,' remembered Charlie Mitten, 'Johnny Morris had gone, Jack Rowley was injured ... we were a bit disjointed.' Jimmy Delaney was also unrepentantly certain that the FA Cup should have been United's. 'Aye, we should have won the Cup that year ... we should have beaten Wolves 4–0 in that replay ... and Leicester were waiting on us playing them in the Cup Final ... we'd have had no trouble. Wolves won from an offside goal with five minutes to go. In the first half we were shooting in ... we hit the bar, the post, everything ... yes, the Cup should have been ours that year.' Allenby Chilton, who had been closest to the start of Wolves' goal-scoring move, shook his head and smiled. 'That Wolves goal ... Jesse Pye was offside ... but we couldn't do anything about it ...'

However many doubts there might have been, the referee's decision was final, and Wolverhampton Wanderers had won the match and a place in the final. Typically, Matt Busby was one of the first to recover from the shock of the defeat as well as to admit to reporters that Wolves were 'well worthy of their victory'. In his programme note of the following week he reflected further: 'While it is upsetting to be beaten by a goal in which there is an element of doubt I do not wish to complain. We are sportsmen – let us remain so.' Tom Jackson in the same programme maintained that 'Wolves deserved the honours, they were the better balanced team ... and it was a tribute to the players' grace in defeat that they were the first to congratulate their rivals at the final whistle.'

History rarely repeats itself in exact detail, so it would be hard to even imagine how circumstances could have allowed United to enjoy the same sort of successful Cup journey as they had enjoyed in the previous season. The team was not the same as the one which had won the Cup the previous year, and certainly most of United's players agreed with Jack Crompton's comment: 'No argument ... no argument at all ... we would have walked it if Johnny Morris had stayed.'

The Cup trail had now ended for United and amid the din of the post-match analysis Matt Busby quietly reminded supporters: '... rather than mourn at our defeat I feel we should rejoice at what the team has already accomplished.' He was right – there was much to be proud of this season, and even more to look forward to.

Some days before the replay with Wolves it was announced that John Carey had been voted Player of the Year by the Football Writers' Association, polling nearly 40 per cent of the votes and only one fewer than the combined votes of the next two players, Raich Carter and Billy Wright. The presentation of the bronze statuette would be made in London at the annual dinner on the eve of the Cup final. It was clearly a popular choice. United's modest and quietly spoken captain was rated as one of the best full-backs in the game. Unfortunately, and against all expectations, he would not be leading out one of the Cup final teams on to the Wembley turf next day.

At this time another piece of news emerged which lifted the spirits of the club and its supporters. Next season, it was announced, senior football would be played at Old Trafford! The Ministry of Works had at last sanctioned repairs, and the rebuilding programme had got under way in January: a temporary roof-less stand of 3,000 seats was to be built on the site of the old main stand, and the terraces would be cleared and concreted. At last, after eight years of soccer at Maine Road, Manchester United would be coming home.

The club was also gradually pulling itself out of the financial plight it was in after the war, and the recovery, by any standards, was remarkable. In November, Manchester United's statement of accounts had shown a profit of £22,329 for the 1947-48 season. The club had taken a record £97,776 at the gates, against which they had to pay £5,000 for the hire of Maine Road; £19,158 in entertainment tax; £24,640 in wages and bonuses; £6,981 in travelling and hotel expenses; and £18,432 had to be earmarked for 'income tax and profits tax'.

Manchester United now had to put the memory of the Cup run behind them and concentrate on the fight for the League Championship: in fact it was still technically possible to win it.

The club was lying seventh in the table, one position below Manchester City. Portsmouth were the current leaders on 48 points against United's 37. Finishing as high up the table as possible was Matt Busby's priority, and the price was a fixture congestion of some magnitude. Because of Cup replays United had been forced to postpone several League matches, and this now meant playing ten fixtures in April, a daunting task for even the fittest of teams.

So a few days after the defeat by Wolves, United began their quest for League points with a match against Huddersfield Town which they lost 2-1. Possibly the side was still suffering a reaction to their semi-final defeat, and their cause could not have been helped by the usually reliable Charlie Mitten who chose this match to record his first penalty miss in senior football.

After eight games in which they were defeated three times, it was clear the Manchester United had forfeited their chance to contest the Championship title, but they found themselves in the thick of a fight for second place with Newcastle United, Derby County and Arsenal.

Meanwhile on Friday, 29 April, John Carey attended the Football Writers' Dinner in London and was presented with his trophy. Then he and Matt Busby caught the sleeper up to Newcastle where United's proud captain helped his team to beat the Tynesiders 1-0.

United's satisfaction at beating Newcastle United that Saturday was tinged with regret. Down at Wembley, Wolverhampton Wanderers, the team United should have beaten in the semi-final, defeated Leicester City 3-0 in the Cup final.

Manchester United's last game of the season was fittingly at Maine Road and ironically against Portsmouth, the declared Champions with 58 points. United had now clawed their way to second place which they shared with Derby County and Newcastle United, all on 51 points. There was everything to play for.

By 4.40 on the afternoon of Saturday, 7 May the picture had cleared. Newcastle had to be content with a goalless draw against Sheffield United, Manchester United had beaten Portsmouth 3-2 in a thrilling match which included a penalty save by Jack

Crompton, and even though Derby County had beaten Stoke 4–1 (Johnny Morris scoring three), United had won second place in the League, for the third successive season, on superior goal average.

The match against Portsmouth brought to an end three post-war seasons at Maine Road where Manchester United had played some of the finest football in their history. As well as winning the FA Cup they had been the beaten semi-finalists in the following season, and were three times in succession the runners-up in the First Division.

# Back Home

There was drama at Old Trafford even before the season had begun. Allenby Chilton, at his own request, had been placed on the transfer list, claiming that his wife's health always suffered during the bad winter months in Manchester, and she had been unable to settle and wanted to return home to the north-east.

It was no secret that Allen Chilton had also been sensitive to the amount of criticism which a section of the home crowd had always given him during and after a game – for being slow or awkward, and for giving away free-kicks and penalties. Possibly he had allowed the criticisms to gnaw away at him more than he should have done, but certainly that section of the crowd who saw little good in Chilton could not be forgiven for failing to remember the solid commitment this likeable Wearsider brought to the game, and how often he had saved the day for United with his strong tackling and powerful headed clearances.

Luckily for United, a replacement was waiting in the wings, so the club did not have to face the same kind of crisis as they had the previous season when Johnny Morris left the club. Sammy Lynn was regarded as Chilton's natural replacement: he had joined United as a junior in 1936, signed as a professional in 1948, and had already made a few impressive senior-team appearances.

But only half a dozen or so games into the season Allenby Chilton walked into Matt Busby's office and asked for his name to be taken off the transfer list. Busby was naturally delighted, and picked Chilton at left-half to play against Liverpool at An-field. He had to be selected for that position, as by now Lynn had established himself firmly as United's centre-half, but a few weeks later Chilton was back in the number 5 shirt, and Lynn was forced to move out to wing-half.

At the end of September another of United's Cup-winning team was transferred – to Third Division Nottingham Forest for

£9,000. It was time for John Anderson to say goodbye to Old Trafford: he had found it hard to stay permanently in the senior team after his marvellous 1947-48 season. The circumstances surrounding his first team debut might easily have been lifted straight from a 'Roy of the Rovers' story, as was the goal he scored in the Cup final to seal United's victory. John Anderson had shared many great moments in his time with United's first post-war team, and he would always be remembered by those who saw him play as a rock-solid and dedicated half-back, and a great reader of the game. John Anderson was to continue for many years in the game with Nottingham Forest and later with non-League Peterborough.

The first match of the season, a 1-0 victory over Derby, featured Sammy Lynn at centre-half and Brian Birch, a 17-year-old from Salford, at inside-left. Matt Busby was already giving promising youngsters a chance, and in the close season had signed up school-leavers Dennis Viollet and Jeff Whitefoot. He had also welcomed in several young full-time professionals, including 17-year-old Jackie Blanchflower, the brother of Barnsley player Danny. Matt Busby's vision was of a young team which would one day grace Old Trafford rich in skill and enthusiasm . . .

The second match was on 24 August, a housewarming 3-0 victory over Bolton Wanderers, which saw United's first League match at Old Trafford for eight years. The crowd and the team were happy to be back home. The long years in exile had indeed produced some memorable football and the FA Cup, and had made Manchester United the top attraction wherever they played. But now at last the club had a home ground, and although there was little covered accommodation and open seating, all agreed it was good to be back.

Just over a week later Manchester United beat Manchester City 2-1, the first 'derby' match staged at Old Trafford for thirteen years. There was a minute left of the game, many of the 48,000 crowd had begun to drift away, when suddenly Henry Cockburn, by all accounts the game's outstanding player, and Billy Linacre, City's lively winger, clashed and were ordered off the field by referee Arthur Ellis of Halifax. It was an unfortunate flare-up and Cockburn, an international player of the highest reputation for skill and sportsmanship, broke down in tears once he reached the

dressing-room. At the FA Disciplinary Committee hearing a
month later, Henry Cockburn was suspended for seven days and
Billy Linacre for fourteen.

Manchester United had played nine games of the new season
before suffering their first defeat, 1–0 to Burnley at Turf Moor
on 24 September, and by the end of December they were second
in the League table and a couple of points only behind the leaders,
Liverpool. International calls and injuries had disturbed but not
unsettled the team which was playing well and had notched up
notable victories over Aston Villa (4–0), Wolverhampton Wanderers (3–0) and Huddersfield Town (6–0). Because he was injured, Jack Crompton's place against Huddersfield Town was
taken by a 21-year-old Irishman called John Ignatius 'Sonny'
Feehan, United's reserve-team goalkeeper who because he had
played Gaelic soccer as a young boy had not handled a soccer ball
until he was 16 years old. He was apparently a spectator for most
of the game, and must have marvelled at the way his team-mates
rattled in their six goals at the other end of the field.

The 'old stagers' were still going strong: eight of the ten players
in front of Feehan that afternoon had passed the century mark in
post-war appearances. Of these, including post-war outings, Jack
Rowley had played 211 times for United, Carey 200 and Pearson
171. Incredibly, Stan Pearson had missed only five matches over
the last three seasons, all because of international duty.

The appearance figures also reflected how, as he had promised
after the war, Matt Busby had been determined to give those
players who had lost six years of their footballing lives a chance
to fulfil their ambitions. They in turn had responded with enthusiasm, and at their peak had produced the kind of football that
rests indelibly in the memories of those who saw them play.

The injury to Jack Crompton was more serious than was at
first realised: he had been playing for nearly a month with a
fractured wrist. Matt Busby was again forced to look around to
strengthen the depth of cover in this position. On their books
United already had 'Sonny' Feehan and Joe Lancaster, the 'A'
team goalkeeper. Because each now had to move up a place,
United had to call upon the services of a young man who worked
in their office to play in goal for the 'A' team. He was 21-year-old
Les Olive (now United's secretary) who this season had already
deputised for Mark Jones at half-back in that team.

Matt Busby had also been alerted to the ability of Third Division Darlington's goalkeeper, an 18-year-old called Raymond Wood, and in a midnight dash up to Darlington, Busby secured Wood's signature. Another 'Babe' had joined the family.

Twelve hours later Ray Wood played at Old Trafford in a 1–1 draw against Newcastle United – a side which contained his boyhood hero 'Wor' Jackie Milburn. Wood thus made the first of the 195 appearances he was to make with Manchester United, and he was the first 'Babe' to make a senior team debut. It was Ray Wood's only senior game of the season and he did not play for the first team again for two years, but from 1953 to December 1957 he was United's first choice goalkeeper until United bought Harry Gregg. Ray Wood also won three England caps, two First Division Championship medals with United, and was a travelling reserve when United played Red Star Belgrade in 1958, and he was one of the survivors of the crash at Munich airport on the journey home.

Manchester United went into their Christmas holiday games with the knowledge that already this season they had used twenty players for first-team duty. International calls, injuries and early season positional problems were responsible for shuffles affecting every department except the two wing-forward positions.

A typical fixture congestion at the end of the year saw United beat West Bromwich Albion 2–1 at the Hawthorns on Christmas Eve; beat Arsenal 2–0 at Old Trafford on Boxing Day; force a goalless draw with Arsenal at Highbury a day later (watched by a crowd of 65,000); and finally see out the 1940s by beating Manchester City 2–1 at Maine Road on New Year's Eve, the fiftieth League encounter between the two neighbours.

The 1950s was a memorable decade for Manchester United and was to bring triumph and tragedy to the club, and the first game to herald in the New Year was the third round of the FA Cup against non-League Weymouth: the long journey to Wembley had begun again.

A train bearing 500 members of their 4,000 strong Supporters' Club made the long overnight journey up to Manchester from Weymouth to watch the part-timers (and 5,000:1 Cup outsiders) from Dorset face a team dubbed 'The Team of the Century' fielding eight of their 1948 Cup-winning side.

The gallant Weymouth team kept their goal intact for thirty-two minutes against a far-from-impressive United display, and went in at half-time only two goals down, scored by Jack Rowley and Stan Pearson. United finally sealed Weymouth's fate with two more goals from Jimmy Delaney and Jack Rowley. Despite their patchy display United had won by a convincing margin and were through to the next round.

Three weeks later, Manchester United faced Third Division Watford at Vicarage Road in the fourth round, and a goal by Jack Rowley only two minutes from the end of the match spared the humiliation of a draw. Don Davies, in typical fashion, reported the team's reaction to Rowley's goal: 'The tender ravishment with which Rowley's colleagues picked him up and pressed him to their bosoms bespoke not so much controlled elation as intense relief at having so narrowly escaped shipwreck. Watford had been a match for United in every phase of the game and as a face-saver Rowley's goal was beyond price.'

It had been a game full of incident and included a penalty miss by Charlie Mitten. Keeping goal for United this time, because Crompton and Feehan were injured and Wood was unavailable, was the club's fourth team goalkeeper, a 19-year-old amateur from Stockport, Joe Lancaster. He had, in fact, already played once for the first team in their 1–0 victory over Chelsea a couple of weeks before and had shown good form, although he had been well protected by his defenders.

So Manchester United were one of the sixteen teams which had won their way into the fifth round and were drawn to meet Portsmouth, last season's League Champions and who like United had been defeated in last year's semi-finals. They were currently lying a couple of places below United in the League table, so all the indications promised a game to remember.

Pelting rain and a near gale-force wind did not stop 53,688 spectators packing into Old Trafford to witness the clash of giants. They were not disappointed. United were two goals up at half-time (from Mitten and Pearson); then Portsmouth scored two goals in two minutes after only a few minutes' play in the second half. Charlie Mitten put United ahead again with a penalty, but with just less than half an hour remaining, left full-back Ferrier claimed the equaliser for Portsmouth with another penalty.

On balance the draw seemed a fair result. Goalkeeper Lancaster's inexperience had given his defenders some anxious moments, and United were not able to sustain much pressure on Portsmouth in the second half, mainly because Stan Pearson, the mainspring of their attack, sustained an ankle injury and had to hobble up and down the wing for the rest of the game, a virtual spectator. United's disappointment at the result was made even sharper by the penalty which had been awarded to Portsmouth (after an unintentional handling by the hapless Allenby Chilton): it was a decision which even the Portsmouth players at the time thought was harsh.

Fears that the replay might turn out to be like the nightmare of that struggle against Wolves last season were groundless. The replay the following Wednesday at Fratton Park saw United win convincingly 3–1, with Feehan restored as goalkeeper and Downie in the place of the still injured Stan Pearson (who had not missed a game because of injury since 9 March 1946). United played at their brilliant best: the forwards in particular produced something of their classic form – their attacks were swift and precise, and rarely had the Portsmouth defence felt so bemused. Goals by Charlie Mitten, John Downie and Jimmy Delaney earned United a place in the next round.

In the sixth round United were drawn to play Chelsea at Stamford Bridge, and the remaining fixtures paired Arsenal against Leeds, Derby against Everton, and Liverpool against Blackpool.

There was guarded optimism at Old Trafford about United's chances. They had beaten Chelsea at Old Trafford in January and the 1–0 victory gave no indication of how United had dictated the play for long periods and how their defence had frozen Chelsea's attackers, especially English international Roy Bentley, out of the game. United had forced six corners in eleven minutes, a fact which merely underlined their supremacy.

Manchester United had hit a patch of consistent success and suddenly the talk was of the 'double'. United were reckoned as Cup favourites again, and because they were only a point behind League leaders Liverpool with twelve fixtures remaining, to win the Cup and League looked a distinct possibility. 'If only they could maintain form' was the hope of everybody at Old Trafford.

Matt Busby chose another young player to blood in the next League match, which ended in a 2–2 draw against Sunderland at

Roker Park. Frank Clempson, an 18-year-old from Salford, played at inside-right instead of the injured Tommy Bogan, and after a nervous start had a good game. Another player would also remember this game with a glow of pleasure: Allenby Chilton, in front of his 'home' crowd, scored the equaliser with a powerful header from a Rowley corner. It was his only goal of the season and his first since September 1946, yet it served to underline Chilton's renewed confidence which everyone, even his critics, were learning to appreciate. He was a pillar of strength in the side and few needed reminding how many top-class centre-forwards had failed to score against United this season. In the days when defenders and attackers were 'paired' so closely, the reason for so many tame opposition centre-forwards was attributable to Chilton's secure dominance of the midfield.

A week later, with Jack Crompton restored in goal after three months' absence, and Stan Pearson back in the side, United beat Charlton Athletic 2-1. The winning goal, a fifteen-yard drive by John Carey, fittingly pushed United to the top of the League table. The double was very much 'on'.

Manchester United could not have been in a more buoyant mood than when they faced Chelsea at Stamford Bridge in the sixth round on 4 March. A victory seemed a certainty, although Matt Busby and his team were too experienced to use the word to one another. Maybe also there is no such a thing as a 'fluke' goal: a shot at goal, however speculative or off-line, is an attempt to score, but after six minutes' play Jack Crompton let in such a goal. A seemingly innocuous shot on the turn from Chelsea's outside-left Campbell bounced in front of Crompton (who perhaps had dived a little too soon) and the ball squirmed between his arms, over his body, and into the net.

The loss of an early goal in such a way seemed to unsettle United. They looked nothing like the brilliant team which had humbled Portsmouth in the previous round, and very few of the 70,362 crowd would have thought they were worthy on this showing of a place in what would have been their third successive semi-final. Only John Aston and John Carey seemed to be playing with any kind of conviction: the rest of the team just could not find any kind of cohesion in their play, and Chelsea's dominance was clear-cut. A brilliantly executed left-foot drive by Chelsea's centre-forward Roy Bentley ten minutes from time put paid to

United's Cup hopes for another season, and sealed a deserved victory for the 'Pensioners'.

A few days later Manchester United met Aston Villa in a League fixture and probably as a reaction to their Cup defeat crushed the Midland side 7–0. Charlie Mitten entered the record books that day, not because he scored four of United's goals, but because three of them were from penalties.

United then went on to beat Middlesbrough 3–2, and broke a nine-match sequence of home wins by the Ayresome Park club. By now, with ten games to play in the League, United were leading the First Division by four points, ahead of Blackpool, Liverpool, Sunderland, Portsmouth and Arsenal. Was this to be the year that United would win that elusive League Championship?

But, incredibly, of those remaining games two only resulted in victories for United – one of which was the last match of the season – and United, to the bitter disappointment of their thousands of followers, allowed the title to slip through their fingers, and they finished the season in fourth place, behind leaders Portsmouth, Wolverhampton Wanderers and Sunderland. The First Division Championship, which they had not won since 1911, had eluded them for yet another year.

After promising so much, the 1949–50 season ended rather disappointingly for the club and its followers. Looking back it was clear that several weaknesses marred the season's performances and without doubt caused United to stumble in the Cup and fade in the League.

The first was the injury to Jack Crompton which had kept him out of the side for three months and had weakened the final defensive barrier; and while Feehan, Lancaster and Wood did their best, none was yet of First Division standard.

There was also a significant loss of striking power, and the need for another sharp-shooter became stronger when Rowley, Mitten and Pearson, who for years had provided United's scoring thrust, suffered a collectively lean scoring spell.

A gradual transition had started to take place in the team, beginning with the loss of Johnny Morris. New players were being tried, but their absorption into such a hitherto settled side took time.

Having tasted the delights of a Cup win in 1948, the thirst for success was growing at Old Trafford (where it remains unassuaged even today) and the lack of success this season was all the more disappointing because United were earning a growing reputation for winning consistency, but as yet it could not be sustained for long enough to secure total success.

Towards the end of the season Matt Busby disappeared from Manchester several times on scouting missions. He knew that the club had to be patient: the Central League team was good, but mostly comprised of young players, and a season or two would see the likes of Mark Jones, Roger Byrne, Dennis Viollet and Jackie Blanchflower pressing strong claims for first-team places. In fact, as well as blooding Frank Clempson, Ray Wood and Brian Birch, Matt Busby also picked half-back Jeff Whitefoot to play his debut game right at the end of the season against Portsmouth at Old Trafford – the youngest player ever at 16 years 105 days to turn out for United's senior team, and the second of his famous 'Babes' to be introduced into the side.

It was to be a busy summer for the United players. Earlier in the season Manchester United had been invited to tour the USA for six weeks – now all the arrangements had been made, and on 2 May the United team and officials set off from Southampton on the *Queen Mary* bound for New York. All but one of the party was to return.

America was still a land of glamour and excitement, but soccer there was a game played mostly by groups of European and South American immigrants. Brazil, coincidentally, was to host the little-publicised World Cup that summer, a competition which England had decided to enter for the first time.

John Aston remained behind with the England party which was to play a couple of warm-up internationals in Belgium and Portugal; he would then fly to America to join up with his United team-mates who by then would be half-way through their tour. Once that was finished he and Henry Cockburn would fly on to Brazil to prepare for their group fixtures against Spain, Chile and the USA.

Aston had actually been England's automatic selection at left-back all season and Henry Cockburn, Stan Pearson and Jack Rowley had also made appearances for England, including a rousing 9-2 victory over Northern Ireland on 16 November at Maine Road. Jack Rowley and Stan Pearson, who knew every inch of City's ground, rattled in four and two goals respectively.

Earlier, John Aston had been the only United player in the England team which was defeated 2-0 by Eire, captained by John Carey, at Goodison Park on 21 September. For the first time in history, England's players had been beaten on their own soil by a team outside the 'home' Associations.

# 1950-51
# So Near... Again

Two summers before, Manchester United had rightly considered itself somewhere near the centre of the sporting universe, and the summer of 1950 was no less interesting. The club and its players found themselves involved in a series of unbelievably dramatic episodes which spread from New York to Colombia.

During those summer months the Manchester footballing public were kept informed of United's fortunes on their tour of North America by news reports in the local evening papers. The *Evening Chronicle* had commissioned John Carey to write a regular series of articles for them which were full of as-it-happened incidents and the tiny details about what players said and did which the true fan relishes. An early despatch described how during the voyage the team had played the crew at table-tennis and darts, 'winning the former 4-1 but losing at darts 6-3. We also joined the passengers' table-tennis competition,' Carey's report continued, 'and Jack Crompton was the winner, beating Stan Pearson in the semi-final and myself in the final.'

Once the United party had docked in New York, Carey regaled his readers with accounts of the warm reception they received wherever they went, and about the food, the neon lights, the famous people they met (including Primo Carnera, the heavyweight boxer, and Henry Armstrong, composer of 'Nellie Dean' and 'Sweet Adeline'). 'The traffic and bustle are tremendous,' United's captain wrote, 'I think it's because they are six hours behind England and they're trying to catch us up!' His teammates were also having a good time. Young Brian Birch indulged himself in a fashionable crew-cut ('He looks like a little shorn lamb') and Jack Warner, Sammy Lynn and Charlie Mitten went to see the horse racing at Belmont, 'where they all said it was easier to back winners than at home'.

Then another kind of news began to appear in John Carey's

reports. In a column headed '£3,500 a year does not tempt us', Carey described how he had received a telephone call in New York telling him that an 'agent' would be contacting him and some of the United players 'to persuade us to play football in Colombia – for a generous salary and expenses'. He was, however, sceptical of the whole business, adding, 'None of the United players would consider such a proposition because it would mean "*finis*" as regards our future in the game in Britain.'

Apparently, the principal football clubs in Colombia – Santa Fe and Millionarios – had broken away from their national association and with other clubs had formed a new league. They were now also outside the jurisdiction of FIFA and as a result did not consider themselves bound by such petty matters as transfer rules and regulations. They were currently making tempting offers to foreign players, mostly Argentinians – and the presence of English players in America with club or international parties was an opportunity too good to miss.

Matt Busby in a transatlantic telephone call to the *Evening Chronicle* agreed with his captain: 'In any case, from the club's point of view I should have no truck with this agent . . . although I could not prevent him from talking to the players if he did contact them.'

But the episode appeared to have been forgotten as the United tour continued – across to California then up to Canada and down to Chicago, before returning to New York to board the boat for home. By all accounts the stay in California lived up to everybody's expectations: beautiful weather, bumping into movie stars like Clark Gable, and lavish hospitality: massive steaks were a welcome relief from the egg powder and ration books of post-war Britain. There was also a day to remember at a ranch just outside Hollywood owned by Walter Tetley, America's diminutive answer to our own 'Wee' Georgie Wood.

Suddenly, events began to move swiftly. After saying goodbye to their team-mates in New York, Henry Cockburn and John Aston flew off to Brazil to join up with the England team who were competing for the first time in the little-publicised World Cup tournament. A few days later John Aston (the first United player to appear in the World Cup) was a member of the England team which suffered one of its most famous and ignominious defeats when they were beaten 1–0 by a team representing the United States of America.

Another player slipped away from the United party to fly south. Charlie Mitten had been approached by an agent from the Santa Fe club of Bogota in Colombia, and United's winger had been invited down to the South American city for an all-expenses, no-obligation look around.

Matt Busby had known of Charlie's interest in playing in Colombia, and had pointed out the serious professional consequences. But Charlie Mitten was the gambler of the team, and like all gamblers had that irrepressible 'go-on-have-a-go' streak, and neither Busby's advice, nor the pleas from his team-mates in a bar on the night he left, could prevent him from going for a look. After all, the United tour was over and there was nothing to lose, he argued.

Charlie Mitten was impressed by the interest in soccer that was being shown in the Americas, and the standard of living which the well-paid enjoyed, and most importantly, the chance of being rewarded for the thing he and others knew he was good at. United's popular outside-left was not the first English footballer to wonder why his wages were so low when attendances were so high, and the financial rewards of football in South America were closer to the ideal Mitten always believed should exist in English League soccer.

It could not have been an easy decision. Charlie Mitten was a Mancunian by adoption and his wife and family were still thousands of miles away in Davyhulme, Manchester, wondering what was to happen. There was also the knowledge that playing football in Colombia might mean the end of football in England if he ever decided to return.

Nobody had long to wait for a decision. Charlie Mitten made up his mind quickly and signed for the Santa Fe club on a year's contract, in return for a signing-on fee, a salary of £5,000 a year (compared to the basic wage of £728 he was earning at Manchester United), bonuses for wins or draws, a furnished house, maids, a gardener and a gleaming de luxe Ford car.

In exclusive articles to the *Evening Chronicle* Mitten offered additional reasons for his decision. 'I am 29 years old and married,' he wrote, 'I have three kids and I find that it is only a mean man who can save for the future . . . in the past few days I have signed up for more money than I've earned in all the fourteen years of being a footballer.'

So Charlie Mitten flew back to England from Bogota, helped his family to pack, placed a 'substantial' order with a Manchester firm for kit on behalf of the Santa Fe club, put his furniture in storage, and with his wife Betty, three-year-old Susan, six-year-old Charlie and nine-year-old John, and his boats burning behind him, set off on the long journey back to Bogota.

Charlie Mitten was not the only Englishman playing football in South America. Several well-known players had already been lured over, the most famous of whom was Neil Franklin, the Stoke and England centre-half, who was there with his Stoke City club-mate George Mountford. Alfred Di Stefano, who was then playing in Argentina, had also been persuaded to play in Colombia.

Within a few days of his signing for Santa Fe, Charlie Mitten was suspended by Manchester United, as Franklin and Mountford had been by Stoke City. Then nothing much was heard of Mitten for a year, except when Tom Jackson or Alf Clarke told their readers of letters they had received from United's exiled footballer. His cheeky optimism was as irrepressible as ever. 'I would really enjoy playing for United again when I come home on holiday from Bogota at the end of their season', he revealed in a letter to Tom Jackson, written only a month after he had started to play for Santa Fe. He concluded with a heavy hint that clanged all around Old Trafford: 'I shall be free November, December and January'. Matt Busby made little comment other than a terse, 'It is not for us to say whether Mitten will be able to play. That is a matter for the FA and Football League.'

The traffic in footballers that summer was not all one way, however. The USA team which had beaten England in their qualifying pool comprised inexperienced nationals and a few foreigners, including their captain Eddie McIlvenny, a Scottish wing-half who had been given a free transfer by Wrexham the previous year. Ironically, Manchester United signed him soon after Matt Busby had seen McIlvenny give an outstanding display for Philadelphia Nationals against United's touring side, and he began the new season as United's first choice right-half. McIlvenny was turning his back on the £30 a week he was earning in America

(£20 as a clerk in a sports ticket agency, plus £10 as a part-time professional with Philadelphia) to receive £12 a week in wages at United, preferring, as he said at the time, 'to play in top-class English soccer'.

That summer, in an attempt to ensure they did not find themselves in the same predicament as the previous season, United had signed a 28-year-old Londoner called Reg Allen for £11,000, the Queen's Park Rangers goalkeeper who was regarded by many as second only to Frank Swift. During the war he had played in Army representative games with Matt Busby and then had spent some years as a prisoner-of-war in North Africa. United had tried unsuccessfully to sign him two years earlier, but now at last they could secure a top-class goalkeeper for a team which was bound to try to win all the honours in the coming season.

Walter Crickmer, who had been holding the fort at Old Trafford, was able to confirm the news of Allen's transfer to Matt Busby and the United party in America, but he also had some sad news for them. Louis Rocca, United's devoted chief scout, who had begun at Old Trafford as a tea boy at the age of twelve, had died at the age of sixty-seven. He had discovered many of United's current stars, and his cheerful smile and countless anecdotes would be missed by everybody at Old Trafford.

At the end of June the United party were at last on their way home, having travelled 16,000 miles and won nine of their eleven fixtures and made thousands of friends.

Henry Cockburn and John Aston and the rest of the England party stayed long enough to witness England's second defeat in their World Cup qualifying pool (Spain beating them 1-0) and flew home, the most seasoned of travellers. Henry's growing interest in travel and languages meant that he now always carried an appropriate phrase book with him as the self-appointed linguist of the United and England party, but sometimes his words were not as accurate as his passes. England colleague Tom Finney once remarked in the dead-pan manner so beloved of footballers: 'Aye, Henry once asked a head waiter what the time was and got a plate of spaghetti.'

The loss of Charlie Mitten had created a vacancy in the United team which had so far not been filled, and Matt Busby was giving his present squad a chance before casting around elsewhere. Most of the names in the trial game were familiar to the Old Trafford faithful, and those who had been to America still sported deep sun-tans. Eddie McIlvenny and Reg Allen were on show for the first time, and the crowd watched Don Gibson and Roger Byrne with particular interest. Gibson was a 21-year-old sturdy ex-Marine Commando from Manchester: he was to feature prominently in some senior games this season, but neither he nor the crowd could have known that a few years later he was to become Matt Busby's son-in-law. Roger Byrne was another local lad from Burnage, but he had another season to wait before his senior debut, and in the all-too-short time he had to play for Manchester United was to become one of the club's best full-backs.

It soon became clear that nobody could do the job that Charlie Mitten used to do, but Matt Busby waited only a few weeks before the ideal replacement became available. He was Harry McShane of Bolton Wanderers, who wanted to move because he did not enjoy playing outside-right for the Bolton team: he preferred the opposite wing but could not command that position because of England international Bobby Langton's brilliance.

McShane had played superbly only a couple of weeks beforehand in Bolton's 1–0 defeat of United at Burnden Park, and he seemed the ideal replacement for Mitten. McShane was a 29-year-old and was married with a son, Ian, who was to become a film actor. The transfer was effected for £4,500 plus the exchange of Johnny Ball who had lost hope of ever playing at full-back for Manchester United while John Carey and John Aston were in such superlative form. And it was, of course, only the merest coincidence that McShane had been born in the same village as his new manager!

Early in the season, Allenby Chilton's deserved and long-awaited selection for England against Northern Ireland in Belfast on 7 October gave 17-year-old Mark Jones his chance to play for United's first team at Old Trafford against Sheffield Wednesday.

Chilton was enjoying one of his best periods with the team and the England selectors had been quick to reward him for a series of immaculate performances. Neil Franklin had been England's regular centre-half choice since the war, but his brief flirtation in the close-season with Santa Fe FC had earned him a suspension

until the first day of 1951. Here at long last was an opportunity
for Allen Chilton to stake his claim.

Alan Hoby reporting on the international at Windsor Park, and
perhaps damning with faint praise, wrote that 'Allen Chilton
started off magnificently and then settled into the usual determined stopper we see in most League games today. But he has
guts, strength and if a shade slow on the turn, was not one of
England's failures yesterday.'

The England selectors must have been thinking on the same
lines because Allen Chilton was not given another England chance
until a year later. His total of two England caps seemed then, as
now, scant reward for a player of his commanding dominance.

After seventeen games into the season United were lying fifth
in the table but even so did not look a completely secure team.
The side had not yet settled – forwards were shuffled and re-
shuffled in the search for the right balance, and still the attack did
not seem sharp enough. The defence appeared solid and confident, having conceded only 13 goals against the 14 of leaders
Arsenal, but the attack had scored only 20 goals against Arsenal's
37.

When the thousands of fans who supported Manchester United
turned to the sports pages of their newspapers on Thursday, 16
November, their hearts sank. Jimmy Delaney had been transferred to Aberdeen.

For weeks beforehand there had been hints in the form of
denials: that Delaney would not become Oldham's player-manager; that he was not thinking of leaving Old Trafford but wanted
to finish his playing days there, and when he did finish he was
seriously thinking of managing a pub in the area.

But there it was in black and white – Jimmy Delaney was going.
Aberdeen had first shown interest in him when Manchester
United had played them in a friendly up at Pittodrie at the end
of September. The truth was that Jimmy Delaney had always
really wanted to finish his playing career in Scotland and Matt
Busby had promised to release him when the opportunity was
right.

The United fans' sadness at Jimmy Delaney's departure, which
broke another link in that dazzling Cup-winning forward line
(leaving now only Rowley and Pearson as the survivors of that

memorable attack), was matched only by Delaney's heartfelt regret. He spoke then, as he speaks now, of the tremendous affection which had grown between himself and the Manchester crowds who loved to see his flying dashes down the right-wing, his canny positional switches with the rest of the forward line, and his diving tumbles in the penalty-area which usually resulted in another spot-kick for Charlie Mitten to whip home.

But after nearly five years at Manchester United he was ready to go. 'At this stage in my career I feel that the Scottish type of football will suit me better,' Delaney said at the time. 'And I am naturally glad, as all Scots are, to return home.'

Jimmy Delaney was Busby's first and one of his best signings and the likeable Scotsman had made a massive contribution to the reputation which was growing around the name of Manchester United.

The 'Good Luck' telegram which the United players sent Jimmy Delaney doubtless helped to inspire him to play brilliantly in his new team's 5-1 victory over Falkirk. A report on the game in Glasgow's *Sunday Mail* concluded, 'Delaney is the best buy Aberdeen have made of its kind ... you cannot keep a fellow like Delaney out of the game. His coolness, positioning and flashing speed made the fans very happy.' Jimmy Delaney was back home.

After Delaney's transfer, United played a few more indifferent games, brightened only by the debut of 17-year-old Cliff Birkett at outside-right in one of them. Even though nearly half-way through the season United were fifth in the League, but they had not won at home for two months which did not indicate Championship or Cup winning form. The old understanding which was the hallmark of United's first post-war team was missing (especially between half-backs and forwards), and while the youngsters in attack were trying hard enough, they obviously lacked the edge which Morris, Delaney and Mitten had provided. Everybody at Old Trafford agreed that a personality capable of holding the forward line together was now a definite requirement. Matt Busby, shrewd as ever, found the link within his own ranks.

For the game against Huddersfield on 9 December Busby decided to move John Aston up to centre-forward in place of flu victim Jack Rowley; and because John Carey was injured a new defence had to be built. Tommy McNulty got his second chance of the season at right-back in the United first team, partnered by Billy McGlen.

John Aston was, of course, used to playing at inside-forward and had led the United attack five times since the war before making a name for himself at club and international level as a full-back. The shuffle was yet another of Matt Busby's calculated gambles which came off: John Aston scored two headed goals in United's 3-2 victory over Huddersfield.

In the next game against Fulham at Craven Cottage, Aston, again at centre-forward, inspired a second half rally by United which secured a 2-2 draw.

Matt Busby now found himself in a dilemma and reflected, 'John Aston at centre-forward surprised me ... his grand work in the last two games makes it difficult to think of moving him from that position.' And, as others were pondering at the time, if Walter Winterbottom was considering Aston for the England team ... would it be at left-back or centre-forward?

But the Christmas period jolted United out of their euphoria. They were beaten 3-2 by Bolton Wanderers at Old Trafford: on Christmas Day lost 2-1 to Sunderland at Roker Park and on the following day at Old Trafford were overwhelmed 3-5 by the same side. In three matches United had conceded ten goals – as many as in the first thirteen matches of the season. The full cost of these results would not be fully realised until the end of the season ...

Obviously the team was going through a period of transition which did not always run smoothly, and Matt Busby continually urged the team's supporters to be patient. Young players were being given a taste of first-team football then slipped back into the reserves to consolidate their experience, and Matt Busby's transfer buys were of necessity modest, though so far quite successful.

When Manchester United met Oldham Athletic in the third round of the FA Cup on Saturday, 6 January the 'Latics' were well beaten 4-1; yet despite the margin, United, according to reports, were not too convincing against their Third Division opponents.

John Aston was still playing well at centre-forward, so when the versatile Jack Rowley returned after illness and injury he was moved out to the left-wing where he was still able to rock opposing defences back on their heels.

In the fourth round United easily beat Leeds United 4–0 with three goals by Stan Pearson and one from Jack Rowley. Even Leeds' centre-half, the 19-year-old Welsh international John Charles, could do nothing to stop the rampaging United forward line which forced their four goals past Leeds within half an hour of the start of the game, thus apparently, as one hard-to-please reporter remarked, 'spoiling the game as a sporting contest and as a Cup spectacle'.

When the names went into the draw for the fifth round pairings, Manchester United had drawn the plum fixture: they were to play Arsenal, at Old Trafford!

Don Davies in the *Manchester Guardian* described United's subsequent 1–0 Cup victory over Arsenal in that round as 'the mother and father of a belting', and echoed all the other reports of the game which particularly praised the brilliant half-back play of Gibson, Chilton and Cockburn, who maintained the firmest of grips on the game. The winning goal came after twenty minutes, when Stan Pearson seized a half-chance in the penalty-area and sent a blistering shot into the bottom left-hand corner of the Arsenal goal.

Arsenal never got back into the game, and United's swiftly moving half-backs and forwards kept up intense pressure and always threatened to run riot at any moment. But one goal was sufficient for victory and when the referee blew the whistle for full-time, United's teenage outside-right Cliff Birkett fainted with excitement, and his team-mates had to pick him up and carry him, unconscious, to the dressing-room!

So in the weekend that Matt Busby completed six years as manager, Manchester United, for the fourth year in succession, were through to the sixth round. They had beaten Arsenal by playing superlative football, and the draw for the sixth round gave them an equally hard task. Birmingham City were a middle-of-the-table Second Division team (having been relegated with Manchester City last season), but their Cup run, with victories over Manchester City, Derby County and Bristol City, had turned them into a fierce-fighting combination. When Matt Busby heard the news of the draw he said, 'We are delighted with

the draw ... and the way we are playing just now we feel we can
pull it off.'

A convincing 2-1 win in the next League match, against
Wolverhampton Wanderers, confirmed Busby's optimism and
Manchester United were full of confidence when they lined up at
St Andrews against a Birmingham side which among others con-
tained the famous Gil Merrick in goal and at outside-left John
Berry, later to become a Manchester United player.

The whistle blew to start the game. Shades of Aston Villa and
1948: within twenty-four seconds the ball was nestling in
United's net! From the kick-off it had moved smartly down the
right wing and was centred quickly. Allen Chilton headed clear,
Don Gibson and Henry Cockburn looked to have the situation
covered, but the ball bounced to the feet of Birmingham's
inside-right Jimmy Higgins and he drove in a shot on the half-
volley from fifteen yards out which Reg Allen, diving to his right
at full stretch could not even touch on its way to the top corner
of his net. 'I never saw it', was Reg Allen's rueful comment after
the game.

Manchester United had faced such an early set-back before,
and there was enough experience in the side to take the loss
calmly and set about the task of equalising, then winning.

But United, yet again, could not find anything of their old drive
which had turned so many seeming defeats into victories and they
failed to make any impression on the Birmingham defence.
United's deliberateness became despair as the minutes ticked
away. The Birmingham players would not let United settle on
the ball and fierce tackles went in on Jack Rowley and Allen
Chilton (each requiring the trainer's attention), and on young
Cliff Birkett who had to be stretchered off with only ten minutes
of the game remaining. Stan Pearson was harried at every turn,
and the resulting inability to find the rest of his forwards blunted
United's attack completely.

Birmingham eventually won a hard, physical game, and never
allowed Manchester United to recover from the shock early
goal which had obviously unsettled the team. It was also obvious
that some of the younger United players had not been able to
find the extra reserves to cope with the physical and emotional
demands of this level of competition. Maybe Anderson, Morris,
Mitten and Delaney would have done the job ... maybe John

Aston's move to centre-forward had weakened United's defence more seriously than everyone, including Matt Busby, had realised ...

But there were no recriminations. It was time to wish Birmingham 'Good luck' in the next round, roll up the sleeves, and get on with the rest of the season.

After their Cup defeat by Birmingham, United could not stop winning: against Sheffield Wednesday (4-0, and the first sight many had of Sheffield's 17-year-old Albert Quixall); Arsenal 3-1; Everton 3-0; Derby County 2-0; Burnley 2-1; Derby County again 4-2; Chelsea 3-1; West Bromwich Albion 3-0; and Newcastle United 2-0.

Manchester United were in contention for the League Championship, but even this remarkable string of victories did not enable them to overhaul Tottenham Hotspur who had headed the table since January. Ironically, since 1 January 1951 to the end of the season, Manchester United had played 17 games, won 14, drawn 2 and lost only 1 - yet they were still unable to catch Spurs. The Reds were paying the price for throwing away too many vital points during their Christmas fixtures.

Manchester United's last appearance of the season at Old Trafford saw them defeat Huddersfield Town 6-0, then in their final League game they drew 1-1 with Blackpool at Bloomfield Road.

It had been another long and tiring season when they had yet again nearly won the League and nearly reached the Cup final. Matt Busby had used twenty-four players this season in his search for a winning blend, and within that number some had been required to play in different positions. The loss of Charlie Mitten and Jimmy Delaney was significant, and to Busby's credit the search for replacements had always begun within his own ranks before he looked around the transfer markets. His belief in the value of carefully nurtured, home-grown young players was still unshakeable and only he and Jimmy Murphy, his reserve team coach, knew how rich the harvest was soon to be. Until then Matt Busby had to rely on slowly grafting young players into the first team which still contained Henry Cockburn, Allen Chilton, Stan Pearson, John Aston and John Carey of the old 1948 team. And, more importantly, Busby was still as calm in defeat as he was modest in triumph: he knew that great days lay ahead.

Seventeen-year-old Jeff Whitefoot and Mark Jones had been
given a few senior-team outings each this season and had profited
greatly from the experience. Roger Byrne had made his debut in
the reserves towards the end of the 1948–49 season and he and
Dennis Viollet had both made regular goal-scoring appearances
for the reserves, and Jackie Blanchflower had also featured prominently at half-back in the same side. Some of Busby's 'Babes'
were already beginning to take their first faltering steps ...


The season ended with United in the all-too-familiar runners-up
position for the fourth season in the last five, 4 points behind
leaders Tottenham Hotspur. No team could claim Manchester
United's high level of consistency in Cup or League, but the top
prizes still eluded them.

The team shared the £440 runners-up 'talent' money, and
United prepared themselves for the two friendly games which
had been arranged right at the end of the season. Then there was
to be a close-season tour of Denmark involving five matches, and
for Henry Cockburn and Stan Pearson some international fixtures.

Manchester United then played host to a team which was to
have a significant though sad part to play in their story only seven
years later. Red Star of Belgrade were touring Britain as part of
the Festival of Britain celebrations which were being held that
year. The Yugoslavian team put on a superb exhibition of smooth,
close 'carpet' passing, and although the game ended in a 1–1
draw, Manchester United were outplayed, and the experience was
further evidence of how far and how fast Continental football had
developed. Most of the United team were surprised by Red Star's
fluent style, and thought themselves lucky not to lose the game.

The Charlie Mitten story had dominated the headlines at the
beginning of this season. What of him now? He was still in Colombia, although his wife and children had returned to Manchester after only six months 'with no regrets about going to
Bogota'. Mrs Betty Mitten had told reporters that Charlie had no
regrets either. They had enjoyed the life over there and the cli-
mate was superb. They had a villa and servants – but she had
brought back her three children so that the two eldest boys could
start school in Manchester in September. Charlie was to remain

in Colombia with the Santa Fe team, and Betty Mitten was to live with friends in Stretford.

In December Charlie Mitten wrote to Alf Clarke telling him that his contract expired in June and that he would be returning home then. 'I will return to United – but whether they decide to transfer me, or keep me, is something I shall have to talk over with the directors. It may be odds-on that I shall be transferred. United may have no further use for me, but whatever happens I shall have to start there.'

Then in February Charlie again wrote to Alf Clarke telling him that he had turned down an offer of £1,000 and £30 extra per week if he would remain in Bogota after his contract expired in June. He had honoured the contract he signed a year ago, but not even the increased financial incentive was enough to keep him there. 'I miss my home life, the companionship of the lads and most of all my wife and family', wrote Mitten.

Charlie knew that on his return he would have to confront the FA and their verdict would have a considerable bearing on whether he could be reinstated by Manchester United. He braced himself for the punishment he knew he would soon have to face.

# 1951-52

## Champions At Last

The 1951-52 season marked the fortieth anniversary of first-class soccer at Old Trafford, and also turned out to be one of the most triumphantly successful in the history of the club.

Charlie Mitten returned home in June to rejoin his wife and children in Stretford saying, 'I want to play for United again and my future in football now lies in England' – and he was still adamant about having no regrets over his year in Bogota, where he reckoned to have made £3,500 profit on his stay.

Mitten's immediate priority, though, was to clear his case with the FA and Football League and apply for reinstatement – before then neither he nor Manchester United could do anything. As ever, he was full of schemes for the future, including a plan to ship stud yearlings from good British racing breeds out to Colombia.

Charlie Mitten knew that most of his team-mates wanted him back and that he was still popular with the supporters, many of whom had written letters to local papers imploring the club to forgive and forget. True, there were some others who said that he had let the club and its followers down by going when he did, and that United should have nothing more to do with him.

Retribution, as he had anticipated, was swift and painful. Mitten was fined £250 and suspended until 31 December; he was to be paid no wages by any club, and worse still, was not even allowed to train with any club until 1 November. A few days later, Manchester United placed him on the transfer list, although nothing could be done about buying or selling him until nearer the time his suspension would be lifted. Justice had to be seen to be done because the football establishment wanted to make an example of him, and Manchester United, despite their 'family' reputation, had to follow suit: their wayward son had to go.

Even then Charlie Mitten was rarely out of the news. A report in early September described how he had turned out at left-half for a Salford pub team in his first game in England for sixteen months. He had apparently gone to collect his family's meat ration from his butcher who was also secretary of a pub soccer team. 'Why not come and have a kick around with our lads?' was invitation enough for Charlie, who was desperately anxious to maintain match fitness. Watched by a crowd of 200 he cracked in three goals in a 5–1 victory.

He had tried to keep quiet about the game, but inevitably word got around. The FA turned a blind eye, but Charlie himself knew the risk he had taken. He told Alf Clarke that, 'It was a friendly game between two scratch sides, and it wasn't an organised match, otherwise I would not have played, of course. So far as I know I have not transgressed any rules.'

Happily, the Football League lifted its ban a fortnight early and allowed Charlie Mitten to train with his former team-mates. He had put on a little bit of weight during his enforced lay-off, but a delighted Mitten said, 'It's great to be back. I feel like a prisoner who has been suddenly reprieved.'

At the beginning of December, Charlie Mitten was transferred to Fulham for £20,000 and his first game for them was to be on 5 January against Chelsea. Manchester United had lost a colourful and skilful winger and many thousands of fans were sorry to see him go, but Fulham in particular and football in general was the richer for his return.

A month into the new season and having played two games a week, Manchester United were leading the First Division table. Matt Busby's first note in the *Review* programmes was full of customary optimism, and not a little prophetic:

Is the Championship trophy to find a resting place at Old Trafford this season? Well, it's United's turn – and if they do succeed it will be the reward of remarkable consistency ... I don't think there is a senior club who would hesitate to applaud United if the Championship is won by us this season. I think we have as good a chance as any other side. Things may go wrong at times – that is football – but I have the greatest faith in my players and they include some young stars coming along apace ready to step in, when necessary, and to acquit themselves well.

Matt Busby knew full well how the Goddess of Hope bestowed her favours generously at this time of the year on every club in the land, and how the Goddess of Triumph was a fickle and elusive creature ... but maybe this was to be the season when she would smile and beckon over the team from Old Trafford.

In this first month of football there had been much for the fans to savour. Jack Rowley had scored three hat-tricks in the first three weeks of the season, still a First Division record. After seven games he had scored fourteen goals, equalling exactly his tally for the whole of last season!

United fans also quickly learned to appreciate the quality of their new right-winger Johnny Berry who had been bought from Birmingham City for £25,000 in the summer. Many remembered the diminutive Berry's speed and skill in the Birmingham side which had beaten United 1-0 in the fifth round of last season's FA Cup. He was also to be a key figure in United's successes this season and was a regular first-team choice for the next five seasons until injuries sustained in the Munich air crash prevented him from playing ever again.

At the end of September the Old Trafford crowd were also pleased to see John Aston rejoin the side. He was back at centre-forward, having recovered from a cartilage operation in the summer, and even though he scored in the second minute of his first game he could not prevent Preston North End from scoring two goals which won them the match. It was the first time United had lost at Old Trafford since Boxing Day in the previous year.

A couple of weeks later Allenby Chilton won his second and Henry Cockburn his thirteenth England cap when they played in a 2-2 draw with France at Highbury. It was an indifferent performance by England, and neither Allen nor Henry found anything of their superb club form which had resulted in their international selection. They were among the six players dropped for the next international against Wales, and neither was to play for England again.

Because of injury neither John Aston nor John Carey featured in United's 5-2 victory over Aston Villa on 13 October, a win which kept United at the top of the table for the second week in succession. The win was all the more remarkable because United were down 1-2 at half-time, but stormed back in the second half in a blistering seven minute spell which saw them rattle in four goals. There was something about these two teams which always seemed to bring out exciting football. A cracking win against Aston Villa had brought Cup success in 1948. Could the same thing happen this season?

But a couple of rather surprising home defeats, and losses away at Chelsea (4-2) and Portsmouth (3-1), meant that United found themselves pushed down to seventh place in the League table. It was time to make changes, so for United's game against Liverpool at Anfield on 24 November, Matt Busby dropped Reg Allen (who had not missed a senior game except through injury since he joined United sixteen months before) and rewarded the ever-patient Jack Crompton with selection, his first appearance of the season. Busby also selected Roger Byrne at left-back and Jackie Blanchflower at right-half for their first-team debuts. It was a goalless draw but none the less one of the most exciting games seen at Anfield all season.

The next game, a stirring 3-1 victory over Blackpool, marked the turning point in United's fortunes that season. From then on they began to climb back up the table, notching up notable victories against Arsenal (3-1 at Highbury) and West Bromwich Albion (5-2 at Old Trafford) and they saw out 1951 as League leaders.

At last it was time for the third round of the FA Cup, and Manchester United, playing well and lying second in the League table could not have been better placed. Matt Busby was able to pick his strongest team to meet Hull City at Old Trafford: Allen; McNulty, Byrne; Carey, Chilton, Cockburn; Berry, Pearson, Rowley, Downie, Bond.

It seemed unlikely that Hull City would provide any kind of opposition to Manchester United. They were lying next to the bottom of the Second Division table, but were looking forward to another battle with their old Cup rivals of three seasons ago to provide some spark to a somewhat depressing season. Some familiar faces graced the Hull team. In goal, for example, was Joe Robinson who had faced United in the Blackpool goal in the 1948 Final, and at inside-right they still had their crafty and seemingly ageless captain Raich Carter.

It was a disastrous game for the home side. United conceded

the first goal after four minutes, Jack Rowley missed a penalty on the half hour, and two minutes before the half-time whistle, Hull scored their second and decisive winning goal.

Hull's win was no fluke: every man, especially Raich Carter, was able to raise his game beyond his wildest expectations, and collectively the whole team fought with real spirit. Manchester United's forwards, who in League games looked so powerful and incisive, had no answer in this, the easiest of fixtures. If Jack Rowley had equalised with the penalty United *might* have gone on to win, but there was no denying that, on the ninety minutes showing that day, Hull deserved to win.

It was the first time since 1939 that United had been knocked out of the Cup at the third round stage, and little comfort could be gained from knowing that Bolton, Preston and last year's finalists Blackpool were also casualties. Northern sides like Everton, Manchester City and Blackburn were forced to replay their ties and of these only Blackburn survived.

So for another year Manchester United, with their Cup fortunes crushed, turned to face the rest of the League season, even more determined to make an all-out effort for the Championship.

The remaining six members of United's 1948 team knew that time was running out for them. Henry Cockburn, John Carey, Jack Rowley, Stan Pearson, John Aston and Allen Chilton were all now in their early thirties and they were beginning to feel the pressures of those young players who had reverently cleaned their boots as apprentices a few years ago, and who now had an eye on their shirts. A League Championship medal was the only other prize they wanted to win to set the seal on their eventful careers.

Their determination was heralded by a 2-0 victory over Tottenham Hotspur which put them at the top of the League again: the team had clearly resolved not to allow itself to start slipping down as it did at the equivalent stage the previous season. A sequence of more exciting victories followed, against Preston (2-1); Derby County (3-0); Sunderland (2-1); and Wolverhampton Wanderers (2-0): only a 1-1 draw against Aston Villa spoiled this impressive winning streak.

Even results such as these, however, did not enable Manchester United to pull themselves away from the following pack, nor were they able to put more than three points between themselves and

whichever club was running in second place. By March, with
only eight games remaining, United were leading the table with
47 points, followed by Arsenal on 45, and Tottenham Hotspur
and Portsmouth on 42.

At that moment United stumbled, losing 2-3 at Leeds Road to
Huddersfield Town, the bottom club in the Division. The Yorkshire team's winning goal three minutes from the final whistle
had ended United's run of sixteen League games without defeat.

In the very next game Manchester United slipped again, losing
1-0 to Portsmouth; they were the first team this season to complete the 'double' over United, and it was the Reds', first
defeat at Fratton Park in post-war football. United were without
Stan Pearson and Jack Rowley who were partnering each other
on England's left flank against Scotland. Their scoring power was
sadly missed, even more so when the news came through that
Stan had scored two opportunist goals before half-time in England's 2-1 win in front of 133,991 spectators at Hampden Park.

With five matches remaining, United, Arsenal and Portsmouth
were now level on forty-eight points, and anxious United fans
combed the League table, looking at the fixtures and permutating
infinite combinations of 'just supposing' results. One thing was
crystal clear - a loss at this stage could mean the end to United's
title hopes.

A 1-1 draw against Burnley on Good Friday: a 4-0 drubbing
of Liverpool (Roger Byrne scoring two) and a 6-1 victory over
Burnley on Easter Monday lifted United two points clear of
Arsenal and four clear of Tottenham Hotspur.

The Championship was now a race between United, Arsenal
and Spurs, and the fixtures they faced could not have made a
better contribution to what promised to be a grandstand finish.
United were to meet Blackpool, Chelsea and Arsenal; Arsenal
were to play Stoke, West Bromwich Albion and Manchester
United; and Spurs were matched against Liverpool, Blackpool
and Chelsea. Possibly the first fixture each was to play would
decide the Championship ... but maybe everybody would have
to wait until United met Arsenal in the last game of the season
for the final showdown.

In the event, on Saturday, 19 April, United drew 2-2 with
Blackpool, Arsenal beat Stoke 4-1, and Spurs drew 1-1 with
Liverpool. On the following Monday, Arsenal were beaten 3-1 at

West Bromwich Albion, and Manchester United beat Chelsea 3-0, a game which many still remember – not least for a spectacular goal by John Carey.

By the time the teams came off the pitch at Old Trafford the calculations had been made. The League Champions of 1952 were Manchester United ... unless Arsenal could beat them by at least 7-0 on the following Saturday!

When the news was announced on the loudspeakers a few minutes after the final whistle, United's thousands of supporters were jubilant, and they could now afford to savour again the game against Chelsea, and especially that second goal scored by John Carey.

In fact the whole game had been fought out at a high pitch of excitement and possibly the shouted news from the touch-line of Arsenal's gradual demise against West Bromwich, spreading man-to-man throughout the team's ranks, was responsible for giving United extra strength. Stan Pearson's twenty-five-yard shot brought the first goal after as many minutes, but it was United's second goal, two minutes before half-time, which sealed Chelsea's fate and symbolically won the Championship title for Manchester United.

John Carey had accepted a square pass from full-back Tommy McNulty, strode ahead with the ball at his feet and let fly from thirty yards. The ball struck the back of the net and rolled back out to the penalty spot: it was the kind of goal which every player likes to score and every spectator loves to see and the crowd were still applauding Carey's effort well after the referee had restarted the game.

Even today, John Carey, whose modesty still prevents him from doing open justice to all his magnificent achievements, could not help a smile of pleasure as he recalled the game and his goal:

I really wanted to win a Championship medal if I could, as time was getting very short for me. We finished up with two home matches, against Chelsea on the Monday night and then Arsenal on Saturday. Chelsea were the sort of team that could throw a spanner in the works. We were winning 1-0 but having a bit of a rough time, and I got the ball and went forward and nobody seemed to come to me so I went on and on and when I got near the penalty-box I hit it with my left foot and it went into the top corner of the net. The crowd did give me a tremendous ovation, but I think it was as much relief as anything else.

The 1948 FA Cup winners. From left to right; *back row:* Busby, Anderson, Whalley, Chilton, Crompton, Cockburn, Aston, Curry; *front row:* Delaney, Morris, Carey, Rowley, Pearson and Mitten.

The Manchester United players beside the swimming pool at Walter Tetley's ranch in Hollywood; taken during their 1950-51 close season tour of the USA.

Relaxing on the golf course. From left to right: Stan Pearson, Tom Curry, Jack Rowley and Charlie Mitten.

John Carey displays the 1951–52 League Championship trophy with Matt Busby.

The Manchester United team celebrate in the bath after winning the League Championship. From left to right: Henry Cockburn, John Aston, Johnny Berry, Tommy McNulty, Roger Byrne, Reg Allen and John Carey – and assistant trainer Bill Inglis dispenses the champagne.

John Aston, the author, Henry Cockburn, Johnny Morris, Charlie Mitten and an old adversary, Joe Mercer, at an Anglo-American Sporting Club dinner in Manchester in 1985.

Jack Crompton.

Jack Rowley.

Jimmy Delaney.

Allenby Chilton.

John Anderson.

John Carey (right) and Jimmy Murphy.

Stan Pearson.

David Meek interviewing (from left to right) John Carey, Jack Rowley, Stan Pearson, Sir Matt Busby and Les Olive for the making of 'The Manchester United Story' video.

Winning the Championship is a tremendous prize ... it lasts forty-two matches compared to the Cup which goes over only six games ... if it's all down to one game the luck can go with you or against you ... that's why we see all sorts of strange teams getting to the Final ... but the team that eventually wins the First Division Championship has really earned it, I can assure you!

A third goal by Henry Cockburn was the final triumphant gesture by United, and when the final whistle blew the Chelsea players dashed across the pitch with congratulatory handshakes, because they too had got wind of Arsenal's defeat. Minutes later the whole of the Manchester United team, cradling cups full of celebratory champagne, were sinking gratefully into their communal bath, champions at last!

Arsenal realised the magnitude of the task which awaited them on the following Saturday, but were determined to make a game of it. Even so, Tom Whittaker, Arsenal's manager, had nobly conceded the Championship title by sending Matt Busby a telegram which read, 'All at Arsenal send you sincere congratulations on a worthy Championship success.' The Gunners' hopes of a League and Championship double this season had been dashed, but they could take some comfort from knowing they still had a chance to win the Cup ... if they could beat Newcastle United at Wembley in a couple of weeks' time.

A crowd of 53,651 turned up to watch the game against Arsenal, the last match of the season at Old Trafford. It had been confirmed that Arsenal had to score seven goals in order to take the Championship, and the record books had revealed that the last time Manchester United had lost a match 7–0 was in the 1930–31 season, against Aston Villa. In the event, the spectators did see seven goals scored on that April afternoon in 1952 – but six were by United, against a single reply by Arsenal!

The Manchester United team was unchanged from the one which had beaten Chelsea the week before: Allen; McNulty, Aston; Carey, Chilton, Cockburn; Berry, Downie, Rowley, Pearson, Byrne. Arsenal fielded Swindin; Barnes, Smith L.; Forbes, Shaw, Mercer; Cox, Goring, Holton, Lewis, Roper.

Jack Rowley scored the first goal after eight minutes' play, then Stan Pearson added another after forty minutes and Roger Byrne after forty-two minutes, ensuring an impregnable lead by half-time. The fourth goal was from a lob by Jack Rowley and the good-natured crowd gave Arsenal a huge roar of encouragement when their outside-right Freddie Cox scored. Eight minutes from the final whistle, after an incident in Arsenal's goalmouth, Jack Rowley scored from the penalty-spot, his third goal of the match and his thirtieth of the season. He had also ended the season as he had begun it by scoring three goals, which he had done in United's opening match of the season at West Bromwich. A minute from the end of the game Stan Pearson drove in a Rowley cross for United's sixth goal.

Jack Rowley recalled his contribution to United's goal tally in that game.

Yes, I scored three goals, and I'll always remember the first one which I scored from inside the penalty area with my right foot and it screamed in. In some of the reports the next day the press wrote 'So Rowley *can* kick with his right foot!' I also scored the fifth goal which was a penalty and I had the cheek to take it with my right foot again. I always remember George Swindin saying, 'You bloody thing Jack ... I didn't know you could kick with your right foot!'

Admittedly, Arsenal had played with ten men for an hour of the game when their centre-half Shaw had to leave the field with a suspected fractured wrist, and while they had conceded the title a week ago, they had wanted to win this game, if only to boost their confidence for the Cup final next Saturday against Newcastle United. They were to suffer another defeat there – and all their hopes of a 'double' were in complete ruins.

Next Monday's *Manchester Guardian* carried a tribute by Don Davies which captured much of the current spirit of Old Trafford:

After an interval of forty-one years Manchester United have regained the Championship of the Football League. The title has never been better earned. Not only has the team, in the five seasons before this one, finished second four times and fourth once in the League and won the FA Cup; it has been captained, managed, and directed in a way that is a lesson to many others. J. Carey, the captain in this period, has been a model footballer – technically efficient, thanks to hard work; a fighter to the last, without ever forgetting that he is a sportsman; a steadier of the younger and inexperienced, an inspirer of the older and tiring, and at all times the most modest of men, though he has won every football honour open to him. M. Busby, the manager, has shown himself as great a coach as he was a player, with an uncannily brilliant eye for young local players' possibilities, whether in their usual or in other positions; a believer in the certainty of good football's eventual reward, and a kindly yet, when necessary, firm father of his family of players. Between them they have built up a club spirit which is too rare in these days, a spirit which enables men to bear cheerfully personal and team disappointments and to ignore personal opportunities to shine for the good of the whole. Moreover, by eschewing the dangerous policy of going into the transfer market whenever a weakness develops and giving their chances instead to the many local citizens on the club's books they have made it likely that this club spirit will persist, since the club today is a Manchester one not in name only but in fact, as far as most of its players are concerned. Manager and captain could never have brought about this happy state of affairs had they not had through these years such full authority and support from the board of directors as must be the envy of many other officials in all parts of the country.

After a lapse of forty-one years and for the third time in their history the Championship had returned to Old Trafford: since the war Manchester United had achieved an undisputed high level of consistent performance in the League, and no other team could rival United's record of having topped fifty points in each of the six seasons since the war.

Amid the noisy scenes of victory, Matt Busby's mind went back to 1945 when he had taken over a club without a ground and with very little money, but full of players rich in talent and enthusiasm. He would leave it to others to remind him of his place in the scheme of things: of how he had suggested positional changes to them and then blended them as a unit, and how his patient belief in the value of young players was beginning to show results. Maybe, though, this team which in recent weeks had rediscovered something of the secret which had made it a matchless football machine in 1948, could be allowed to run for a little longer ...

The Championship title had been won by a total of twenty-four players who had made senior appearances this season, but the team itself had been mainly drawn from: Reg Allen, John

Carey, Tommy McNulty, Roger Byrne, Allenby Chilton, Henry Cockburn, Johnny Berry, Stan Pearson, Jack Rowley, John Downie, Ernie Bond, John Aston, Billy Redman and Don Gibson. Allen Chilton in fact was an ever-present this season with forty-two League appearances. Harry McShane, Jack Crompton, Frank Clempson, Jeff Whitefoot, Mark Jones, Billy McGlen, John Walton, Brian Birch, Lol Cassidy and Jackie Blanchflower had made fewer, but nevertheless essential, contributions to the collective effort which had made Manchester United the most successful team in the Football League, and one of the most exciting to watch.

Near the end of the season Manchester United announced they had bought The Cliff training ground at Lower Broughton where they had recently installed floodlighting. The Cliff had also been used to play 'A' team and Colts fixtures and as the training venue on Tuesday and Thursday evenings for juniors and the part-time professionals.

Those floodlit games were to illuminate the potential of many young players who were later to make an indelible mark on United's history. Next season, for example, in the second round of the FA National Youth Cup, United beat Nantwich 23-0, with a goal by Albert Scanlon, five from David Pegg, and five by a powerfully built young lad from Dudley called Duncan Edwards.

# 1952-53
## The Old Order Changes...

Six players who had won League Championship medals in 1952 – John Carey, Allenby Chilton, Henry Cockburn, Stan Pearson, Jack Rowley and John Aston – had also won FA Cup medals in 1948. Four of them were pre-war signings and at the moment they were all holding their places on merit, but they knew it was only a matter of time before they would have to give up their places to one of the many talented youngsters whose skills they themselves had helped to exercise and encourage in the training sessions at The Cliff.

A poor start to the 1952–53 season (fourth from the bottom of the table after only six games) had caused concern in many quarters. The players themselves appreciated the situation, but others had less patience and understanding. At the annual meeting of the Manchester United shareholders, Matt Busby paid tribute to the players for winning the League Championship and also re-assured the members that in his opinion the young players on United's books were worth hundreds of thousands of pounds. 'In a couple of years time we shall have wonderful young material when it is needed most', he added.

In fact, during the course of the 1952–53 season Matt Busby introduced David Pegg, Bill Foulkes, Tommy Taylor, Duncan Edwards and Dennis Viollet into the first team, although the 'Old Brigade' at the moment, including Jack Crompton (who had recently restablished himself as first-choice goalkeeper) could still consider themselves first-team players.

Overall, this was an indifferent season for Manchester United, even though it had begun in promising fashion with a 4-2 Charity Shield win over Newcastle United at Old Trafford. United's Cup run had ended prematurely when after having beaten Millwall 1-0 in the third round they had allowed themselves to suffer the humiliation of a 1-1 draw with non-League Walthamstow Avenue at Old Trafford in the next round, then managed to beat them 5-2 in the replay at Highbury, only to lose 1-2 to Everton in the next round.

At the end of the season Manchester United were in eighth place in the League table, their lowest position since the war, but while their Cup and League performances had been disappointing, the season had still offered many memorable moments.

Right at the beginning of the season, Duncan Edwards had played in the junior match which preceded the senior public trial match and few could have failed to notice the power and skill of this 15-year-old with a man's physique. His prominence as a schoolboy footballer had attracted the notice of many League clubs, but Duncan Edwards had wanted to come to Manchester United, attracted by their fame, and because they played the same kind of creative, direct football he wanted to play.

A series of brilliant displays in United's youth and reserve sides convinced Busby at the end of the season that Duncan Edwards was ready for the first team. He appeared at Ninian Park in a 4-1 defeat by Cardiff City on 4 April 1953 and only two years later became the youngest player ever for England at 18 years 183 days old.

It was also during this season that the term 'Busby's Babes' began to be used with increasing frequency. Of the debutants this season Duncan Edwards was fifteen; David Pegg, signed as a schoolboy winger from Doncaster, was seventeen; full-back Bill Foulkes was twenty and forward Dennis Viollet was nineteen. Tommy Taylor was a 21-year-old centre-forward signed from Second Division Barnsley in March, the most expensive of Busby's signings to date at £30,000, and he flourished immediately in Old Trafford's unique atmosphere. After only eight games of First Division football Tommy Taylor was chosen for the England party (along with Johnny Berry) which would be touring South and North America in the close season.

Matt Busby had also given a chance this season to Eddie Lewis, a 17-year-old centre-forward; Johnny Doherty a 17-year-old inside-right, and John Scott, an 18-year-old winger. And a glance through the Central League and Junior sides that season reveals more familiar names who were to play their part in the United story of the years to come like Ian Greaves, Eddie Colman, Ronnie Cope and Colin Webster.

Leslie Olive at twenty-four was the oldest of the season's debutants. He was then assistant secretary to Walter Crickmer and
on Saturday afternoons had been keeping goal in the Central
League side, although in times past as an outfield player with the
junior teams had proved himself a successful goal-scorer. At the
end of November Jack Crompton was declared unfit, Ray Wood
had a fractured wrist and Reg Allen had been absent for several
months because of illness. So Les Olive was picked for his first
senior appearance, a 2–2 draw against Newcastle United at St
James's Park, one in which, as a report described, 'all he had to
do he had done well'.

The goalkeeper's jersey had been worn by some unlikely
characters this season. In the game against Bolton Wanderers at
Old Trafford, Jack Rowley had laid on the pass from which
Johnny Berry had scored the single deciding goal. Then, ten
minutes from the end of the game, Jack had to don the goalie's
jersey because Reg Allen had been forced to leave the field with
an injured finger. By all accounts Jack had made a good job of it,
and grabbed, clutched, or fisted away everything that had come
his way. When Reg Allen had returned after treatment he was
given a role in the forward line and the crowd really got their
money's worth, because in the last few minutes of the game a
grinning but rather lost looking Reg Allen made two first class
passes but conceded four free-kicks!

John Carey had also been given the chance to wear the goalkeeper's jersey although he had already had a spell as United's
'keeper after Jack Crompton had been carried off unconscious at
Chelsea in December. John Carey remembered:

I have played in ten different positions for Manchester United; the
only position I was never selected to play in was at outside-right. I
played in goal because Jack Crompton had a very bad bout of flu which
only became apparent after we'd reached Durham on our way to play in
Sunderland. So I started and finished in goal. We couldn't get a replacement; the kick-off was at two o'clock; the doctor didn't see Jack until
about ten o'clock so that left only four hours to send for somebody. So
Matt looked at me and said, 'You'll have to play in goal.' We drew 2–2
which wasn't at all bad . . . I was very pleased with myself. I couldn't do
anything about the first though, which was an own goal by Allen Chilton
– a real rocket header into the bottom corner of the net, miles away from
me. I was responsible for their second goal, I admit, which was a lob

over a crowd of players. So there I was very pleased with myself, but
Tom Curry brought me down to earth: he said to me when we came in,
If it had been a load of hay going through the goal you wouldn't have
got two handfuls!'

If this transitional season had been disappointing for United,
football in general rejoiced in May. Stan Matthews, playing
the game of his life, had at last, on his third attempt, secured
a Cup winner's medal when Blackpool beat Bolton Wanderers
4-3.
    Stan Matthews's Cup medal was one of the many achievements
that summer which heralded the New Elizabethan Age, cele-
brated by the Coronation of Queen Elizabeth II in June 1953.
    A renaissance had also begun at Old Trafford. Manchester
United's supporters had been prepared for the departure of John
Carey, because an article by Tom Jackson in the *Manchester
Evening News* right at the end of the last season had begun:

> There is an odds-on chance that this will be John Carey's last season
> as a player. Within the next few days the Manchester United captain,
> who has achieved every honour in football since he started his career
> as a junior at Old Trafford in 1936 is to decide whether or not to re-
> sign for next season. Carey, the most popular captain in United's
> history, has of course been offered terms for 1953-54 but he told me
> today, 'My future as a player hangs in the balance. I am not getting
> any younger (he is just thirty-four), and I don't intend to become a
> has-been in the game which has been my life.'
>     United, anticipating that he might not be available as a player next
> season, have already offered him a job on their coaching staff. It is
> also known that several foreign clubs would value his services as a
> coach.

The news was no easier to bear when John Carey made his
decision that he was ending his career as a player known in May.
He had decided to retire after seventeen seasons with Manchester
United 'because I do not feel capable of playing the United brand
of soccer for another year'.
    There was, of course, a great deal of speculation about what
John Carey would do next, but just before the 1953-54 season
began, Second Division Blackburn Rovers announced that they
had appointed John Carey as their manager. He was to bring to

the task of managing the same shrewd and thoughtful skills that he had brought as a player – and was to lead the Rovers to third place in the League table by the end of the season. Characteristically, he absorbed himself fully into his new life with Blackburn, though he was never to lose his links with Old Trafford and Manchester. He had been the first of the 1948 team to make his senior debut way back in 1937, and his retirement as a player was the first move in the final dismantling of that great team.

The 1953–54 season began without transfer-listed Reg Allen, and John Downie who was later to sign for Luton Town. Stan Pearson was appointed captain and one of his first tasks was to welcome two starry-eyed juniors called Bobby Charlton and Wilf McGuinness to the club. Bobby Charlton had kept the promise he had made himself when he had listened to the broadcast of the 1948 Cup final: he was now a Manchester United player.

It was again an inauspicious start to the season, exacerbated by a knee injury to Stan Pearson in the opening fixture with Chelsea, and National Service demands on Tommy Taylor and Dennis Viollet. The first six games had produced three defeats and three draws, and with John Carey gone and Stan Pearson injured, Matt Busby's hand was forced: some bold changes had to be made.

If there was one game in which the 'old' finally gave way to the 'new', it would probably be the match against Huddersfield Town at Leeds Road on Saturday, 31 October 1953. A few days beforehand, Manchester United had played a floodlit friendly game up in Kilmarnock: Stan Pearson and Jack Rowley had stepped down 'because of slight knocks' to make way for Jackie Blanchflower and Dennis Viollet. It was an easy 3–0 victory for United, marred by an injury to Henry Cockburn which was later diagnosed as a broken jaw.

For the game aginst Huddersfield, Matt Busby again selected Blanchflower and Viollet, and he also picked Duncan Edwards in place of Henry Cockburn. These players joined Ray Wood, Bill Foulkes, Roger Byrne, Jeff Whitefoot, Allen Chilton, Johnny Berry, Tommy Taylor and Jack Rowley in the 'new look' United side, in which seven of the players were twenty-one years of age or younger. Even though the game ended in a 0–0 draw Matt Busby was pleased with the way the young team had settled.

The same side held Arsenal to a 2–2 draw a week later, and in the next game an unchanged side outplayed Cardiff at Ninian Park in a 6-1 victory, and then went on to a dazzling 4-1 victory over Blackpool. The 'Babes' had arrived.

Allenby Chilton had taken over the captaincy from Stan Pearson and the new responsibility added a further dimension to his presence as the classic centre-half pivot, around whom attacks were initiated and defences were organised. He readily assumed the fatherly mantle of the departed Carey, and ushered his young team through this transformational period with style and inspiration. Jack Rowley, 'the sole survivor of an immortal trio' as Don Davies described him, and with Chilton the only other survivor of the 1948 team, had kept his place on the forward line and in that capacity complemented Allenby Chilton's influence as a wise old head among United's eager young forwards.

Elsewhere, another old order suddenly found itself taken by surprise, when at Wembley on a foggy afternoon in late November, England were 'outplayed, outgeneralled, outpaced and outshot' by Hungary in a 6-3 defeat, their first ever against a Continental side on British soil. The face of British football was about to change.

Manchester United's 'new' team was growing in strength and confidence, and their 3-1 defeat at the hands of Chelsea in the middle of December was their first for two months. But they were also to learn their first powerful competitive lesson when they were beaten 5-3 by Burnley in the third round of the FA Cup at Turf Moor, an unhappy baptism for five of United's young players who were playing in a Cup tie for the first time.

Stan Pearson and Henry Cockburn were beginning to realise that their days at United were numbered. It had been an unhappy season for Stan: he had been injured in the opening game of the season and had subsequently not been able to find anything of the form that had made him one of Old Trafford's most consistent players. He was having to play reserve-team football while Dennis Viollet, who had inherited his number 10 shirt, was consolidating his own position with a series of brilliantly opportunist displays. Stan had several talks with Matt Busby: he was thirty-four years old and knew he was still good enough for first-team football, but both men knew how difficult it would be for him to get back into United's current line-up.

In early February, to the regret of the thousands who had seen

him at his brilliant best, Stan Pearson was transferred to Second
Division Bury for a modest fee. So ended a brilliant career with
Manchester United, the club he had joined as a lad in 1936: yet
another of the 1948 side had moved on to fresh pastures.

If the story of the 1948 side had to end anywhere it should really
be at this point, but Henry Cockburn, Jack Rowley, Jack Crompton, Allenby Chilton and John Aston were still at Old Trafford
when the 1953–54 season ended with United fourth place in the
League. Then Henry Cockburn left in October 1954 to join Stan
Pearson at Bury; Jack Rowley left in February 1955 to become
Plymouth Argyle's player-manager; and Allenby Chilton left a
month later to be player-manager with Grimsby Town. John
Aston was still with Manchester United in 1955 when illness
forced his retirement, and Jack Crompton (kept on to understudy
Ray Wood) was released by United in 1956 to become Luton
Town's trainer. Both John Aston and Jack Crompton, however,
were to become reconnected with the club in various coaching
and scouting capacities, and for a brief time Jack Crompton was
United's manager in the interregnum between Dave Sexton and
Ron Atkinson.

As Matt Busby had promised, the transition from the side
which won the Cup in 1948 and the League in 1952 to the side
which had become known as his 'Babes' had been effected
smoothly over a couple of seasons. The spirit and comradeship of
the players in those teams, and their loyalty to the club had allowed the transition to be made painlessly, apart from the inevitable disappointment which older players always feel when they
realise (or are told) that it is time to give way to younger men.

The nature of the game dictates that too much time cannot be
spent lingering over past glories – what is happening to his team
*now* is what preoccupies the supporter and the player. But Jack
Crompton, John Carey, John Aston, Henry Cockburn, Allenby
Chilton, John Anderson, Jimmy Delaney, Johnny Morris, Jack
Rowley, Stan Pearson and Charlie Mitten gave Old Trafford its
first taste of success and created that indefinable aura which now
surrounds the name of Manchester United. It was by their example and on their achievement that all the other great Manchester United sides were to build.

# Where Are They Now?

### Jack Crompton

Matt Busby once described Jack Crompton as 'perhaps not the greatest goalkeeper ever to play for United, but he was the sort of player rarely noticed even when doing a fine job of work.'

Jack Crompton did do a fine job of work for United as their regular goalkeeper between 1945 and 1950 and even when he lost his place to Reg Allen at the beginning of the 1950–51 season he patiently practised his craft in the reserves, waiting for a chance to win back his place, which he did two years later. In all, Jack made 191 appearances for Manchester United, having signed for them as a 20-year-old junior in 1942.

His finest game for United was undoubtedly the 1948 Cup final, and even today his team-mates sing Jack's praises for his performance on that April afternoon. It began badly, of course, when Jack let in the first penalty awarded in a post-war Wembley final. From then on Jack's contribution was flawless. Not only did his throws and kicks keep the ball away from Stanley Matthews, but he also saved a certain goal attempt by Walter Rickett, and it was his miracle save from Stanley Mortensen and his swift throw out to John Anderson which led to Stan Pearson's winning goal. It was Jack's proudest moment when he collected his Cup winner's medal from King George VI, less than three years since he had been a member of the very first United team selected by Matt Busby, along with team-mates Henry Cockburn, John Carey and Jack Rowley.

Characteristically, after the ballyhoo of the Cup success had died down, the shy Jack Crompton slipped away for his summer holiday, and with £15 in his pocket and rucksack and tent on his back, hitch-hiked through France, Italy and Switzerland for five weeks.

Jack is still adamant that his days as a player at United, parti-

cularly as a member of the 1948 side, were the happiest in a long
and varied career:

Why were we so good? Firstly, discipline ... we'd all experienced discipline in the forces ... we were easy to handle. Secondly, we had beautiful
balance ... we could all do our job well. We had a stable defence of
destroyers, and a forward line of creators ... they were a forward line
without equal ... they all had skill and pace: they were all so positive
and they couldn't wait to get to the opposition goal. And physically we
were all very strong, which was important in those days. It was a side
which would have won credit in any era.

But even as a professional footballer Jack's mind was never
very far from outdoor pursuits: as a member of the YMCA he
spent most of his spare time climbing and walking the Derbyshire
hills, and later he organised groups of young people on climbing
and touring trips abroad.

When Manchester United won the Championship in 1952 the
regular goalkeeper was Reg Allen, but the following season saw
Jack's return although as the season went by he had to make way
for young Ray Wood whose goalkeeping skills were developing
rapidly.

My wrist was fractured in the 1949–50 season and I was three months in
plaster, and it never really healed. I stopped a free-kick from Dickie
Dorsett at Villa Park in October but the ball 'took' the top of my thumb.
I'd saved the goal but I often wished I hadn't. I wished I'd missed it
completely ... it might have made a difference to my whole life ... but
it was just one of those things.

I tried to make a come-back for a spell but by then United had bought
Ray Wood and Reg Allen to replace me ... I played for the first team
only now and then. I played quite regularly in the Central League side,
but I was always struggling in the first team from then on ... the bone
in my wrist never really mended ... I only had to catch my wrist against
something and it was agony.

Jack's last appearance at Old Trafford was his only appearance
in the 1955–56 season: from there he went to Luton as their
trainer-coach. His return a few years later was occasioned by one
of the most tragic events in United's history:

I was still at Luton as first-team coach and I lived next door to Allan Brown (the ex-Blackpool player) in Dunstable. I was driving home about tea-time when I saw Alan's car coming up very fast behind me and I thought, What's that lunatic up to? and he came screeching up behind me as I pulled up my drive. I said, 'What the hell's the matter with you?' and he said, 'United's been in a plane crash and I've been trying to get you at the ground but you'd left. I think it's serious.'

So we went in and had a cup of tea and listened to the radio ... it was heart-breaking because I'd known so many of them ...

I think the pre-Munich side would have been the greatest side United ever had, mainly because they were so young but very experienced ... they were playing European football at a very early age. They also had depth which our 1948 team didn't have ... Matt could have had three of that young side sick, but he could still manage to produce a winning side.

Jack was summoned back to Old Trafford by Jimmy Murphy to organise the training of a shattered club, and thus began thirteen more years with United as first team coach, in which the resurrected club twice won the First Division Championship, the FA Cup and the European Cup.

He left Old Trafford again in 1971 when Matt Busby retired, and became manager of Fourth Division Barrow, then coach at Bury, and finally a coach to Preston North End, which at the time was managed by Bobby Charlton.

Towards the end of the 1973–74 season Jack was offered the post of reserve-team manager and coach at Manchester United again, under Tommy Docherty ('it's always a pleasure to come back to Old Trafford at any time'). There he remained through the managerial reigns of Docherty and Dave Sexton, and even managed the club himself in the short interregnum between Sexton and Ron Atkinson in the summer of 1980. After that Jack left the world of professional football, to which he had given nearly forty years' service.

Today Jack is still fully occupied with numerous local coaching commitments, as well as holding the positions of Secretary and Match Organiser of a six-a-side Unemployed Football League in Salford. He is also the Manchester Alliance Sunday League's first President.

It is a testament to Jack's enthusiasm and commitment that he is still putting so much back into the game at a level where it must be nurtured if it is to continue in any kind of a healthy state. Even so, Jack maintains that:

The game has lost a lot since those immediate post-war days – but it reflects life in general ... people are not as dedicated to a purpose as they used to be.

At school level they now offer many more sports than they used to and this is bound to affect the game. Years ago most boys played football, and that's not happening today. It's all very well talking about wanting exciting football today, but you've got to have good players to produce exciting games ... and the sources are drying up. And the emphasis on money and success has not done the game much good either.

There's no doubt that play is more negative and ultra-defensive today: actually it's the fear of failure rather than the desire for success which characterises today's game. Results are more important. Chances to score goals don't come as easily as they did, but forwards today don't seem to look as hard for those chances.

Maybe one day football will see one or other of Jack's three young grandsons playing the game their grandfather still loves so much. What football already knows is that Jack Crompton will always be remembered as one of the most loyal and dependable players ever to grace Old Trafford.

## John Carey

John Carey can look back on nearly fifty years' connection with Manchester United, and his achievements as one of their greatest players are superlative by any standards.

He played at Old Trafford for eighteen seasons, making 304 Cup and League appearances, and figured in ten different positions, including goalkeeper. He brought to his game a combination of the footwork and ball-skills of an inside-forward and the creative ability of a half-back, and it was his fine sense of positional play which made him look unhurried, even under pressure. A wasted pass by John Carey used to bring gasps of disbelief from spectators.

As well as his League and Cup honours John Carey was capped 29 times by the Republic of Ireland and played 7 times for Northern Ireland. He also captained the Rest of Europe team against

Great Britain in 1947 and was voted Player of the Year in 1949 and Sportsman of the Year in 1950.

But there is more to the man than mere facts and figures: his qualities on and off the field made him a natural leader, and very early on in their acquaintance Matt Busby saw him as the man he wanted to be the captain of the side he was going to manage.

When John Carey decided to retire in 1953, the directors of Manchester United invited him to the boardroom to express their appreciation, and the last sentence of the minute which recorded the tribute said everything about John Carey's contribution to the Manchester United story: 'By his outstanding personality as a true sportsman, the honours he had won as an international and in club matches, he had covered his career with glory and set a shining example to all who follow him.'

At the time I retired [John recalled] I knew deep down I could have played on for another two or three years. I was thirty-four when I finished playing but I was very fit and Matt would have liked me to continue at Old Trafford. But I looked at the tremendous career I'd had ... the six years of the war had taken a lot away from it, but from 1946–53 I'd had seven years at the top and I'd set a standard and I felt that the only way I'm going is down. I also felt it wasn't quite fair for all the people who looked up to me and wanted to tell everybody what a good player I was. I didn't think I was going to enjoy playing Second or Third Division football. I looked at Manchester United and thought, There's no way I can keep my place in this team ... or maybe only on reputation, and I didn't want to keep it on that.

In 1953 United were so well equipped that you could see the club bulging with talent ... Duncan Edwards, Roger Byrne, Dennis Viollet, David Pegg, Bill Whelan, Jeff Whitefoot ... they were all there by then. The whole club was all geared up. Unfortunately there wasn't a position for me at the club ... Jimmy Murphy was there doing a tremendous job, Walter Crickmer and Les Olive were there on the admin. side. What Matt wanted was for me to stay on as a player and do a bit of coaching with the youngsters and gradually work my way into that side of the club's activities – but rightly or wrongly I decided that I would try my luck and see if I could make my name as a manager and as it happened I went to Blackburn Rovers where I had six tremendously happy and successful years.

John Carey did make a name for himself and, although his

career as a manager was slightly shorter than as a player, his list of achievements is no less impressive.

Five years after taking over at Blackburn he led them back into the First Division in 1958. By 1963 he was managing Leyton Orient and he brought them into the First Division for the first time in their history. Then Nottingham Forest enjoyed one of their best seasons ever under his leadership: in 1967 they were declared runners-up in the First Division and reached the semi-finals of the FA Cup.

Eventually John returned to Blackburn as general manager, then team manager in 1969. But during the past fifteen years even the peerless John Carey had suffered the indignity of being sacked three times, usually (and classically) without much warning. Publicly he accepted his fate with the dignified and philosophical calmness of the truly wise man, and even today maintains that he has no regrets and bears no malice.

In 1971, John left football management and at the age of fifty-two began work with a textile machine company, eventually retiring in February 1984 from a post in the Treasurer's Office of Trafford Borough Council.

John and his wife Margaret now live in Bramhall, Cheshire, with time at last to enjoy the lively company of their four children and eight grandchildren. When he is able John escapes to the golf-course to indulge his passion for the game where he now plays off a handicap of eleven.

All the world loves a story teller, and John has a deep fund of footballing stories which he retails in his famous gentle brogue. His hilarious account of a supposedly diet-conscious director of a club John once managed, ordering a lethal-sized meal in a restaurant is matched only by another which begins, 'I always suspected this goalkeeper of having dodgy eyesight and it was confirmed after a night match when I saw him feeling his way up the steps of our team bus ...' When he was a player he often led the team sing-songs, and his rendition of 'Patsy Fagan' in a rich baritone was always very popular. But he is still full of admiration for the less musical efforts of one of their party. 'One evening around the piano this chap was asked to have a go. He cleared his throat and began ... and it was only when he got to the chorus did we all realise that Matt Busby was singing "Glasgow Belongs to Me"!'

Settled in his armchair John Carey looked back on the best days of the 1948 team:

I used to enjoy watching our attack because I was standing at the back and could see all they were doing ... the forward line was tremendous and they could all really play. Defenders realised that they didn't have to mark just one or two of the forwards, *all* United's forwards needed watching. Sometimes it would be Charlie Mitten who'd get three goals, sometimes it'd be Jack Rowley or Johnny Morris or Stan Pearson, and while Jimmy Delaney didn't perhaps score as many as the others, he made lots ... they were all pretty formidable.

As players we weren't perhaps as showbiz as players are today – we were just professional footballers in a very successful team. Our wages were modest and fixed, with a minimum and maximum amount. However outstanding you were you got the same as every other player in your team.

We enjoyed our football tremendously, more so than now. I don't think today's players get the same enjoyment from playing ... they have so much more pressure on them today. But make no mistake, they're ten times fitter and better organised.

The crowds were marvellous and tolerant and they were also there to enjoy themselves ... there was always pressure in our day of course, but we were playing for the team, and not so much for the money. Football in our day was more entertainment, possibly because we made more mistakes. There were more goals for the simple reason that goalkeepers weren't as good as they are today. And Matt Busby always encouraged flair. Sometimes it went wrong and he was always watching in case it did go wrong, but he always gave you the authority to express yourself on the field.

If I had to make comparisons between all the post-war sides at Old Trafford I'd have to say I don't think the 1948 team was nearly as good as the 'Babes'. When the 1948 side played, having regard to the conditions and facilities of the time, we were outstanding and everything we achieved reflected that, but we wouldn't have lived with the 'Babes'. We had six or seven really good players but the 'Babes' had eleven and many more beside. They had power, strength, ability, skill – not just in certain places, but everywhere.

After the crash I went to Munich to see them and I kept in touch with Jimmy Murphy and we discussed one or two things but really there wasn't very much I could do, much as I wanted to help. I saw their first match back against Sheffield Wednesday and it was a very emotional game for us all.

# John Aston

On the morning of 20 December 1972, an announcement from Old Trafford declared that Manchester United had sacked its manager Frank O'Farrell, as well as trainer Malcolm Musgrove, and the chief scout and coach John Aston. For John Aston it was a particularly bitter moment as it ended thirty-four years' connection with the club.

John's last full season as a player (1953–54) had also been full of disappointments. From the outset he had been out-of-form, then dropped; in October he had fought his way back into the first team but had then broken his arm, and he could only watch from the sidelines as many of Busby's next young generation of players began to establish themselves as first-teamers. In that season the luckless John Aston only made twelve senior appearances.

I played in the last League game of the 1953–54 season and we'd drawn 2–2 with Sheffield United (I got our first goal I remember) and we were all in the bath arguing about whether or not we were going to be able to pick up a bonus for being fourth in the League Championship table. I'd felt very drained during the game, and for some time after: then I went on holiday with the family to Jersey and I was coughing a lot.

When I got back the doctors diagnosed TB and the club asked me to go into a private clinic. Thinking of the expense I asked the club doctor to negotiate a bed for me in the Sanatorium at Abergele belonging to Manchester Corporation. I suppose there's a bit of a contrast with the way today's players would be treated ... when I went to Abergele I got off the train and had to walk miles up a hill lugging a big suitcase! I was in that hospital for seventeen months, and of course I never played a League game again.

It was only at the end of September 1954 that the *Manchester Evening News* revealed that John Aston was undergoing 'special treatment' in a North Wales hospital. As a tribute to his outstanding service to the club which he had joined as a 16-year-old, it was proposed by the directors of United to re-sign John for another season on full pay, which was then £14 a week. However, he refused, because he thought it was more or less a gesture of charity. After much persuasion by club officials and friends, John eventually agreed to re-sign, on condition that his wages were reduced to £9 a week. His pride wouldn't allow him to accept full money while still a bed-ridden patient.

John Aston was then granted a testimonial match which was played on 25 April 1956, a few days after United had been declared the season's First Division Champions (for the fourth time in their history). The game featured the current United team playing against an All Star XI which included Frank Swift, Tommy Docherty, Tom Finney and Nat Lofthouse, and some of John Aston's old team-mates like John Carey, Henry Cockburn, Jack Rowley, Stan Pearson and Johnny Morris.

It was a great night of football and a chance for the crowd of just over 40,000 to say thanks to a popular and loyal clubman who had made 290 League and Cup appearances for Manchester United, won seventeen England caps, and was the club's first World Cup player. He had abundant skills in every department of the game, and the club would always be indebted to him for sacrificing his regular left-back selection for England when he took over as United's centre-forward after an injury to Jack Rowley at the end of 1950.

United continued to keep in touch with John after his testimonial game, and Jimmy Murphy, anxious not to lose the skill and experience of a player of Aston's calibre, asked him to do some scouting and coaching for the club. John thus became one of United's indispensable back-room staff and in the 1960s travelled miles to watch likely prospects and spent hours coaching and advising young players. He was around to watch at close quarters how the blend of Law, Best and Charlton helped to create one of the most remarkable and exciting teams of the 1960s, culminating in the European Cup win of 1968. It was also in that match where he watched his own son John play the game of his life on United's left-wing in the thrilling 4-1 victory over Benfica.

John Aston was then appointed chief scout in 1970 following the retirement of Joe Armstrong. Two years later United were in turmoil. The retirement of Matt Busby and the subsequent attempts of Wilf McGuinness and Frank O'Farrell to cope with the slide in United's Cup and League fortunes, against a background complicated by the capricious behaviour of George Best, created more tension than had ever before been experienced at Old Trafford.

In such a situation there was little room for sentiment and the almost brutal speed with which the United board acted on that

December morning in 1972 denied John Aston and Manchester United time for a proper leave-taking of each other.

Understandably, it is an episode which John Aston is reluctant to linger over, and he much prefers to talk about happier days at the club. 'Let's just say I was a little disillusioned ... but even so United are still the number one love of my life after my family.'

After many years in Glossop, John Aston (a real countryman at heart), and his wife Lilian have moved back to Manchester. The Astons have two daughters Lilian and Jill, and of course son John, who has two children Mark and Faith. The Aston name might continue to live on in the game: by all accounts young Mark shows real promise ...

A distance of forty years, and the hundreds of games he has played and watched cannot dim his memories of that famous 1948 team.

We blended well and played for each other, and the confidence in the team was amazing. It was a good blend because we had one winger, Jimmy Delaney, who was direct, and the other winger Charlie Mitten was good on the ball; Stan Pearson was the general ... he could play one-touch football but he could also dwell on it; Jack Rowley was very strong and direct; Johnny Morris was a great individualist ... he could do it on his own ... he was a strong little devil ... we only had to give the ball to the forwards and they'd do the rest.

Busby always used to preach to us to hold on during the first quarter of an hour. 'They'll come at you, and come at you', he'd say. Lots of games were like that, particularly at the beginning of the season ... it was all helter-skelter. 'After the first fifteen minutes or so,' he used to say, 'is when you can start playing your football.' His maxim was always 'Keep playing football'.

Busby didn't have a ready-made team, as some used to say at the time. Most of the players were there, but they needed organising, and that's what he did. He was a good player himself when he became United's manager ... he was only in his mid-thirties. He could have been in the side ... actually, he would have made an ideal right-half for us.

The financial side of football used to puzzle me at the time. As winning finalists we were only paid what we were entitled to (our wage and a £20 bonus) plus some tickets.

We organised a players' brochure which made a tiny profit for us, but these things were in their infancy then. We should have had somebody to organise it all for us, like they do today. The lads got together and we

asked the Press for a donation to the brochure and they refused ... their
attitude was 'You need us as much as we need you'.

So on press day none of us wanted to be photographed and I thought
that was rotten for the public. But all the time the Press had been selling
thousands of team photographs and action photos of individuals and so
on, at a couple of bob a time, and we weren't getting anything ... so we
were right in my opinion.

I say good luck to players who are getting big money nowadays,
although I do think that the sizes of some of the wages we've been
reading about over breakfast over the last few months are ridiculous.
... It's too much for playing football ... it's getting out of all proportion.

Football today is too commercialised ... the game itself as a spectacle
isn't as good as it used to be, is it? I try not to be biased ... but I haven't
watched a game for a couple of seasons now ... there's no pleasure ...
if there had been I wouldn't have stopped going. The games are drag-
ging, and I only used to enjoy fifteen out of the ninety minutes ...
they've killed it with negative coaching. I don't even watch it on TV
... if there's something good on the other side, I'll have that on.

I was about twenty-seven when I got my first cap ... I got seventeen
altogether ... so I suppose I did well having lost six seasons, as the
others had, through the war. I'd have liked to have got a cap as a
centre-forward ... that would have been final proof that I'd made it as
a forward. But at the time I went playing up front I was enjoying my
football, but I wasn't fully fit ... I had knee trouble, having damaged
my cartilage in my second or third game as centre-forward in 1950 and
I played the rest of the season limping. I took over as centre-forward for
United when Jack Rowley was injured, so maybe that did mess up my
chance of keeping my left-back place for England ... but I enjoyed
playing centre-forward better than playing full-back! I wasn't full of
nerves like I used to be a few years before. I was confident and I used to
think, I'm going to have a go ... I really enjoyed it. As a full-back in
that 1948 side I was a spectator half the time ... sometimes I only used
to get an occasional touch of the ball ... but at centre-forward you were
on the move all the time.

Walter Winterbottom did come and look at me once as a centre-forward when we played Birmingham in the sixth round in 1951. But I was
limping from the cartilage trouble ... I used to run with a limp in those
days. We were beaten 1–0 and I should have scored that day against Gil
Merrick. Late in the game the ball came down and it just needed nodding
in and I was on the six-yard line watching it come down ... I thought
Merrick was bound to come and get it but he didn't ... I realised too
late ... I should have scored. Actually, I shouldn't have scored ... the
bloody goalie should have got the ball. By the time I realised he hadn't

come it was too late to do anything about it. It was a chance gone ...
and it must have looked bad from the stands.

I played in that England game when we were beaten 1-0 by USA in
the 1950 World Cup. It was a diabolical result ... we should have won
six or seven-one. They scored a fluke goal, but we murdered them. The
ground was atrocious ... it was like a sponge ... the ref. was diabolical
... but you can't make excuses ... we should have beaten them. I was
dying to get up front ... Morty was clean through I remember, and this
centre-half, Colombo I think he was called ... he used to play with
gloves on ... dived at Morty in the area ... the ref. gave a free-kick well
outside the area! The Press crucified us, of course, and rightly so!

I've given this question of comparing the great United sides a lot of
thought over the years, because I've seen them all through, so to speak.
I think the 1948 side was the best side of all to watch. I think the team
that was killed at Munich would have matured into a better side than
the 1948 side ... we were eleven players, but in that pre-Munich side
there were twenty-two not eleven players who could play. Matt Busby
could draw on two players for each position, like either Pegg and Scanlon
on the left wing, and either Morgans or Berry on the right. The year
before the Munich crash Jeff Whitefoot couldn't get in the second team,
and he'd been in the first team as a 16-year-old in about 1950! Busby
had Eddie Colman, Duncan Edwards, Mark Jones, Jackie Blanchflower,
Freddie Goodwin ... every one of them class half-backs. Jeff Bent was
a sterling full-back ... he could have walked into any side, but Roger
Byrne kept him out.

I was in the back of my little shop when a pal of mine rang up about
the Munich crash ... and I knew by his voice that it was serious as soon
as he spoke. I knew they were flying back that day ... I knew what had
happened even before he told me.

That same night I vowed that through God's grace my son would go
on to become a first-teamer and I'm proud of the fact that he did so, the
only son of a 'Forty-eighter' to make the grade, as it were. Lots of players
dream of their sons becoming pros and I'm proud to know that young
John and I are, to my knowledge, the only father and son to have won
First Division Championship medals with the same club. It was a pity
he broke his leg within weeks of his team winning that European Cup
final.

# John Anderson

John Anderson will always be remembered at Old Trafford for
his story-book debut for the team, and for the goal he scored four

months later at Wembley in the 1948 Cup final to seal United's 4–2 victory over Blackpool.

His fourteen appearances in the following season (the last being an unhappy one at inside-right against Wolves in the first of the two semi-final replays which United eventually lost) perhaps reflected the precariousness of his place in the team. Henry Cockburn then Tommy Lowrie played at right-half for the remainder of the season and John began to realise that his chances of sustained senior football at Old Trafford were receding fast.

In October 1950, Third Division Nottingham Forest, quick to see the value of this stocky and strong-running half-back, paid £9,000 for him.

It was right for me to go when I did. Once Johnny Morris had gone I suppose we all thought, That's the end of the team, anybody could go now. I can still remember the boss saying, 'You don't have to go Johnny' ... but I decided to. I got a full gratuity because I'd been with the club five years ... it was £750 less tax which was a lot of money in those days. I'd just remarried and the money furnished the house which Nottingham Forest had provided for us ... and I bought a little car ... and I had a bit left over.

I had a good three years in Nottingham. Billy Walker was building a pretty fair team there and they played the same attacking sort of football that I was used to at United and I fitted in a treat there.

A couple of years after I'd gone to Nottingham we were promoted to the Second Division. I stayed with them another year then was put on the transfer list: I was thirty-one years old then. I had lots of offers but I eventually chose to go to Peterborough: Jack Fairbrother had taken over at Peterborough which was non-League then. He came to see me ... he shouldn't have done but he did. I'd been on £14 a week at Forest, but Jack promised that he'd put me on £11 a week for only being part-time ... so that, plus my wages in the job I was found down there, made me better off than if I'd been playing as a full-time pro, even in the First Division!

I had fifteen very happy years at Peterborough: as a player, trainer and coach under Jack Fairbrother, then George Swindin, then Jimmy Hagan. There were quite a few United old boys around the area ... Johnny Morris was just around the corner at Corby as manager, and I used to see quite a lot of Charlie Mitten who by then was manager at Mansfield.

John Anderson moved back to Manchester with his family in 1969 and found a job as a night telephonist with the GPO. A friendly and hospitable man, whose name is probably better known than his face, John still has a sharp memory for names and incidents, prompted by an old briefcase full of photographs and cuttings, mementoes of his years as a footballer.

That 1948 side was a good side that tried to entertain by playing attacking football. We all enjoyed changing positions during the course of the game. If Johnny Carey went past me with the ball, I dropped back to cover his position. I knew that when I had the ball and was going forward, Johnny Morris would either be taking men away from me by making diagonal runs, or he'd be staying back to keep an eye on the inside-left I was supposed to be marking. Jimmy Delaney made my job very easy. Just before my first game he said, 'When you see me running past the full-back you just get the ball in front of me, and I'll make it into a good pass' ... he really was a great player.

And that summer of 1948 we used to play cricket matches for charity all over the area. John Aston and me used to vie with each other for tenth and eleventh places in the team. I bought a full set of whites and said to myself, 'This will definitely get me a place in the team!'

And we used to take the Cup to the matches and to hospitals and dances and so on ... that Cup's been under all sorts of strange beds I can tell you! There's all sorts of security people around it now but in those days whoever finished up with it at the end of the evening took it home with him and brought it back in next day.

Very few of John Anderson's generation of players made enough money out of the game to live in the style of today's professionals, and once his playing days were over, it was back to work.

I'm still a night telephonist and I suppose I've a couple of years more to go before I retire, but I'll keep going as long as I can ... who can afford to pack in work nowadays!

The family are still in the area: Joyce and I have three children, and of course there's my eldest son John, who was one year old when my first wife died, but Joyce brought him up as her own. John's living in Peterborough with his wife and three daughters: he showed real promise as a player and got as far as Peterborough's 'A' team, but as his trainer and his dad I was much harder on him than on most of the other players ... looking back he might have done better to have moved to another club and not have had me on at him all the time!

We've got nine grandchildren altogether and they keep us active: otherwise I like to keep the garden tidy and watch a bit of TV. When we

first moved back to Manchester we used to live in a house right next to
Maine Road but I never went to a game ... do you know there's nothing
about football today that excites me, and I'd certainly rather watch a
good film now than 'Match of the Day'.

I have to smile when I hear of the money players are getting today.
Have you seen what some of them make on their testimonial games?
They gave me a testimonial game when I left Peterborough and we
invited Stan Matthews to turn out, which he did of course for the usual
£100 fee. When they'd paid all the other bills I got a cheque for £98!

Some of those who became known as the Babes were just juniors when
I was about to leave Old Trafford, but anybody could see how good they
were going to be. When the news of the crash came through I was at
work ... in the despatch department of an engineering firm owned by
one of Peterborough's directors. Like lots of others I just could not
believe the news at first, just couldn't believe it ...


# Allenby Chilton

Allenby Chilton was always a player's player, and must take responsibility for inspiring a little lad from Collyhurst who dreamed
that some day he would also become a famous United player. 'He
was one of my heroes,' Nobby Stiles said, 'I used to sit on my
dad's shoulders and watch him ... I used to call him Sir Allenby
de Trafford ... he was a mighty centre-half.'

Matt Busby, notoriously reluctant to compare the merits of any
of United's great post-war sides, also showed that Chilton was a
manager's player when he allowed himself to pick a United All-
Star XI for his *Manchester United Scrap Book*, published in 1980.

Busby noted four contenders for the number 5 shirt: Bill
Foulkes, Mark Jones, Jackie Blanchflower and Allenby Chilton,
his eventual choice. 'Nothing seemed to beat him in the air, and
the longer he played, the better he seemed to get', Busby wrote.
'Chilton was truly a stalwart, and I don't mind confessing that
when I realised he was coming towards the close of his career, I
worried a bit about his successor. Even while he was still playing
and I was bringing in youngsters around him, he nursed them
along, and I knew I could rely on him to make it easier for them
while he was still coping with his own job.'

When Allenby read of Busby's praises he chuckled and said:

I always knew he had good judgement. He always used to let us have our say when things weren't going right ... he knew just when to ask us. He knew we had to sort out the difficulties on the field because we were the players. I remember once when goals weren't being scored and we had a team discussion and I decided to speak up. 'We've got two first-class full-backs,' I said, 'but when the ball comes to them they want to take the lace out and then beat the winger. I think the full-backs should be hitting the ball much quicker ... our forwards are moving into position and are free from the defenders, but they're not getting the ball ... we're making it hard for them.' And I remember Johnny Carey, with his pipe and his cap and this dry sense of humour he had, saying to me, 'Is that what you want us to do then, Allenby?' And I said 'Aye, we've got five forwards up front who can catch pigeons.' It seemed to work because the goals began to flow again. It was really great to watch those forwards switching positions ... it was a team with a good blend and fire and we all wanted the ball.

Allenby and his wife Anne now live in quiet retirement near Sunderland, with a framed photograph in the hall of him lined up with the 1948 Cup side and shaking hands with King George VI as the only visible memento of his life as a professional foot-baller. And like Jimmy Delaney, his old team-mate, Allenby is troubled by an arthritic hip, 'but on a good day I can usually manage a walk by the sea and a pint in the local'.

After a total of 353 appearances for Manchester United, Al-lenby left Old Trafford in March 1955 – in his last three full seasons at United he had played in every League match.

I left Old Trafford to become player-manager of Grimsby. It was frus-trating and a bit lonely being a manager. You rely on your players out there ... if things are going badly you start to lose sleep and it starts affecting your health, so after four years with them (and we'd gone up into the Second Division while I was there) I knew it was time to pack it in.

We had a pub in York for a while, but it meant we were working for the brewery; then I looked after Wigan FC for eight or nine months – they were non-League at that time. After that we moved up here and took a little shop, but after five years or so we were finding that local supermarkets were taking away a lot of our business, so we got out. I got a job at the local steel works and I worked there happily for fourteen years, booking in raw materials like steel plates and so on, and I took early retirement in 1981.

Was he disappointed that in his long career with one of the best clubs in the First Division he played only twice for England?

I wasn't disappointed ... annoyed is a better word. I played my first international against Ireland in October 1950 ... we won 4-2 and I can remember the team: Bert Williams; Alf Ramsey, John Aston; Billy Wright, myself, Jimmy Dickinson; Stan Matthews, Wilf Mannion, John Lee, Eddie Baily and Bobby Langton. At half-time Walter Winterbottom said, 'You're playing well, Allenby', but he didn't need to tell me ... you always know when you're playing well.

Charlie Buchan then wrote a report on the game and he said how well I'd played, and how the position, long overdue, should be mine. But the next game I was out and I didn't play for another year ... it was against France at Highbury and we drew 2-2, and after that I never played for England again.

But in 1954 I was called to train with the England party at Roehampton. I was in the peak of condition and playing well for United, but I found out later that I was just being used in practice games to offer a bit of resistance to forwards like Nat Lofthouse and Ivor Broadis, there was never any intention to include me in the final party. When they left for a European tour they took Sid Owen of Second Division Luton Town as England's centre-half.

They were beaten 1-0 by Yugoslavia, 7-1 by Hungary, drew 4-4 with Belgium, won 2-0 against Switzerland (and Billy Wright was playing centre-half by then) and finally lost 2-4 to Uruguay in Basle. Roger Byrne and Tommy Taylor were on the tour, and Roger was furious when he got back. 'Allen, you should have been with us,' he told me, 'you should have been the centre-half.'

But for all his strength in the tackle and power in the air, Allen Chilton also had the reputation at Old Trafford for giving away free-kicks and penalties. As the classic stopper centre-half, his was often the last and characteristically vigorous tackle in the penalty-area. As Matt Busby once wrote, 'Allen was sometimes unlucky ... whenever he made a mistake, the team paid for it.'

Agreed, but I'll tell you something else, [Allen rejoined] being a centre-half wasn't the easiest position on the field. I remember once being full of cold, and Matt Busby asked Johnny Carey to play centre-half. When he came off he said, 'Allenby, you can keep that position ... the centres are coming in from all angles ... you've got to watch the ball and the man, and you're getting knocked all over the place.' You see, as a full-back he always knew where the touch-line was ... it was like a reference point. But the middle of the field was always full of forwards cutting in from all sides, and he wasn't used to it. I tell you, if the centre-forward scored, I took it personally ... maybe that was my trouble!

The critics on the terraces got to him once, and at the beginning of the 1949–50 season he asked to put on the transfer list. But Allenby Chilton was never one to walk away from difficulties ... after a few weeks he was off the list and back in the team. Two years later he became United's captain and Busby's right-hand man on the field.

Time has perhaps dulled the memories of the more painful criticisms, but Allenby did bring to mind one particular incident. 'We never normally bothered when the crowd was getting at us. Somebody once threw an apple at Charlie Mitten. He picked it up, took a bite out of it, and threw it back. Man, the crowd loved it!'

Did he think today's players suffer similar sorts of pressure?

It makes me laugh when they talk about pressure today. If there is any pressure, it's caused by the weight of the bags of money they're taking to the bank every week. The pressure would be on if they had to get up at quarter to six to go to bloody work every morning. The rewards are all out of proportion, and there isn't the happiness in the game that there used to be. They don't know how lucky they are. It's healthy life ... it's work you like to do and you're being paid for keeping fit. You get every medical attention ... you're paid in your holidays, you travel ... everything's arranged. There were no fancy clubs and fast cars and such in those days. When we'd finished playing on a Saturday, Jimmy Delaney and I used to go up to the Seymour Grove Hotel for a pint. I used to admire Matt Busby for that ... he'd never stop us from having a beer, because he knew it relaxed us.

The money in the game now is unbelievable. Apparently, even players who play in somebody's testimonial are asking huge fees. I can remember four or five of us piling into Johnny Carey's car to go to somebody's testimonial ... a lad who'd played eleven years at Crewe. Joe Mercer was playing as well, I remember. Anyway, the lad got a canny gate and was overjoyed that we'd turned up and after the game he said to us, 'How much do you want for playing?' And Johnny Carey says, 'Do we want anything, lads?' And we all said 'No.'

There's obviously a different atmosphere in the game now, nobody seems to be playing with much happiness. It's all serious now, because of the money, I think. They seem to be worried that they're going to do something wrong, and that's when they do things wrong.

Allenby Chilton is still the gentle giant he was thirty-five years ago, and his laughter and laconic North-Eastern wit still punctuates every conversation. He also looks back on his time in Manchester with great affection, and is always eager to know all the latest news from Old Trafford.

The memories of his last months with the club are happy ones, inevitably tinged with regrets. As a central defender of immense experience he proudly watched as the younger players around him, full of life and energy, established themselves as United's new generation of heroes.

As everybody knows, the game against Huddersfield at the end of October 1953 marked the end of our old side. Busby put in Blanchflower and Viollet and Duncan Edwards ... there was only me and Jack Rowley left of the old-timers. The referee was Bob Wood who actually lives just down the road here and I'll always remember him saying to me after the game, 'Hey, Allen, you've got some really good youngsters here.' I was still managing to hold my place, and Matt knew that as long as I was there he could try out a new defender and maybe a full-back because I could still cover them. Duncan was a good player ... and Roger Byrne ... perhaps he was a bit moody sometimes ... but he was a good clean kicker of a ball, and he had terrific speed. I used to play war with him on the field. If a ball was hit down the wing, instead of getting up and heading it, he'd just duck and let it go over his head and run back because he knew he had the speed. I used to say to him, 'One of these days, Roger, you'll meet someone faster than yourself!' Then came Munich, of course ... what a tragedy ... we never saw the best of those lads.

## Henry Cockburn

The game which effectively ended Henry Cockburn's career with Manchester United was the friendly against Kilmarnock on Wednesday, 28 October 1953, a game arranged to celebrate the installation of floodlights at the ground.

Henry scored the first goal with a twenty-five yard-shot which one report unkindly described as 'speculative', but tragedy finally struck when his legendary heading ability against taller opposition forwards led to a terrible injury.

'Floodlights weren't all that common in those days,' he began, 'and I went up for a ball with a Kilmarnock player ... the lights were in my eyes as I jumped ... our heads banged together and that was it, a broken jaw. Duncan Edwards took my place for the rest of the game and I never really got it back off him.'

In fact, Henry played only another five first-team games during the rest of the season, spending all the other Saturdays in the reserve side. He realised that Matt Busby's head had to rule his heart, and that he could never win his place back on reputation or sentiment.

Henry Cockburn was to play only once more for Manchester United, in the next season against Wolverhampton Wanderers. A 21-year-old full-back called Ian Greaves made his debut for United in that game and their paths were to cross many times in the next twenty years. 'Yes, in my last game for United we were beaten 4–2: I "scored" their last goal as an own goal when Jimmy Hancocks smacked the ball against my legs and it was deflected into our goal. What a way to end your last game!'

A fortnight later Henry was transferred to Second Division Bury and joined up again with his former team-mate Stan Pearson. Never again would the Old Trafford faithful see their popular little defender tame the biggest and the best of the opposition, and Henry's 13 England caps and 243 appearances for United bear sufficient testament to this skilful and tenacious player.

Henry spent a couple of seasons with Bury then moved on to non-League Peterborough (where he linked up with another old team-mate John Anderson), and Corby Town. He then returned home to Ashton, his footballing days apparently over, where he opened a grocery shop, but Jack Rowley, who by then was manager of Oldham Athletic, got in touch and invited Henry to be the club's trainer. A few years later he moved a short distance across the Pennines to Huddersfield to work as their senior team coach under his old United colleague, Ian Greaves. Once he had finally retired from the game, Henry got a job in a sports goods firm in Huddersfield, where he still works, 'and I'll keep working for them as long as they want me'.

Today, Henry Cockburn lives near Huddersfield, 'growing old slowly but gracefully'; sadly, his marriage of twenty-five years ended quite recently in divorce, but he keeps in regular touch with his five children, two of whom have moved away from the area: a son in the Fleet Air Arm and a daughter who lives and works in London. In spite of the mixed fortunes which life has

given him, Henry has the twinkling eyes of a man still full of life
and energy which is seen at its best when he tells his stories about
his United days, complete with actions and imitations:

I live by myself now, but I've got my health and some great memories
to look back on. I used to like gardening and going to the pictures but
I don't do any of that now. I was never one for the bright lights, always
a bit careful. Just after the war my wages were £14 a week in the season
and £12 out of season, it was good money at the time. After a couple of
years I bought myself a little car. I was beginning to be recognised
wherever I went. I was so involved in football I thought, I've got to look
after myself, so consequently I had to cut myself off from going out with
the lads. So nearly every night I used to go to the pictures, 6.30 to 9.30,
then home. That was it ... I just lived for my football.

Religion is and always was a great help to me. I've never sought it but
it's always been there, you know. I used to go to the sportsmen's services
with people like Frank Swift and Bert Whalley ... I'd probably read a
lesson and Swifty would give a short address ... I used to look forward
to those services.

I loved to travel and in my time at Old Trafford we had two tours of
America in the close season ... six weeks at a time ... Busby loved to go
there because he had relatives over yonder. We had some great times
over there ... We met Jerry Lewis and Bing Crosby, Bob Hope and
Richard Montalban. They had the equivalent over there to Wee Georgie
Wood called Walter Tetley ... he had an English mother I believe. When
we were in Hollywood he invited us over to his house. It was a beautiful
day. There was a swimming pool and lots to eat and drink. We were there
all day, swimming and relaxing. In the evening there was a party, with
a bar and dancing. I picked up with a big six-footer, 'Big Mo' they called
her. The lads were always kidding about me and her. It was very warm
and sultry and I was drinking Coke and there must have been something
else in it. I began to feel a bit dodgy so I went for a bit of a stroll in the
dark. Tetley lived in a sort of ranch house and he kept horses, but as I
was walking up and down in the dark taking deep breaths I got worse
and fell over. So I stumbled back to where the lights of the party were
and I could see Stan Pearson standing near the open door. I whispered
'Stan! Stan!' He came over and said, 'What's up?' I said, 'I'm not very
well ... I've had too much to drink.' I felt like dying. So they sat me
down and gave me black coffee. We all then went back to our hotel in
taxis, to the Plaza on Sunset Boulevard in Hollywood. I was in a taxi
with Tom Curry and Matt Busby. They sat me in the middle. 'Now
Henry,' said Matt Busby 'when we get to the hotel, try and look respect-

able.' They put me between them and we walked across the lobby shoulder to shoulder ... them just about holding me up!

Why were we such a good side? We linked together as a team ... we were comrades. We were a good side ... we played some good stuff ... we were so enthusiastic and full of running. The way we played was never to stop the ball. Busby used to say, 'The ball is round to go round, so don't stop it, keep it rolling.' They call it one-touch nowadays ... that's how we played it then. The game was so fluent, you never saw the ball stopped like it is now. Players used to run into positions ... it was bloody great to watch from the back. In the days when we had wingers there was no finer sight than to see them running with the ball, taking players on, going past them, crossing balls, inside-forwards coming in and hitting the ball ... wham! They just don't seem to play with width any more.

We were a very close team really. That summer of 1948 we got a cricket team together to show people the Cup. Hundreds of people used to pay to watch us and we got officials to take the Cup around the ground. We played all over the area ... Levenshulme, Longsight, somewhere up near Rochdale. Charlie, Stan, Jack Rowley and Johnny Morris were good cricketers. I once wore my international cap when I was fielding but the lads said, 'Put it away, you big-head', so I had to!

I always felt that it was a shame that people like Stan and Jack had relatively short international careers because I don't think they ever played as well for England as they used to for United and it was the War that took a lot of time out of their lives. They would have had longer international careers than I had, I'm sure. There were a few players competing for the left-half position ... me, Harry Johnston of Blackpool and Jimmy Dickinson of Portsmouth, and even Billy Wright. I took over from Joe Mercer of course ... As I said I was a bit surprised to get a cap so soon because I hadn't been in the game ten minutes ... I was still working as well – I got in because they were so short of players straight after the War.

In those days you got £20 a match and a cap and probably they would give you your shirt. I remember one occasion playing for England at Highbury against Switzerland and there was me and Johnny Hancocks (who was about five foot nothing) ... we were the two smallest players in the team and the shirts were made all the same length, so the two of us stood there with our shirt laps down to our knees ... so we had to turn them up and the England trainer who was Jimmy Trotter from Charlton had to put strips of Elastoplast on the hems to keep them up!

We all had set roles and if you look at the record books you'll see it was rare for us defenders to score goals. When Johnny Aston played behind me he used to like going down the flanks a lot and I used to have to say, 'Hey, bloody hell, Asto, where are you going? Get back behind me and look after that winger!'

Most of the 'Busby Babes' as they called them were still apprentices when I was nearing the end of my time at Old Trafford. They were all good lads. Roger (Byrne) played behind me a couple of times, in place of John Aston. I always thought the 1948 side was a good one because we'd been together for so long ... maybe the 'Babes' would have been even better if they'd had the time to develop together.

I was with Peterborough United at the time of the Munich crash. It was a non-League club then, of course. I had a job as well. I was the first professional player they'd signed - it made all the headlines. I worked for the local paper in Peterborough ... I used to make out the placard headlines for them, you know, for those boards outside newsagents' shops. They supplied me with a little car and I used to take these placards around to the selling points. It was a great little job after I'd finished training.

The sub-editor used to phone the news down to me. I was just writing out placards like 'Local Girl Gets Married' and 'Man Found Stealing in Supermarket' and the phone rang. 'Henry,' he said, 'there's something happened here. Get this down ... "Manchester United Plane Crash ... Many Feared Dead".' I had to make these bills out and take them round. Then it was coming through the tele-type every so often ... who was dead and who was injured. I went to a couple of funerals up here in Manchester ... it was awful ... awful.

# Jimmy Delaney

The financial rewards in soccer at the highest levels today allow a player to save and invest for the time when his footballing days are over. When it was time for Jimmy Delaney's generation of professional footballers to retire, most of them, unskilled and unqualified in anything except soccer, became ordinary working men. The maximum wage system also ensured that even Jimmy Delaney, a Scottish international and one of the five gems in Manchester United's glittering 1948 forward line, took nothing out of the game except medals and cups - and a rich store of memories.

But Jimmy Delaney feels no jealousy or resentment against today's players, some of whom earn in a week what he did in a year, even when he was at the peak of his career.

'Good luck to them, I say. We enjoyed ourselves ... it was a

great time to be in the game. I've a lot to look back on and that's
reward enough. Do you know, if I'd have been given a pound for
every handshake from people who've come up to me and said,
"Hello, Jimmy, how are you doing?", I'd have been a millionaire
today. Nobody can take that away from me.'

Today Jimmy is as dapper and cheerful as ever, troubled only
by the arthritis which prevents him from taking the long daily
walks he used to enjoy so much. He and his wife Anne live in a
neat modern terraced house in Cleland, a small mining village
near Motherwell. Jimmy was born in that same village nearly
seventy years ago, and Joe Jordan, the ex-Leeds and Manchester
United player and Scottish international is another of Cleland's
famous footballing sons.

He looks back on his time in Manchester with obvious pride
and affection.

I soon got to love the city and the people and my time there was very
happy. I still think that Manchester people are the greatest I ever met in
all my travels. We were a great team under a great manager ... we were
a family. Matt Busby never gave you abuse. If you didn't play well he
left it until Monday morning ... he never said anything during or after
the game or at half-time. He'd see you in the office, just the two of you
and you'd sort it out. He'd always say, 'Is there anything bothering you
... have you any worries?' A good long chat and you'd got everything
sorted out.

When I went to United the club had very little money and I'm certain
it was Mr Gibson who actually paid my transfer fee out of his own
pocket. I never regretted going over the border to play in England. It
was after international games when the players got together for a drink
and you got talking to the English players that I was told about the wages
and opportunities and realised how much better I could do in England.

I was part of a great forward line at United, and I think we perfected
the art of interchanging positions in a way no other team had done
before. I was at United for nearly five years and if I had to pick any one
game, out of all the ones I'd played for Celtic and Scotland and Manchester United, it would be the 1948 Cup final at Wembley ... the
atmosphere of an English Cup final is the greatest in the world.

I suppose all Scotsmen want to return home eventually, and even
though I loved being at United I always knew that one day I'd go back.
There was a chance actually that I'd go back to Celtic, but it wasn't to
be. I knew when it was the right time for me to move ... I didn't like

the idea that Matt soon might start picking me for the team out of sentiment.

I knew Scottish football wasn't as fast as English ... so when Aberdeen put in for me I couldn't miss the chance. Matt didn't really want me to go, but there it was. I met Matt a few months later and United were having a bad run and he told me that in one of the team chats about why things were going wrong Stan Pearson had said, 'We're missing the old man ... Jimmy used to give us heart.'

I moved to Falkirk from Aberdeen, then on to Derry, then Cork. I'm in the record books as the only player who's won Scottish, English and Irish Cup winners' medals. I'd won a Scottish Cup medal with Celtic when we beat Aberdeen 2-1 in 1937; an English Cup medal in 1948 of course; a Northern Irish Cup medal with Derry when we beat Glentoran 1-0 in 1954, and I nearly won an Eire Cup medal with Cork in 1956. We were winning 2-0 in that final but then got beat 3-2! The boys used to joke about all these Cup winners' medals and they used to say, 'Have you ever thought of going to Wrexham for a crack at the Welsh Cup!'

I finished up playing for a wee club, Elgin City, in the Highland League in 1957, and that's where my football career ended. My only other

record is an unofficial one for United I think. I've got eleven grand-children ... a full team!

I still watch every Celtic home game, they leave a ticket out for me. It's a very different game today and I think too much coaching has ruined modern football. Good players can read a game, they just need trainers and coaches to get them fit. The likes of Kenny Dalglish, George Best, Bobby Charlton, Denis Law, Duncan Edwards ... no coach in their right minds could tell them how to play ... they were born with an abilty to play the game.

The team that was destroyed at Munich would have lifted everything for the next ten years ... they were so young ... so brilliant. I saw them when they played Bilbao in the 1956-57 season, in that second leg game at Maine Road, when they won 3-0. They'd lost the first leg 3-5. When Johnny Berry scored that third goal ... they say you could hear the noise up here!

When I first heard the news of the crash I was so shaken. I'm going to tell you the truth: I just cried like a baby when I heard about Matt and those young lads. I was working in a factory just down the road from here and we had the radio on all the time. I couldn't concentrate on my work ... I could hardly speak to anyone ... and I couldn't wait to get home at the end of each day. It hit everybody up here just as hard, you know ... that young team was so well-known ... everybody loved them.

## Johnny Morris

Johnny Morris was the first of the triumphant 1948 Cup winning
team to leave Old Trafford. In March 1949 he was sold, swiftly
and unexpectedly, to Derby County for a record fee of £24,000.

Any conflict which existed between himself and Matt Busby
has been forgotten, at least publicly. To this day most of Johnny's
team-mates affirm that United would have reached the Cup final
for the second consecutive year if their inside-right had not left
at such a vital stage in the 1948–49 Cup campaign.

Matt Busby, as always, keeps his own counsel, but his praise
of Johnny Morris's footballing skills is always very fulsome, and
he invariably concludes, 'It was a sad day for me when Johnny
and I found that we had to agree to differ.'

Although Johnny Morris had actually been at Old Trafford for
ten seasons, having signed as a 15-year-old in 1939, it was from
1946 to 1949 that he established himself as a United player. When
he left Old Trafford he had scored 32 goals in 83 appearances,
then continued his career at Derby County where he made 130
appearances and netted 44 goals between 1949 and 1952, as well
as winning three England caps.

Johnny's career as a League player ended at Leicester City
where he spent six seasons and made 206 appearances, and won
two Second Division Championship medals in 1954 and 1957.

Johnny's memories of his playing days centre very much
around his all-too-brief time as a United player:

In 1948 there was no better team in the country than Manchester
United as far as I was concerned. It was great to play with them. We
started off after the War with more or less average players and there were
about six or seven local lads in the side. The best signing in our day that
Matt Busby ever made I think was Jimmy Delaney who was a fabulous
winger to play with. It was a privilege to play as his inside-forward. To
me he read the game so well ... I would say he was the best outside-
right I'd ever played with, apart from someone like Tom Finney. Tom
Finney was the best all-rounder and Stanley Matthews was the best
individual winger and probably the best I've ever seen, but he wasn't as
easy to play with as Jimmy Delaney was. Jimmy was always on his way
before you got the ball. You didn't have to look up ... you could send
it first time. Jimmy didn't hold the game up like Stan did, which suited
our type of play.

Every game was alike ... it was just great to play with the lads we had in the team. I never used to worry about the score when we were on the field ... we just used to *go* for ninety minutes ... if we scored six goals we scored six goals ... if they won one-nowt they won one-nowt.

It was only since the start of the 1947-48 season that we started to really play – all due to one man in my opinion ... Allenby Chilton. He dictated the play. Allen was a hard man ... some of us like Henry Cockburn, Allen Chilton, Jack Warner, myself – we'd go through a brick wall for a £2 bonus. I put it all down to Allen Chilton though, because he dictated the play with his attitude to the game. He wasn't a shirker and he didn't like anyone else shirking. When they talk about the 1948 side they talk about the forward line. Why don't they talk more about Chilton, or Warner, or Cockburn? They were the ones who made it easy for the forward line.

We had a great method of playing and I don't think there's anybody in this country who could tell you how we played. In our tactics the king pin was the centre-half and he made the full-backs play and he was good enough to cover the full-backs – not the full-backs covering him. Allenby Chilton was never rated as highly as he should have been and it was a sad day for Manchester United when he finished.

Our understanding of each other was so natural – for us it was a natural way to play football. Stan Pearson was one of those fellows that could help a ball on first time without stopping it ... always trotting into an open space in the penalty-area ... exceptionally good with his head. We had Charlie Mitten who was one of the best, most accurate kickers of a ball I've ever seen ... and he could beat a man. We had Jack Rowley who had one of the hardest shots I've ever seen as a centre-forward. If you put a ball on the 18 yard line for Jack Rowley and he let fly the goal keepers never saw it.

That's what I mean ... the way this team played they made players. They could have put my daughter in the team and she'd have played well! There was none of this standing still waiting for a ball. The only person you could give a ball to who was standing still was Charlie Mitten. We were a mixture, but our play was free and easy ... we enjoyed our game.

I think the lad who made me a footballer, quicker and earlier than probably would have happened was Jack Warner. He was playing behind me as wing-half, during the War it was, and I was only a kid of sixteen or seventeen and I used to think that all I had to do was what I used to do at school ... if you're a bit above average you can beat three or four ... you can be a George Best ... but playing with United the lads knew more and the opposition was a bit better ... if I was fiddling the ball around a couple, then it was being taken off me and I was getting the team into trouble. This went on for a couple of games. The next game

though, Jack Warner left the ball, came over to me and got hold of me
by the scruff of the neck, right in the middle of the park, and said, 'If
you don't get rid of that ball sooner than you are doing, I'll knock you
over that wall!' From that day on I could play ninety minutes without
any trouble because I made the ball do the work. He was the one who
made me a player before my time, really.

The way we played in that Cup winning season ... we could have
played with ten men and beaten any First Division side. One regular
player out of the team didn't make much difference. There were no
substitutes then. If we were 1-0 down and an injured forward went off
for treatment, by the time he'd returned we were often 2-1 up.

Like many of United's players Johnny often contemplates the
reasons why his prowess was only rewarded three times by the
English international selectors. Admittedly he was in competition
with two brilliant inside-forwards, Stan Mortensen and Wilf
Mannion, but there might have been other reasons:

I only became an international when I moved to Derby. I sometimes
wonder why my international career wasn't longer. I only got three Caps.
I was asked to go to Australia on a summer tour but I had business in
Derby and at that particular time I felt I couldn't go on the tour and so
I turned the offer down. Now whether that had any bearing on the fact
I don't know, but I think it may have.

Then I got appendicitis when I was playing at Derby ... just after I'd
got back from an England tour on the Continent, funnily enough. We
were still rationed in this country, but abroad we could eat and drink
pints and pints of orange juice. This might have led my having to have
an operation. So all this did interrupt my career for almost a season.
That's my excuse anyway!

The time came under Walter Winterbottom when I remember they
had far too many players playing for England in one season. In our day,
if you saw an international footballer once in twelve months it was great.
When Winterbottom took over there was a bloody international in every
street you went down! It's been the same ever since. There's an international footballer in every town you go in now. At one time there were
only eleven internationals and they all lived in different towns. Take an
England side in those days. In one season England would only pick about
twelve players throughout a season. Admittedly they didn't play as many
games. For footballers to get selected for England in the days when your
Lawtons and your Carters were playing (because they were first choice
for years) - to break that was something. England hardly ever used to
lose a game then, you see.

As an inside-forward Johnny possessed many remarkable qualities. He could tackle hard, dribble well, and was difficult to dispossess. Best of all he had a quick brain and swift reactions: his lightning free-kick which led to Jack Rowley's headed goal in the 1948 final began a second-half revival which Blackpool could not contain.

He was an essential component in one of United's best-ever forward lines which was dedicated to attacking football, and this in no small way accounts for his disaffection with today's game:

There's a lot that disappoints me about football today – that's why I've not much interest in the game now. There's some good 'uns playing today ... but I'll tell you what, there's some bad 'uns ... all the trouble's come through coaching, I believe. Put that on bloody record! Coaches have spoiled the game, make no mistake. There are some comics now, aren't there? I never went on a coaching course, although Stan Pearson, myself and Jack Warner were asked to coach the English Olympic squad at Old Trafford in 1948. Then they wanted us to go Loughborough College to tell us how to coach. And all the coaches were the lads who couldn't make it with a club as a player. Now I'm not saying that the best players make the best coaches or the best managers. But I think that's what's spoiled the game and it's gone worse ever since. I'm not against coaching, so long as it's done right.

You've got to give Matt Busby credit for one thing – letting the players get on with it – he didn't tell you how to play. Little bits of advice, yes, but how can you tell a side that's winning how to play football? I've had team talks from Walter Winterbottom when I played for England ... I've given team talks ... and you've got eleven or twelve players there and the coach or manager can say something to the team which can be quite complicated and they think that the team understands what they're talking about and they'll say to one of the players, 'Do you follow, Jimmy?' and he'll say, 'Yes, boss'. He's not going to say 'No, I don't follow' just to be embarrassed in front of his mates! And that's what happens even at international level. There's probably seven of them won't understand what's being said, but they're fabulous players on the field. And if they listen and try to change they can't play their own game then. I could name you internationals who are very good players but know nothing about tactics. In every team I've played in there's been five or six blokes not even interested in the talk because all they want to do is get out on the field and play in their own way.

I hope all the successful teams that came after us enjoyed their football as much as we did when we played, that's all. There wasn't a bloke on our side when I was at United that didn't enjoy playing. We enjoyed

training because we had a terrific trainer in Tom Curry. He didn't have
a whip or a stop-watch – but there was no fitter side than us on a
Saturday. They talk about the game being faster now than it used to be.
What rubbish! It takes them ten minutes longer to get to the opposition
goalmouth now – so how can it be faster?

If I knew a young lad who wanted to be a footballer I'd let him be one
– there's lots of money in the game now, I wouldn't worry too much –
after all, half the managers today wouldn't be able to tell whether he's
had a good game or not! It's so complicated the way they play now – all
on a sixpence – they could almost cut the ground space in half and give
the other to the spectators and sell another 40,000 tickets if it was Wembley.

It's so disappointing the way the game's turned out … so disappointing. It was such a good game and still could be …

After leaving Leicester in 1958 John had spells of managing non-
League Corby, Kettering, Great Harwood and Oswestry. He has
now retired and he and his wife Marian live near Bury. They
have three children and nine grandchildren. John, the 1948 team's
best golfer, still plays off a creditable eight, and his spare time is
fully taken up now as Assistant Sectretary of the Manchester and
District Golf Alliance, where he helps to organise competitions
among the hundred Alliance clubs within thirty miles of Manchester Town Hall.

In 1958 Johnny Morris was still a Leicester player but living
in Derby where, like many soccer players of that era, he ran a
newsagent's business.

I was working in the shop when news came through of the crash at
Munich Airport. I can't count the number of customers who rushed
around to the shop to tell me the news … they were worried that I
hadn't heard … it was a sad time for the whole of football.

Football has been Johnny Morris's life and even though he's
critical of many aspects of today's game he still maintains, 'I'm
a fanatic'. He was the youngest of Manchester United's 1948
team, and Matt Busby doubtless saw in the ebullient Johnny
Morris where the future lay – in finding young players who were
full of skill and running who could be blended into another team
to remember …

## Jack Rowley

Jack Rowley and his wife Vi live near Oldham, but any visitor to the Rowleys' front room would look in vain for evidence of Jack's long and distinguished career as a professional footballer. All his caps and medals and trophies are safely locked away, 'and my three children and grandchildren have already decided who's getting what'. Jack and Vi have six grandchildren and they still listen with great delight to each other's stories of their achievements and misdemeanours.

Jack still retains his Wolverhampton accent which characteristically broadened as he talked about his childhood and his footballing father and brothers. Younger brother Arthur scored 434 League goals for West Bromwich, Fulham, Leicester City and Shrewsbury, and he and Jack share a unique record. They are the only two brothers to score more than 200 goals each, and by a chance in a million each scored his 200th goal on the same afternoon, both in away matches in the Second Division. On Saturday, 22 October 1955 Arthur scored for Leicester City at Fulham, netting his 200th goal in the 53rd minute of the game. Twelve minutes later, Jack scored for Plymouth Argyle at Barnsley to reach the same total!

After a long and distinguished career at Old Trafford, where he had scored 175 goals in 359 appearances, Jack went to Plymouth Argyle as player-manager in February 1955. He retired as a player in the close season of 1957 but continued as manager until 1960. Jack then managed Oldham Athletic for three years, coached Ajax of Amsterdam for a year, then had spells as manager of Wrexham and Bradford before returning to Oldham for another year's tenure before finally retiring from the game in December 1969.

For many years Jack and his wife ran a local newsagents and sub-post office, then he worked for a local mail-order firm before retiring in October 1983.

He still maintains active contact with the grass roots of the game as the proud President of the South-East Lancashire Amateur League, and Jack's legendary bluntness only emerged when the talk moved on to the modern professional game. His contempt for defensive play, and 'the prima donna attitudes of too many modern players and their so-called skills' is complete and undisguised. He's earned the right to his opinions, because Jack

Rowley isn't just a 'Now-in-my-day' critic, but he knows his football and he's played the game at its highest levels. Jack recalled:

In the United team I rated Johnny Carey very highly because he could play anywhere. When he came back after the war he played right-half, outside-right, then they pushed him to full-back ... he looked as though he'd been made for that position. It didn't matter what game Johnny played he was magnificent at it – golf, snooker, billiards. He was a natural ball player and a very educated fellow. When we were in America on tour he used to send articles back and he wouldn't have any ghost writers. I used to share a hotel room with him then and I used to have the radio on and he used to go mad because he was trying to write these articles to send home.

The way we used to play at that time was fantastic. I don't think any of the players who played in that team could explain it because you can't coach that that type of football. For instance, the ball would come to me and I'd be facing my own goal and then I'd just flick it, then I'd turn round and it was amazing ... it always went to one of our own players. I always remember we went to Wolves once and we hammered them 6–1 and I never had a shot at goal and I didn't score one, yet all the goals were scored by someone from the centre-forward position. I mean even Charlie [Mitten] got two from the centre-forward position (and that's saying something for Charlie!). Two of their defenders followed me so what did I do? I went lying deep so there was a big gap in the middle of the field and everything went through the middle.

I played for England six times – in every forward position except outside-right. The most memorable international was at Maine Road against Ireland when I scored four. We beat them 9–2, you know. I came in as a late choice and it was the only time I ever played centre-forward for England. I'll always remember something that happened before that game. We met at Southport and we were in the hotel and I think it was the Chairman of Southport who came in as we were having breakfast and he said, 'Morning Tom [Finney]. ... Morning Neil [Franklin] ... and who the hell are you?' he said, looking at me! For me it was an unlucky period because there were too many good centre-forwards about such as Tommy Lawton, Jackie Milburn, Stan Mortensen. People have often said I should have had a longer international career: I don't know where it came from, but I think I had a bad name for hard play, I don't know. But I can honestly say that I never went out to injure any player. Now I was taught the hard way – if somebody hit you, you hit them back to stop them. If you didn't then they'd hit you all the more. I always remember that my first League match was for Bournemouth against Walsall. It's only a small ground with a wall around it and there was an

old West Brom player playing full-back against me. At that time I used
to show the full-back the ball and go past him. I went past him a couple
of times and he said, 'Son, don't bloody do that again.' I said, 'I beg your
pardon?' He said, 'Don't bloody do that again.' I thought, 'What's he
talking about?' Then the next time I gets the ball and goes past him and
suddenly I'm into the wall. I thought every bone in my body was broken.
I thought, 'I know what he means now.' Going off at half-time my father
said, 'Son, hit him back, he won't hit you any more if you hit him back.'
In the second half he had a go at me and I had a go at him and hit him
back and stopped him ... and it always stuck in my mind that if someone
clobbers you, you clobber them back ... and I can honestly say that I
never clobbered anybody with the intention to injure them permanently,
but to let them know that I could do it if they did it. I play to win, that's
the only way I could play: even in friendly matches I played to win. The
game isn't as physical as it used to be. You can't even look at a player
now but it's a foul. You can't even go into a tackle now and take the ball,
they blow for a foul. When I played and a goalkeeper held the ball on
the goal-line he went in the back of the net ...

I think footballers are born, not made. It is a sad affair if you have to
tell players in their twenties how to play football. I mean you can help
them a little bit by saying 'You should be running here ... or over there',
but this should already be in them. I think they get set in their ways
from sixteen onwards, but you can help them in positional playing and
tell them when to release the ball and when not to. So you can accelerate
development in a player that's already got it basically. Coaching can do
a certain amount but he's got to have ability to start with.

It's a sorry state of affairs to have to say this but I think at the present time there's too many managers who are afraid to lose their
jobs. They've got to get results. I don't think it was as bad as that
when I played but now if you don't get results – it does not matter
whether you've got a contract or not – if you're not getting results you're
out.

I don't go to football now ... I don't watch now for the simple reason
that I can't stomach defensive football ... I've never been used to it. I
always remember before I went to Ajax I went over there for an interview
and I said, 'Before we go any further, what style of football do you like?'
and they said, 'Attacking football', and I said, 'That's the sort I coach –
I won't have anything to do with defensive football ... if you want
defensive football you're wasting your time with me.' And on that I got
it. Let's be honest, who pays the wages? It's the spectators. Look at the
price they have to pay now ... so you've got to entertain the public who
keep you alive ... and defensive football does not entertain the public.
It's not sour grapes but I think footballers today are prima donnas. I

hate the petty things that happen now. I sometimes watch football on television but I certainly don't watch on Sunday afternoons.

I was at the ground at Plymouth and the press reporter at Plymouth rang me up and said, 'Jack, have you heard the sad news?' I said, 'No, what is it?' and he said, 'United have crashed'. So I went home and left the radio on and listened. When they started bringing the bodies back and everything I said to the board at Plymouth, 'Look, I call Manchester United my home. They were good enough to let me come here on a free transfer and didn't ask for any money so I would like to go back and see what I can do for them.' They said, 'Yes, we'd like you to go.' I came back and I was up here for about two weeks helping out. I remember I had to sort out Johnny Berry's wages because his wife had come to the ground – she wanted some money. When the coffins started coming back they pushed them in at Old Trafford ... I mean the place was like a morgue and I went to as many funerals as I could get to because I knew these lads. It was a terrific blow. I still say it ... this would have been the greatest side in the world if it had been left to mature, because when you consider they were all nineteen ... twenty ... twenty-one years of age. You could keep Real Madrid ... to me this would have been the greatest team ever.

Roger Byrne was one of the great young players who were beginning to get in the side before the Munich tragedy. Roger was a bit fiery when he came but he got quietened down a lot and it didn't matter where he played, he was a good outside-left and when he went to full-back he was one of the best I'd seen ... he matured very quickly ... he really was a great full-back. Eddie Colman ... I always remember little Eddie Colman when he first came to Old Trafford. We used to have him out and get a wet ball and put it on the eighteen-yard line and he could hardly hit the back of the net, so we used to send him to the Gorse Hill Hotel to get his dinners to feed himself up. This little fellow, what a dribbler ... he used to send us all ways. You'd go for the ball and he'd be coming toward you ... and he'd be past. He had some speed that lad ...

## Stan Pearson

Stan Pearson left Old Trafford in February 1954 when he was transferred to Second Division Bury, where he played for a few seasons before joining Third Division Chester. After a couple of seasons he became their player–manager, then manager, until he left Sealand Road and the world of professional football in November 1961.

Those who saw him play will never forget his talent. He had scored many important goals for Manchester United: his contribution to the goal tally in United's journey to Wembley in 1948 was immeasurable, and the goal which broke the 2–2 deadlock in the final is always reckoned as one of his finest. He was famous for a lethal shot, his clever headed flicks, the sweeping passes he made out to the wing, his control in the dribble and the tireless energy which guided his fellow-forwards into Cup and Championship winning success. The bare statistics of his achievements – 8 England caps, 304 League appearances and 125 goals for Manchester United – tell nothing of the pleasure he gave to the many thousands who marvelled at his skill and footballing intelligence.

Stan now lives above the newsagents/post office he runs in the picture postcard Cheshire village of Prestbury. His wife Elsie died in April 1985: for both it was their second marriage, having been widowed within a few years of each other. Elsie had known the 1948 team 'when they were all so young and handsome' and she had remained a devoted United fan all her life.

Once he had left Chester, Stan was on the look out for a newsagents business (he had already run one in north Manchester) when he heard about the shop in Prestbury. But active football had one last demand to make from him. Some players retire at the top, others, like Stan, cannot and do not want to leave the game, even if it means playing at successively lower levels.

'One day the local stationmaster Mr Greenwood came to see me and said, "You know, Stan, Prestbury used to have a football team in the East Cheshire League, shall we start it up again?" So we did, and I played, but by then I was in my mid-forties and the old legs used to get very tired!' His son Stephen, however, a keen sportsman and Cheshire County standard tennis player, carried on the Pearson tradition and for many years was a member of the village team his father had helped to revive.

As a season ticket holder ('which I pay for') Stan Pearson is the only player of the 1948 side who still watches every home game at Old Trafford from a seat in the stand. He is also one of the very few of that side who has any admiration at all for the modern game:

These lads can play a bit – they are quick and skilful and it's modern tactics which bog the game down in the middle of the field. In my day lots of full-backs were often players who used to be half-backs or forwards – they'd just got older and slower so it was easy for us forwards to get past them. Nowadays the backs are just as fast and skilful as the forwards.

Yes, we seemed to score far more goals then than we do now. To be honest, I think it's because the professionals have now got hold of the game. When I first started at United, Scott Duncan was the manager. He was an office bloke, we never saw him on the field. All the managers now are ex-footballers and unfortunately now it's so easy to organise a defence to make it hard for anybody to score a goal if that's the way they want to play it. It's much harder to organise an attack. There have been spells when I've been bored stiff watching teams coming to Old Trafford and playing for a draw by leaving eight men in defence. It's spoiling the game. Teams would get murdered now if they went at the opposition like we used to because they'd leave themselves open at the back. In the days when we were playing we were lucky ... in all the time I played for United I can never remember at any time going anywhere and playing for a draw. No way. We went to win and that was the attitude of all the teams then. Teams came to Old Trafford then and they had a bash at us and if they lost they lost ... it was a proper football match. Two defeats in a row today and they start talking about relegation and sacking the manager and all that business. The only matches really worth watching now are often Cup ties. It's all very short-sighted ... they are forgetting the spectator ... if they forget him they might as well pack up.

The style of football in our day was people getting forward as soon as they could. Unlike today, we were never afraid of giving the ball away and we didn't take as long to build up an attack as they do today. As an inside-forward you'd get the ball from the defence and float it over the full-back for the winger to run on to. He might get it ... he might not. The full-back might turn and be as quick as him. But at least we'd try it.

We used to release the ball much more quickly than they do today. I could get a ball from John Aston, gather it on the half-turn, and nine times out of ten I had no need to look because I knew darn well that Jack Rowley would be coming away from the centre-half ... I'd just slip it along the ground – he'd get it, perhaps play it to Charlie Mitten who'd be a bit further up. In the meantime Johnny Morris would be diving into the gap that Jack had left. Jack was a terrific centre-forward, you know. I remember him once scoring against Wolves at Maine Road. He collared it in the centre-circle and he set off. Somebody came and leaned on him but he finished up on the floor. That happened twice! Then he got to the edge of the box and by then the ball was twice as heavy as when we'd started, and he walloped it in ... no bother. He could head a ball as well ... like when he scored at Wembley from Johnny Morris's free kick. When you see the pictures of that ... Jack's way up in the air and he heads it in like a shot.

There's good players and international-class players and there's another standard that only covers the best few there's ever been. Matthews was one on his own, so was Bobby Charlton, so was George Best. I would have hated to have played with Bobby Charlton because I've never seen him play a first-time ball yet, which was my way of playing. He used to get the ball and then turn round on it. He knew what was behind him then and he'd set off and devise something completely on his own and perhaps finish up with a bang at goal. He could also sling a ball, like Jack Rowley could, and pin-point a forty-yard pass without any bother. I used to like the one-touch stuff. Push it – go – get it back – push it somewhere else – get it back – everybody moving ... that's the only style of play where you can't be stopped. But the class above involved players like Charlton, Matthews, Finney, Best. They could take the ball themselves and go past people as if they weren't there. I'd have also hated to have played with Best, because he used people. He had people going into positions, and what happens gradually if the others don't get the ball? The team-work breaks down and they say, 'I'm not running because I never get the bloody ball!' But when somebody like Best finishes up sticking it in the back of the net you forgive him, don't you?

We were a very well co-ordinated side ... it's difficult to talk about who was outstanding ... we all had particular strengths. We had players like Allenby Chilton ... perhaps not as good a footballer as some of the others, but he was just what we wanted in the particular position – a big, strong lad, good in the air and no frills. Jack Rowley could play anywhere on the forward line and give you a good match. Johnny Morris could go past people ... he could beat people. My strength was that I could plonk a ball to advantage very quickly ... I could see chances. Johnny Carey was very versatile ... perhaps he never had a lot of pace (neither did I for that matter) but his positional play was outstanding. He had the ability to jockey wingers and more often than not they'd finish up giving him the ball.

It's difficult for me to compare how good the 1948 side was with the other great United sides that followed on. I've seen better individual forwards at Old Trafford than we were – fellows like Charlton and Law and Best ... but I've never seen a better forward-line than we had.

Perhaps without realising it – and without talking about it – we had developed a sixth sense. You don't do it consciously. Our understanding of each other's game was amazing. For example, if Charlie [Mitten] saw me getting the ball in a certain situation he'd already be on his way and I'd know he'd be on his way and he knew the same about me ... it was a kind of instinct.

Matt Busby was a man you wanted to play for ... he made you want to play for him. He was fair and he knew how to handle men. An incident which shows this was once when the team sat down, as we always did, to discuss the next match which was against Preston at Preston. We always used to talk about the previous match and then the coming one. I was always very placid about everything ... but Busby suddenly turned to me and said, 'We drew last week and that was a match we should have won and we needed to win, but we didn't because we got a bit lacka-daisical, and Stan, I think it was partly your fault as well.' And I said, 'What way?' and he said, 'Well, not getting the ball away quickly enough' ... and I said, 'Well, as far as I'm concerned it was Jack ... normally I can find Jack without looking, but when I looked up and he wasn't where I thought he'd be, I had to hold the ball and try to stop people getting it off me.' Jack said, 'Rubbish!' Then Johnny Morris said, 'Stan's right ... it was the same with me ... I got the ball and I don't want to dribble all day and Jack was never there' ... and Busby's not said a word and me and Rowley and Johnny Morris and Henry Cockburn who chipped in, were all having a go at each other and suddenly Busby says, 'That's enough now, forget it ... we've got to win our next game at Preston.' You should have seen Jack Rowley in that game! We beat them 6–1 and Jack had scored two in the first twenty minutes. He was flying about all over the place. Busby had obviously picked on me ... if he'd have a go at Rowley himself, Jack might have sulked a bit, but that day he just rolled up his sleeves and slaughtered them all on his own!

I never had a cause to be against Busby ... I might have been if he'd left me out a few times but he never did. I thought he was a good manager because I was always happy under him. I'd have played any-where, even full-back if he'd asked me. He knew we could play ... more often than not he'd say, 'Go out and enjoy yourselves.' He knew what we were driving at as a team and he let us get on with it ...

I played with a few of the 'Babes' before I left United, and I played with Roger Byrne a couple of times with him on the wing. In one of the games there was a ball coming over from the right and I'm moving in on it and getting ready to jump and head for goal and something flashed past me and jumped about a yard higher than I could have jumped and knocked it in, and I thought, 'Bloody hell, who was that?' It was Roger! He was also a fantastic full-back, of course.

I had a shop in Prestwich when the news of the Munich crash came through. It was a terrible tragedy. They asked me to go on TV that night. I didn't really want to, but I did, and I can't remember what I said now. Now there's a team that would have set a standard . . .


## Charlie Mitten

'Cheeky' Charlie Mitten's was the last name in United's famous forward line – an immensely fit and confident winger who could cut inside the full-back at speed, or centre a ball on a sixpence, as they used to say at the time.

For the two seasons following the Cup victory Charlie was an ever-present member of the side, and it was also in the latter season that he created a record which only two other First Division players have equalled. On 8 March 1950 Charlie scored a penalty hat-trick against Aston Villa – actually notching four goals in United's 7-0 victory. Was there any truth in the story that before each penalty Charlie told the goalkeeper where he was going to place the ball?

'I didn't tell him the first time,' chuckled Charlie, 'in case he thought it was a fluke . . . but I told him where the next two were going. My fourth was a header . . . that was the goal I really remember . . . I could see it coming in so up I went . . . it hit me on the ear and flew into the net . . . a real beauty!'

And even today, despite the differences they might have had in America in the summer of 1950, Matt Busby thought highly enough of Charlie Mitten to give him the number 11 shirt in his 'Scrapbook' All-Star United side, along with team-mates John Carey and Allenby Chilton.

It was, of course, on that famous close-season tour of America that Charlie and Manchester United parted company. The trip was all but over and the players were relaxing for a few days in New York before sailing home to prepare for the new season.

We were in the Astor Club in New York and I got a phone call from Neil Franklin in Colombia and he asked me if I'd be interested in playing there. I said 'Yes' and he said, 'There'll be a ticket around for you in a couple of days' time . . . come on down, and if you don't like it then there's no harm done, you can go home. So I saw Matt and I told him

I was going to have a look ... I said, 'Well, boss, we've won everything except the Boat Race and I've got nothing.' I went down to Bogota and had a look at the set-up and I liked what I saw. So I signed, came home, picked up my wife and children and put the furniture in store.

The living conditions were magnificent. We had a beautiful detached house, fully furnished ... it was in a lovely area. We had a maid who did the cooking and cleaning, and a big, de luxe Ford car.

They thought the world of me. We had a good side ... every time we won (and that was most of the time) we got a £35 bonus ... compared to £12 a week at United. I got £2,500 for signing on ... my year's salary was £2,500 ... and I got a £1,500 bonus when I left, having honoured my contract for the year.

The big mistake I made was coming back to England. Most of what I earned in that first year went on buying things and setting up our house in Bogota. If I could have had more years on that kind of money, more would have gone into the bank. I should have gone on to Real Madrid with Alfred Di Stefano and Hector Rial ... I was offered £20,000 to go ...

There was no money in the game then ... only when you look back do you realise that we didn't know our own value. For instance, I guested for Chelsea in a wartime Cup final and we each got £2 10 shillings ... and that was a War Bond Certificate ... we didn't even get a medal!

That's why I went to South America ... when we went on that tour in 1950 I was hearing about players who were earning ten times more than we were – only because they were playing football in a different country.

All of us were beginning to wonder what we'd do when we finished in the game. I realised early on that if I didn't do something about it myself, nobody else would. The Players' Union today is now quite strong ... we had one in our day but it wasn't up to much.

I played with some brilliant footballers when I was in South America including Rial, Di Stefano, and a goalkeeper called Chimorro who'd give Frank Swift five start. They were all so young and so skilful.

Uruguay won the World Cup in 1950 you'll remember, and soon after me and Neil Franklin and George Mountford played for Columbia against them in Bogota, and we beat them, yes, the World Champions 3-1! Mind you, there was some blood flowing that day ... they had some hard players but they were good, even brilliant. At the end of my year in Colombia Di Stefano was about to go to Real Madrid and he said, 'Charlie, come on, come with us to Real Madrid', and I said, 'Where the bloody hell is Real Madrid?' Eventually I told him: 'No, my contract's finished and I've got to go back to England.' It was one of the biggest mistakes I made ... I should have gone to Madrid with them ... I just wish I'd known someone who'd known the set-up over there who could have advised me. If somebody had told me that it was a big club and it was only a couple of hours' flying time from England I'd have gone. But there we were, thousands of miles from home ... not really knowing what was what ...

So Charlie returned, not much richer but very much wiser, and many of his friends could only speculate about how United would have fared had he remained with the club.

Many people regret that Charlie Mitten was never an England player, apart from being picked for the Bolton Disaster Fund international in August 1946. The other four members of that legendary forward line were all eventually to win international honours. Bobby Langton and Tom Finney dominated the left-wing spot for many seasons, and Jimmy Mullen, Johnny Hancocks and Jack Froggatt were all given chances as England's number 11. But in those days Manchester United, let alone England, could never countenance reinstating Charlie Mitten after his 'illegal' year in Bogota.

Yes, we came home to all the ballyhoo, it was disgraceful. You know the story. I was fined £250 and was suspended for six months which niggled me because I knew that what I'd done was right and my contract with United had expired when we were in the USA. I wanted to be well rewarded for playing a game I was good at, and to make a decent living for my wife and family.

I trained in the park and played for pub teams to keep fit ... and eventually I was bought by Fulham who looked after us very well.

So Charlie Mitten, one of United's pre-war signings, and who scored a total of 92 goals in his four post-war seasons with them, was transferred to Fulham in December 1951. He had been bought to help keep them in the First Division but even the tireless Charlie Mitten could not stop Fulham's slide into relegation. He made 156 appearances for the 'Cottagers' between 1951 and 1955 and enjoyed his time in this most sociable of clubs under the chairmanship of Tommy Trinder with a team full of characters like Bobby Robson, Eddie Lowe, Bedford Jezzard and Johnny Haynes.

Charlie was still as irrepresible as ever, and Bobby Robson still remembers the time when he and Johnny Haynes, both still teenagers, were having some treatment and Charlie came in carrying a black greyhound.

'Come on Haynesey,' Charlie said 'Get off that table. The dog has a sore fetlock and needs some heat treatment on it.' Johnny Haynes, in some awe of the famous Mitten, dutifully made way for the dog. Frank Penn, the trainer, strapped on the equipment and gave the animal some short wave treatment and the greyhound duly won his next race!

At the age of thirty-one Charlie moved to become player-manager of Third Division Mansfield Town. Having served his managerial apprenticeship, he went up to Newcastle to become their third post-war manager.

I was in for a bit of a shock. Things were in a mess when I took over ... they had half a ton of scented sòap but they hadn't got a new ball to start a match with, just forty or fifty old ones lying around ... they had no drying room for the kit ... the players were wearing the same gear they'd had for three years ... they'd had to buy their own boots and the groundsman wouldn't let them on the pitch to practise ... what a set-up!

Even Charlie's managerial career was full of incident, including a situation which matched the one he himself had faced as a player. George Eastham, Newcastle's star inside-forward took his club (and Charlie Mitten) to the High Court to free himself from his contract and with the help of the Players' Union, won the case.

After nearly five years at St James's Park, Charlie was fired and the family moved back to Manchester. A series of jobs followed, including assistant manager of the White City Stadium in Manchester where dog racing (still very close to Charlie's heart) used to be held. He also became a licensed UEFA agent and helped to organise the travel and accommodation arrangements of football teams all over the world.

Since 1961 I have travelled the football world visiting over sixty-five different countries promoting football. The most popular team from Great Britain used to be Arsenal FC but since 1957 the best-loved and most popular team is Manchester United, made famous by great players and a great manager in Sir Matt Busby. All players who served under his leadership love and respect him, surely a sign of greatness and human understanding.

Charlie has now retired and he still lives in the house he bought after he left the professional game. His wife Betty died in 1980, but two of his children (daughter Susan and son Charles) still live in the Manchester area. His eldest son John (a schoolboy international and once on United's books) lives in Devon and has a daughter Sarah who is a very promising tennis player ('and she's got the best left foot of any of my grandchildren'). Charles's sons, Daniel and Paul are also ensuring that their grandfather's supreme sporting ability lives on because they are also very talented young sportsmen. Charles senior helps his son (who was also a registered United player) to coach the boys and their team-mates on a Saturday morning before he goes off for a round of golf.

On and off the field Charlie Mitten made the best of every chance. Always an opportunist, he braved it out in Bogota, knowing that the reality did not always quite match the expectation, and if he had any regrets at all it is that 'I didn't earn enough money to make a decent living here in England, which was amazing when you think of how many people were paying to watch us entertain them'.

But most important of all Charlie Mitten today still retains the cheeky directness and infectious sense of humour which made him such a popular figure and one of United's best ever players.

I've always loved Manchester, after all I'm one of its adopted sons when I moved down here as an office boy at Old Trafford before the war. I was still manager at Mansfield and I was sitting in my office when the news of Munich came through. I made a couple of phone calls just to check because I couldn't believe it at first. When I was told it had happened I put the phone down and had a little cry. It was a terrible loss . . .

## Sir Matt Busby
## and the Old Trafford Staff

The reasons for the success of the 1948 and 1952 Manchester United teams lie deeper than the moment when Stan Pearson scored the winning goal at Wembley, or when John Carey finally lifted the Championship trophy after forty-two gruelling League games. Many could rightly claim to have been part of the success story of United's first great post-war side, the foundations of which had been built years beforehand.

If the story begins anywhere, it should be with Louis Rocca, who was a player with the club at the turn of the century and was appointed chief scout in 1907 until his death in June 1950. He spent many hours on cold and windswept touch-lines watching out for those sometimes indefinable qualities in young players which indicated a potential United could develop. It was Louis Rocca who first brought to Old Trafford many of the players who eventually won the Cup in 1948, and his recommendations, and the young talent from the Manchester United Junior Athletic Club, as well as local clubs like the Goslings, ensured a steady supply of players to Old Trafford during and just after the war.

From then on, the contribution of Jimmy Murphy, the reserve team manager, Bert Whalley, the youth team coach, Tom Curry, the trainer, and Bill Inglis, his assistant, permeates every detail of life at Old Trafford before and after the war, until the tragic deaths of Bert and Tom at Munich.

Jimmy Murphy and Matt Busby worked together from 1945 until 1971, in a partnership which won five League Championship titles, two Cup finals and the European Cup. Jimmy was made assistant manager in 1955 and he took charge of rebuilding United's first team in February 1958 when Matt Busby was fighting for his life in a Munich hospital, spending sometimes eighteen hours a day at Old Trafford in a quest to find players who could continue United's League and Cup commitments.

Jimmy, as forthright and honest as ever, still believes that the team which was destroyed at Munich was the best ever United team, but of the 1948 team he once said: 'They were an attacking side and a brilliantly entertaining side ... this mature team was our golden asset, because it gave us time and breathing space to look around and build for the future.' Matt Busby also has only praise for the 1948 team and dislikes being asked to compare the merits of each of United's three great post-war sides. Comparisons, as he kindly but firmly points out, are irrelevant:

They were all great teams, the best of their own time. You get a great deal of satisfaction from knowing you've helped to create these sides, but I never want to start talking about which was the best ... I keep that within myself. But I will say that we had a great team spirit in that 1948 team ... everybody played for one another ... everybody fitted in ... if one was having a rough time, the others would try and help him out. They were a very entertaining side, win, lose or draw. I was all for encouraging creative football and I had in my mind that at the end of the day it was all about scoring goals ... so you had to have players who had the ability to create and the ability to score. The 1948 side had those sort of players. Jimmy Murphy, Joe Armstrong, Bert Whalley and his staff, they all played their part in our successes in 1948 and 1952 ... it was a very happy period for us all ...

On 15 February 1985 Sir Matt Busby completed forty years' association with Manchester United. As the club's President and Old Trafford's elder statesman he can look back on nearly half a century of triumph and sadness which began when he turned up at Old Trafford in his demob suit on that cold February day in 1945. The magnificent stadium which is the Old Trafford of today is vastly different from the piles of rubble and twisted girders which greeted him then, and it is a fitting tribute to the man who has done so much for the club that the last section of the rebuilt stand will incorporate the Matt Busby Suite, and a bust of Sir Matt will be given pride of place at the entrance to the new museum which will be housed there. Less tangible, but no less important for all those who saw them play, are the memories of the great teams Matt Busby fashioned over a period of twenty-five years. Their supreme achievements under his wise and imaginative leadership ensure a permanent place for them all in the history of Manchester United.

# Index

*Index*